AMERICAN PRAGMATISM

AMERICAN ACADEMY OF RELIGION REFLECTION AND THEORY
IN THE STUDY OF RELIGION SERIES

SERIES EDITOR
Mary McClintock Fulkerson, Duke University

A Publication Series of The American Academy of Religion
and Oxford University Press

AAR

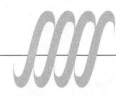

American Pragmatism
A Religious Genealogy

M. GAIL HAMNER

UNIVERSITY PRESS

2003

OXFORD
UNIVERSITY PRESS

Oxford   New York
Auckland   Bangkok   Buenos Aires   Cape Town   Chennai
Dar es Salaam   Delhi   Hong Kong   Istanbul   Karachi   Kolkata
Kuala Lumpur   Madrid   Melbourne   Mexico City   Mumbai   Nairobi
São Paulo   Shanghai   Taipei   Tokyo   Toronto

Published by Oxford University Press, Inc.
198 Madison Avenue, New York, New York 10016

www.oup.com

Oxford is a registered trademark of Oxford University Press

Library of Congress Cataloging-in-Publication Data
Hamner, M. Gail, 1963–
American pragmatism : a religious genealogy / M. Gail Hamner
    p. cm.—(The American Academy of Religion reflection and theory in the study of
religion series)
Includes bibliographical references and index.
ISBN 0-19-515547-5
1. Pragmatism.   2. United States—Religion.   I. Title.   II. Reflection and theory in
the study of religion
B832 .H36 2002
144'.3'0973—dc21   2002022024

9 8 7 6 5 4 3 2 1

Printed in the United States of America
on acid-free paper

To my parents, William F. Hamner, Jr., and
Jane Freeborough Hamner, in love and gratitude

Acknowledgments

The seeds for this project were sown years ago, when I was a seminary student at Boston University School of Theology. I wish to thank Harold H. Oliver for introducing me to A. N. Whitehead and the Boston personalists, and Robert C. Neville for introducing me to Peirce. Their mentorship and friendship sparked my interest in the connections between "cultural dispositions" and "philosophical formations," and endeared me to life in the academy despite its many pitfalls and roadblocks. Also from my years at BUSTh, I wish to thank Paul J. Sampley for his sharp wit and equally sharp critiques and Katheryn Pfisterer Darr and Jennifer L. Rike for their charismatic teaching and for providing needed models of women in the academy.

On moving to my doctoral work at Duke University, I was fortunate to find colleagues among both faculty and graduate students. Of the latter, there are not words of thanks enough for Joerg Rieger (now at Perkins School of Theology) and Frank Crouch (now dean of Moravian Seminary). My conversations with Joerg kept me sane and helped me work out a much-needed framework for my doctoral research. Frank and I read through much of Peirce's *Collected Papers* and secondary Peircean scholarship together, and he read (suffered) through almost all of the early drafts of this work. His comments and suggestions were, and are, invaluable. I also wish to thank Karen Trimble Alliaume, Randall Styers, and Audrey West for their supportive friendship and intelligent conversation over the years.

Among the faculty at Duke, I am blessed to have Kenneth J. Surin and Elizabeth A. Clark as my teachers and friends. Their constant encouragement, brutal editing, late night conversations, lessons from the trenches of teaching and scholarship, general availability, and gentle prodding made graduate school a wonderful experience and literally provided the material ground for this book. I continue to be blessed by their loyal friendship. I also wish to thank Judith Farquhar (University of North Carolina, Chapel Hill), Michael

Hardt, Stanley Hauerwas, Bruce Lawrence, Dale Martin (now at Yale University), Tomoko Masuzawa (now at University of Minnesota), and Tom Tweed (UNC, Chapel Hill) for time you gave, lines of thought you inspired, and lessons you taught me, sometimes simply through witnessing your actions. I am also deeply grateful to the Duke-UNC religion and culture reading group, which was begun by Ken Surin and further sponsored and facilitated by Liz Clark and Tomoko Masuzawa. We met once a month for years to discuss hundreds of pages of current theory, anthropology, cultural studies, and religious studies; it is an experience I sorely miss.

During my three years at Syracuse University, I have been extremely fortunate to have congenial and supportive colleagues. My deepest thanks go to David Miller, Patricia Cox Miller, Richard Pilgrim, and James Wiggens for regularly attending a monthly departmental reading group and standing ready with what seems to me an unending arsenal of encouragement and sound advice. I am grateful to Deborah Pratt and Carol Williams for their smiles and for their efficient and patient administrative assistance. Thanks also to Laura Auerbach, Claudia Klaver, and Monika Wadman for solidarity in our shared task of being a feminist academics and mothers.

My thanks and gratitude to the AAR series editor, Mary McClintock Fulkerson at Duke University Press, for her enthusiasm and support of my work, to Stacey Hamilton and Theo Calderara at Oxford University Press for their astute editorial advice and assistance, and to the anonymous reviewers of my manuscript for their pertinent and useful comments and criticisms.

To Maggie and Michael Bennett, and Al and Jane Boyers: thank you for always being there and for having more confidence in me than I have in myself. And to Dan, Elena, and Seth: without you (your constancy, your clarity, and your love), none of this would matter in the least. I dedicate this book to my parents, in remembrance of my father rocking Elena to sleep while I typed away, and of my mother nudging me out the door to work and giving me her labor of child care and cooking in return. Both of you have consistently supported my long journey from laboratory to ivory tower; thank you.

Contents

AMERICAN PRAGMATISM

Introduction

Context

This book is about American pragmatism, a way of thinking that has enjoyed renewed attention in the 1980s and 1990s. Recently, philosophers, social theorists, legal theorists, and literary critics have mined the rich texts of classical pragmatism (C. S. Peirce, William James, and John Dewey) for new perspectives on contemporary problematics.[1] Richard Rorty, for example, takes from classical pragmatism a suspicion of correspondence theories of representation and hones it in ways he thinks can extricate classical pragmatism from its ties with crass empiricism and crass utilitarianism.[2] To give only two other recent applications of classical pragmatism: Frank Lentricchia elicits from his study of William James a perspectival epistemology that enables his literary criticism,[3] and historian James Kloppenberg views pragmatism as a valuable means of articulating the possibilities of democracy and human freedom in the age of postmodernity.[4] In general, what seems to attract contemporary thinkers to American pragmatism is everything it purports to be *against*: ostensibly, it is anti-universalist, anti-authoritarian, anti-Cartesian, anti-essentializing, and antirepresentational. One could surmise that this *anti-* character of American pragmatism resonates with the *de-* and *post-* prefixes favored by many current philosophical and social theories.

This book, however, analyzes something that pragmatism *is*, something quite taken for granted: "Pragmatism is the only unique contribution American philosophy has made to the tradition known as Western philosophy."[5] Pragmatism is "thought to be a distinctly American product."[6] "Pragmatism is justly regarded as a distinctively American philosophy."[7] Pragmatism is "the major contribution of America to the world of philosophy."[8] Pragmatism is "the most distinctive American contribution to philosophy."[9] Pragmatism is "America's 'first indigenous philosophy.'"[10] But what *is* American about American pragmatism? In some way, the question might seem banal. Pragmatism is American in that its organizers and proponents were (and are) primarily American. At the same time, the fact that this question has never received sustained attention is surprising. Despite a long history of American cultural criticism, the more recent development of Americanist discursive terrains, and numerous attempts to correlate national temper and philosophical pursuit, no pragmatist or commentator has attempted fully to clarify and discuss the American character of pragmatism.[11] By analyzing the works of two classical pragmatists—Charles Sanders Peirce and William James—and their continental interlocutors, this book asks what is distinctly "American" about the only philosophical movement indigenous to this country. In forming an answer to this question, this book takes the form of a double project. First, American pragmatism marks a repositioning of British and European science, especially psychology, within theories of human knowing and being that emphasize the purposive and disciplined production of the self through habits (Peirce) or will (James). Second, the engine of this repositioning is something I term America's slippery but persistent "Puritan imaginary." Put differently, I attribute the American quality of pragmatism to an insistent, nondoctrinal Puritan legacy that operated during the mid- to late nineteenth century. The two aspects of the project come together in narratives about subjectivity, since applying the methods and assumptions of natural science to the human self (in psychology) highlights the limitations and aporias of those methods and principles and, for the early pragmatists at least, underscores the necessity of religion. For these reasons, the chapters on Peirce and James dwell on their accounts of subjectivity.

Organization of the Book

The prologue offers a brief look at the meanings of *Puritanism* and *Puritan imaginary*. It clarifies what is meant by these terms, how they affect my reading of the pragmatists, and how the meaning of *Puritan* changed over the course of the nineteenth century. Parts I and II (chapters 1–4) examine the pragmatists' continental interlocutors (Wilhelm Wundt and Hermann von Helmholtz in Germany and Alexander Bain and William Hamilton in Scotland) and elucidate the strands of their philosophies that were picked up and mutated by Peirce and James. Part III (chapters 5–6) turns to the pragmatists themselves, describing how the continental thinkers were transposed on to American soil and demonstrating the specific connections between those European concepts and the legacy of American Puritanism. The chapter on conclusions ties these readings of Puritanism directly to a discourse on nationality and to a discussion of the place of the religious today, both within culture and within that part of culture called "theory."

Situation

As stated at the outset, this book investigates what is "American" about American pragmatism. The primary, question-setting interlocutors of Charles S. Peirce, William James, and their philosophical friends and students were not American, but European.[12] Moreover, the nexus of thoughts and events that coalesced in the philosophical stance of pragmatism can be strongly correlated with the changing attitudes toward, and the growing societal dominance of, the natural sciences. A word should be said about the latter.

The relation of European scientific developments to the genealogy of American pragmatism is an important story. Just as in the nineteenth-century philosophical arena in America, the theoretical questions of natural science were posed—and the bulk of its experiments and publications occurred—on the European Continent and in Britain. The new land of America was designated (and complied in its role) as a gold mine of data and information, but it was commonly presumed even by American data collectors that the fruits of their labor needed to be tested and categorized by the time-honored laboratories of Europe. It is thus no surprise that most of the funding for science in pre–Civil War America came from established European sources such as universities and scientific associations. What little indigenous funding existed initially came from private individuals with specific, personal goals. Though Thomas Jefferson had authorized the Coast Survey in 1807 and though the American Academy for the Advancement of Science (AAAS) had formed in 1848, broad interest in and support for American science were generated primarily through the exigencies of the Civil War.[13] Thus it was not until the period of Reconstruction and the beginning of the second wave of industrialization that increasingly persistent calls for public (that is, government) funding arose. These appeals were fueled by well-attended public lectures given by successful scientists,[14] who effectively disturbed the European image of the scientist as "expert" and began to portray scientific questions as ones of general interest and practical value both for individuals (especially entrepreneurs) and for the nation.

The lecturers were able to depict science as not simply predictive but also inherently purposive. The emphasis on purpose in science aided the formation of a peculiarly American disposition toward science as at once a specialized knowledge that generates technological advances and as an application of common sense that encourages efficiency and discipline. A paradox is embedded in this disposition for it suggests that investigations are properly theoretical only if they produce visibly practical results, and it suggests that common sense is inherently tied to quite uncommon notions about the way a self acts in the world. As this book will make clear, the material conditions of this American paradox are transformations of European attitudes, the roots of which lie in English Puritanism and the fruit of which is American pragmatism.

Peirce and James experienced an intense desire to be faithful both to the residually "Puritan" ethos of their fathers and to the scientific, empirical ethos of their own day. According to general historical accounts, American Puritan communities of the seventeenth and eighteenth centuries had little suspicion or fear of scientific progress. On the contrary, their theocratic cosmology approved of all endeavors to understand the world as attempts to understand God and to model one's life according to the Divine Will. This very precept, however, while allowing unlimited curiosity and experimentation, also narrated the uses to which science was put. Puritan ministers studied Locke and Newton, not for understanding the world in itself, but rather "for the sake of the moral and theological lessons to be drawn from nature."[15] Such Puritan purposiveness illuminates the tension between what were termed *science* and *religion* in post-1859 America, that year marking the publication of Charles Darwin's *Origin of Species*. At root, Darwin's arguments for evolution were less troubling to American intellectuals than the growing influence of a notion of causality devoid of final causality (teleology) and a notion of consciousness devoid of spirit. Such trends shocked many well-bred and philosophically trained New England thinkers and provoked a struggle to accept the guidance and successes of the natural sciences without relinquishing the guidance and successes of inherited Christian traditions. The importance of this claim for a genealogy of American pragmatism is highlighted by the fact that the members of the Cambridge Metaphysical Club—C. S. Peirce, Chauncey Wright, William James, Francis E. Abbot, John Fiske, Oliver W. Holmes, Jr., and others—were reading and admiring *European* texts.[16] The answer to this book's guiding question—what is *American* about American pragmatism?—thus centers on the specific ways in which European scientific concepts and dispositions were transfigured in America in an attempt to maintain faithfulness to a Puritan past.

From one perspective, the European roots of pragmatism are well known. For instance, pragmatism is said to have arisen both from Alexander Bain's associationist psychology and from Wilhelm Wundt's and Hermann von Helmholtz's functionalist psychologies. More broadly, pragmatism is said to have developed out of a critique of British empiricism's stringent utilitarianism. And many students of classical pragmatism take for granted the shaping force of evolutionary theories, especially the role of Herbert Spencer's theories in rampantly spreading Social Darwinism through America's changing (and intensifying) capitalist landscape. While each of the above origins is true in part, however, none is true alone, and even when combined, the story line remains too simple. For the purposes of this book, the issue is not how certain European modes of thought influenced or caused American pragmatism as much as how they became repositioned in the American context through specific mutations of the questions addressed by those modes of thought.[17]

To amplify, consider that nineteenth-century French, German, English, and Scottish thinkers alike were pondering questions such as the following: What is the relation of natural science to other ways of knowing? What is a "scientist?" What is it "to know?" How can we trust the process of coming to know something? In this book I neither answer these questions nor determine to what extent they caused analogous enterprises in America. Instead I address how questions like these resonated differently among the nineteenth-century

American intelligentsia and how those differences led to suppositions that eventually (by 1898 or 1905) were perceived to be American pragmatism.

I show that the differences reside within the ideologically Puritan Christian culture of late nineteenth-century New England, a culture and area of monumental importance in the formation of America's mythic or ideological identity. As the prologue will clarify, what I term the Puritan imaginary trickled through the Unitarian years of Jeffersonian republicanism and took on new life as the generation preceding Peirce and James responded to the upheavals of the Second Great Awakening.[18] As the phrase *Puritan imaginary* evokes, "Puritanism" is not, and never has been, one entity. Even within American Puritan communities of the seventeenth and eighteenth centuries the meaning of 'Puritan' was contested and shifting, and Puritan clergy continuously pointed to other times and other places for the material example of a 'true' Puritan community. Certainly by the late eighteenth and nineteenth centuries, *Puritan* encompassed a range of religious sentiments and values that undoubtedly would have been thought quite foreign by the likes of John Winthrop or Cotton Mather. From the first Puritan's step onto New England soil, Puritanism has been a concept fissuring from within. Nevertheless, the concept of Puritanism consistently has sustained mythic portraits of America as a uniquely religious country with a God-given mission and constituted by God-intoxicated persons. The understandings of the words *religious*, *God*, *mission*, and *person* shifted considerably between 1620 and 1890; but America's "Puritan" mythos spoke to and encompassed those shifts. I thus prefer to call this Puritan legacy a Puritan "imaginary," invoking the Lacanian sense of the imaginary as "that which is tied up with our self-*image*, with the image we have of who and what we are."[19]

Not just the purposiveness of pragmatism, therefore, but broader and murkier religious concerns, habits, and priorities guide the ways in which the science of Europe is read and assimilated by the pragmatists. As Peirce and James attempt to reconcile the growing dominance of empirical, scientific truth with the nonscientific, religious truths held by their fathers, they increasingly emphasize the embeddedness of human knowing in bodily action and social interaction, a scrutinizing attention to the consequences of our habits of knowing and being, and an insistence on the value of scientific inquiry for treating matters of the heart.[20] I will suggest that the nineteenth-century natural scientist becomes inserted into and altered by the American pragmatic terrain, that the construction is centrally Christian, and that it assisted the formation of a mythos of America under which we still exist. The primary threads of this story belong to the classical pragmatists themselves (Peirce and James), to Scottish philosophers and psychologists (Bain and Hamilton), and to German psychologists (Wundt and Helmholtz).

Methodology

What might be a pragmatic approach to the question of what is American about American pragmatism? My answer is first to analyze concepts that were important to the pragmatists and then to ask how those concepts acquired a different saliency as they were reappropriated in different intellectual contexts. "Religion" enters in the second phase of the investigation, in the manner in which shared intellectual concepts come to mean different things, to signify differently, in the different spaces.

In their reading of European philosophy, natural science, and psychology, Peirce and James acknowledge, appropriate, and employ concepts that were common to American, German, and Scottish intellectual spaces. Concepts such as consciousness, causality, will, and action were shared by classical philosophers, budding psychologists, and laboratory physicists alike. Naturally the sharing was not precise. As is always the case with the interpretation of signs, the concepts were plastic and in flux. Even so, it is possible to establish some boundary lines according to the ways the concepts were used in the different spaces and thereby to map, however sketchily, the spaces they inhabited. After producing such maps (in this case, of German psychology, Scottish philosophical psychology, and classical pragmatism), questions can be raised about the status of those boundary lines. What is at stake in anchoring, for example, consciousness in *this* way and causality in *that* way? What might enable will and action, for example, to be shaded in one direction in Germany and in quite another in America? Pursuing this type of question leads the investigation to the investments that work in textual production. That is, I shall determine what forces or predilections make consciousness and causality, or will and action, concepts of such importance. Initially, the investments will be elaborated in terms of other concepts. In American pragmatism, the stakes circle around purpose and its cosmic or divine extensions, as well as around issues of personal ethics, especially the roles of habit and self-discipline in character formation. At this point, I ask, what other prevalent intellectual spaces (or discourses) encompassed these concerns? In America, those spaces were named "religious" and had an imaginary (ideological) connection to the narratives of mission and American uniqueness that were attached to the notion and legacy of "Puritanism."

The American nature of pragmatism, then, is its connection with these narratives, its insistence that the task before Americans is cosmically oriented and personally exacting, and its equal insistence that America clearly position itself in communication with but as different from its European past. American pragmatism is one of many articulations of the story of American identity and mission. It is an articulation that arose out of the privileged upper middle class of Brahmin Boston and that, through William James, spoke convincingly to the growing middle class of intellectuals and professionals from New England to California. Because its proponents occupied the class that wrote books, filled public offices, and taught the next generation, the story about America told by American pragmatism was broadcast widely and deeply.[21] Even today, the media regularly tell consumers that we are a "pragmatic" nation. Although all philosophical subtlety has been removed from this assessment, this notion of pragmatism conjoins classical pragmatism's foci on purpose, action, effects, and personal accountability. Also, in less acknowledged ways, it connects to a mutated but still echoing Puritanism, something that today has devolved into the presumed Christian religiosity of America (as well as the presumption that "religion" means "Christianity"). The Puritan element of American mythology persists as a part of the American identity that is inevitably encountered and negotiated, a reality frustrating for the segments of America that consciously reject Christian hegemony.

My method proposes a three-part investigation that begins with a philosophical analysis of a few concepts (consciousness, causality, will, and belief) and, in the end, ties the operation of these concepts to discourses that help illuminate the way the religious force of the Puritan imaginary constructs the culture of America pragmatism. The first task of the book is to examine how the concepts of consciousness, causality, will, and belief signify differently in German psychology and Scottish psychology (chapters 1–4). In analyzing the historical and cultural differences of signification between these shared concepts, the first four chapters also encapsulate the professionalization of psychology during the second half of the nineteenth century and highlight the questions of human knowing and being that enable and strengthen that professionalization. During this time, epistemology becomes self-reflexive (how do we know that we know? how do we know ourselves?), a crucial turn for the development of pragmatism. The second task of the book relies on this initial investigation in order to demonstrate certain American transformations within networks of concepts. The primary focus here is how the pragmatists transformed the European intellectual maps in the American context, thus producing the map of American pragmatism (chapters 5–6). These chapters focus especially on how notions of habit and purposiveness affect the pragmatic transformation of the fluid concepts listed above. At stake here is *ascesis*, Foucault's term for the movement between issues of subjectivity and issues of ethics. The third task of the book is explicitly pragmatic. Drawing from the analysis of transformations of non-American concepts, I examine the changes wrought on the American plane and question how those changes enabled production of America's "only indigenous philosophy."

In Jamesian terms, this book will explore what difference the American difference makes to the understanding of the natural sciences, especially as the latter reflect on human being and the human capacity for thought, and will argue that the Puritan imaginary is that difference. In effect, the book develops an extended pragmatic reading by asking both what interests or concerns enable the priority of these concepts in the works of thinkers (who themselves stand as cultural types) and to what ends and effects the concepts are put. The unfolding process provides the necessary context (what Peirce calls the "ground of inquiry") through which to understand the importance of the concepts and the assumptions that steer their use.

Prologue

The "Puritan": Mirror of America's Self-Understanding

As early as the 1640s, scholars of Christianity pleaded for the eradication of the term *Puritan*.[1] The word was thought to be too general and employed too variously and too contradictorily to be useful for description or interpretation. The passing centuries have only reinforced this conviction, as evinced by the harsh and steadfast criticism of historians and scholars of religion, with recent decades being no exception. Raphael Samuel, for example, calls the word "unstable," noting that "Puritan" can refer to anything from the president's "covenant" with the people to the fashions of Laura Ashley and even, oddly, Islamic fundamentalism.[2] More radically, Margo Todd calls Puritans "mythical creatures of modern academics."[3] And moving from critique to new constructions, Darren Staloff suggests abandoning the term for the new phrase "'precise' Protestantism,"[4] while Peter Lake acknowledges Puritanism as "a distinctively zealous or intense" Protestantism that exhibits a certain aesthetic ("synthesis or style").[5]

Despite criticism of the term, there is continued scholarly interest in the notions of "Puritans" and "Puritanism." A crucial consideration here is the very ambiguity of these notions. The looseness of the concept of Puritan(ism) ensures that its meanings extend beyond their initial semantic anchorage in the "Puritan" narratives. As a result, the changing meanings of Puritan and Puritanism have everything to do with changing understandings of being religious, being American, and being morally and/or politically effective. I argue this by identifying some of the ideological issues central to debates about Puritan(ism), especially as that term is used in the nineteenth century. As indicated in the introduction, I trace the American character of American pragmatism to the nineteenth-century persistence of a Puritan imaginary, an ideological formation that negotiates meanings of self and nation and that enables the American pragmatists to appropriate and revise for their own purposes a number of important scientific concepts with a provenance in nineteenth-century European thought.

In his *Imagined Communities*, Benedict Anderson famously defines a nation as "an imagined political community—and imagined as both inherently limited and sovereign."[6] By "imagined," Anderson means the simple fact that "the members of even the smallest nation will never know most of their fellow-members, yet in the minds of each lives the image of their communion."[7] Beyond this basic mental projection of the whole from the part, Anderson does not theorize *imagination*. Lacan, on the other hand, discusses the imaginary as one facet of a tripartite, structuralist theory of the human psyche.[8] The details of his theory are complex; suffice it to say that, for Lacan, the imaginary develops through the "mirror stage." which can be thought of literally as the time an infant first recognizes (and, at the same time, misrecognizes) itself in its mirrored reflection, or figuratively as the ontological moments of self-constitution through and by the images of the nonself. The ego, or understandings of the self, can form only by conjoining three moments: a moment of recognition (which is also a misrecognition), a moment of displacement, and a moment of mediation.[9] The moment of recognition occurs when a baby grasps that the image in the mirror is indeed an image of itself. Analogously, the moment of recognition occurs when a person identifies with a nation's flag. For both examples, the recognition is always also a misrecognition. The image in the mirror is not actually the baby, and the flag is not actually the person. (Mis)recognition thus entails a displacement that is necessary for understandings of the self to congeal: the baby comes to a sense of itself only through the displacement of the self in the mirror image, and citizens come to a sense of themselves only through displacing their particularities for the unifying character of the flag. Importantly, Lacan theorizes that (mis)recognition and displacement also require mediation. The baby always has someone (usually the mother) holding it up and naming the image and event ("See that baby? That's *you*! Do you see [Annie] [Billy]?"). Adults have various and multiple mediations for the objects with which they identify. Consider the numerous places and events that include a nation's flag and the stories and songs about it. All of these are mediations that enable citizens to claim the flag as who they are ("I am American," or, as my four-year-old says whenever she sees red, white, and blue together: "That's America right there; those people are America"). By Puritan imaginary, therefore, I wish to evoke the changing connotations of the term Puritan and how they make visible the various mechanisms of recognition, misrecognition, displacement, and mediation whereby nineteenth-century citizens understood themselves to be American.

In order to establish the cultural force of the Puritan imaginary, this chapter will examine the context and means by which the American pragmatists took hold of and reinvented certain European scientific concepts. By examining the appeals to Puritanism from the Second Great Awakening to the Civil War and from Reconstruction to the Gilded Age, I will show how at different times and on behalf of particular causes different stories about the history and destiny of America were inflected in selective and specialized ways by this or that understanding of Puritan and Puritanism.

Constructions of Revivalism, Principles of Moral Action

My account draws on Joseph A. Conforti, *Jonathan Edwards, Religious Tradition, and American Culture*,[10] and Jan Dawson, *The Unusable Past: America's Puritan Tradition, 1830–1930*.[11] Conforti makes the theoretical assumption that traditions are constructed and that they speak to and about larger cultural ideologies. He attempts to demonstrate the ways in which the writings of Jonathan Edwards were selectively appropriated for the construction of American narratives about Puritanism, revivalism, and exemplary individualism. Dawson, on the other hand, resists the notion that Puritanism and the Puritan tradition are mere intellectual or cultural constructs, and she presumes that these "authentic historical phenomena" are accessible to anyone willing to read about them.[12] Dawson, though not sharing Conforti's theoretical perspective, nevertheless does accept the fact that the concept of Puritanism continually shifts in meaning and application throughout the nineteenth century. Taken together, Dawson and Conforti demonstrate that both traditional and postmodern scholarship agree on two points, namely, that the term *Puritan* was significant in the nineteenth century and that it referred not just to seventeenth-century immigrants but also to the fluid contours of America's imagined community.[13]

Dawson and Conforti begin by reflecting on the early nineteenth-century debates between New England Calvinists and Unitarians. These cultural debates arose from more narrowly theological tensions between the so-called New Divinity professors of Andover Theological Seminary—intellectuals who prided themselves on continuing the traditions of Jonathan Edwards—and the less consistently Edwardsian thinkers of Yale and Harvard. The tensions grew into a battle over which group of theologians could claim to be the true and proper heirs of Puritanism. The spark that ignited the battle was the 1805 appointment of a Unitarian, Henry Ware, to the traditionally Calvinist chair in theology at Harvard. In response to this perceived usurpation, the Calvinist New Divinity men quickly deemed it imperative to reiterate Jonathan Edwards's condemnation of Arminianism.[14] The Unitarians, their culture's "Arminians," responded to this Calvinist provocation by portraying Edwards's life as a failed response to the attractions of a culturally dominant deism. The stories were initially told in theological terms, but they rapidly evolved into morality tales of the region's religious history and, depending on the storyteller, New England's loyalty or disloyalty to that history. Where the Calvinists claimed Puritan authority by taking Edwards's side against Arminianism, the Unitarians argued that *they* were the rightful heirs of Puritan theocracy by virtue of their current "ecclesiastical, civil, and cultural leadership."[15] According to both Dawson and Conforti, these debates inspired and fueled the so-called Second Great Awakening, though Conforti draws a more daring conclusion from them. "The [first] 'Great Awakening,'" he writes, "needs to be recognized as the deus ex machina that it is: a nineteenth-century cultural artifact invented by second Great Awakeners, who created an Edwardsian revivalistic tradition to resolve contemporary religious conflicts."[16] By Conforti's account, the nineteenth-century legacy of Puritanism cannot be divorced from its encompassing, ramified ideological field.

Dawson does not seek or find such ideological features in the history of Puritanism, but she does argue that the second "Awakeners" provide historical evidence of Puritanism's continuing influence. Colonial Puritanism mostly died out in the eighteenth century, she maintains, but "its original elements did not necessarily lose their ability to guide and mold American civilization." Not speculating on what these "original elements" might be, Dawson observes that nineteenth-century debates presumed a unified Puritanism and not simply a "fragmented" Puritan legacy.[17] Put simply, for Dawson, it is evident from the texts themselves that Puritanism functioned as a unified tradition for those who wrote about it. Conforti, in contrast, regards the Puritan writings as constructions of the past for particular, current debates. He points to the printed pamphlets, journals, and novellas that formed the material battleground of these debates and concludes that each side had a rhetorically pertinent and powerful motivation to present a unified Puritan tradition and then to demonstrate that the other side was obviously failing to live up to it.

Conforti contextualizes this print war by pointing out that the publication of Puritan and Edwardsian tracts had nearly disappeared in this country during the latter half of the eighteenth century.[18] The early nineteenth-century debates, the bicentennial of the Plymouth Rock landing in 1820, and finally the revivals and theological furor of the Second Great Awakening each occasioned a sort of resurgence of appeals to Puritanism and witnessed a flurry of publications by and about those early Americans. To underscore the crucial role played by these print wars in constructing a tradition about Jonathan Edwards and revivalism, Conforti quotes Yale president Ezra Stiles's 1787 prediction that within one more generation, Edwards's writings would "pass into as transient notice perhaps scarce above oblivion."[19] Conforti suggests that without the historically contingent, early nineteenth-century need for those writings, Stiles's prediction would likely have come true. As it is, we can hardly consider American religious history without mentioning Edwards's life, writings, and influence. His stature, Conforti argues, arises not from his own life and times but from the use made by a later generation of his reputation and his theology. The meaning of Puritanism and the semiotic resonance of "Jonathan Edwards" within that wider and more encompassing use thus feature in cultural debates that supersede theology and religious history. These terms enable in significant ways the imagined community of America and function as the enabling matrix, or imaginary, for the constitution of the notions of religion, nation, and history.

Like Conforti, Dawson notes the dependence of the early nineteenth-century debates on an earlier body of printed material. What interests her, however, is not how the print wars materially constituted the legacy of Jonathan Edwards and Puritanism but rather how the writings especially stress the moral character of Puritanism and how this particular quality attracted the notice of literary and philosophical Romantics. To Dawson, the Romantic encounter with Puritanism revalued the "traditional Puritan tension between individual free will and providential fate" through a vital interest in "individualism, perfectability [sic], and progress."[20] Indeed, Dawson claims that the Romantic "brooding" about providence is "the true legacy of Puritanism to antebellum American culture."[21] In the end, Dawson places more weight on the Romantics' ethical revaluation of Puritanism than on the northeastern debates between Calvinists and Unitarians by framing this ethical emphasis as a crisis of national identity. For Dawson, the regional squabbles over Edwards's legacy carried less weight in perpetuating the Puritan tradition than the failure of the French Revolution, an ideological failure that pointedly begged the question of how and why the American Revolution had succeeded. According to Dawson, pre–Civil War America commonly presumed that the success of the Revolution lay in what she calls John Winthrop's "liberty to do good,"[22] or what might be called the moral force of Puritanism. No less than Conforti, though perhaps against her stated intentions, Dawson's research indicates how the use of the term Puritanism had far less to do with "authentic" historical or theological phenomena than with the struggles of Americans to understand who and what they are.

Dawson paints a picture of the years leading up to the Civil War as a time in which the "liberals" (Unitarians) and "conservatives" (Calvinists) relinquished their dependence on the *theological* force of Puritanism (a notion of God's providence) and clung instead to a Puritan *disposition* that highlighted social and personal morality. The liberals battled slavery, the conservatives crusaded against drinking, and the revival fires of the 1820s and 1830s spread across the Northeast and the southern bible belt. All were united under the imaginary Puritan banner of moral perfection. Dawson argues further that these two poles of Christian citizenry came together in the 1840s by both emphasizing God as the end of all moral action. Then, by the 1850s, the meaning of *Puritan* shifted again. The traditionally Unitarian social activists and the traditionally Calvinist crusaders for private morality formed another alliance by agreeing that their Puritan ancestors sought to erect not a democratic republic but a Christian commonwealth.[23] These reformers applied their desire for a Christian commonwealth to the social and political struggles leading up to the Civil War, arguing that only a return to the historical and theological project of their Puritan ancestors could redeem the country from its contemporary woes. Dawson summarizes: "The use of political power to achieve moral ends, when these ends are dictated by a higher law that is not only ethical but also historical, is what an American commentator would most likely have meant by the adjective 'Puritan' and the noun 'Puritanism' at mid-century."[24] This meaning is somewhat removed from its seventeenth-century semiotic antecedents.

Conforti's and Dawson's accounts demonstrate in different ways the gradual mutation of the term *Puritanism* in antebellum America. Early in the century, it functioned as a nexus of theological concepts that articulated a region's history, memory, and self-image. Later, it became a nexus of historical and moral concepts that justified specific forms of revivalism and social action. Finally, by midcentury, it served as a mosaic of theological, historical, and ethical forces that coalesced into the ideology of America as a Christian nation with a Christian mission.[25] Dawson devotes two full chapters to examining the function of Puritanism as upholding particular nationalistic images, though she would not describe her task in quite those terms. To Dawson, it simply is the case that the rhetoric of Puritanism is "deeply entrenched" in American consciousness,[26] so that learning and analyzing that rhetoric is the necessary first step of any sustained cultural critique. Her discussions of midwestern Catholics and Copperheads and her engagements with the southern Romantic traditions (non-Calvinist and non-Unitarian) both revolve around this necessary negotiation of America's Puritan past. To me, however, Dawson does not underscore enough how these debates centered on the very notion of who and what was (fully, purely, truly) American. In the nineteenth century, a particular understanding of American identity could be guaranteed or justified by making a selective appeal to the history and example of Puritanism.

The Puritan imaginary is elaborated more fully by Conforti's narrative of the changing shape of "Puritan tradition" in the context of events of national and historic moment. For instance, he stresses that Andover Seminary became the focal point for Edwardsian theology not because of any straight and ostensibly true lineage of theologians faithful to the seventeenth-century minister, but because that institution responded astutely to the groundswell of popular interest in revivalism. Seminary officials worked earnestly to stimulate and manipulate popular interest with a view to securing their own power and authority,[27] in the hope that they would be considered the more authentic storytellers about Puritanism and about America. More broadly, Conforti connects the persistent interest in revivalism (and Edwards's legacy within that interest) to the general solidification of seminary training and the institutionalization of the training of pastors.[28] In a profoundly ironic move, Conforti notes, professional theological institutions legitimized themselves through the legacy of Edwards, despite the fact that Edwards himself valued a non-institutional, apprenticeship model of learning the pastorate and, moreover, was exiled from the prosperous congregations of eastern Connecticut to an isolated Native American reservation. Conforti explains the irony as an attempt by the developing Presbyterian and Congregational professional ministry to rein in and domesticate the democratic and lay-oriented effects of America's revivalistic tendencies. Edwards's Puritan credentials were used to specify in a delimiting way who could be a minister and where and how he (and, rarely, she) would be permitted to operate, questions that intensify as the social and cultural role of the church becomes acutely circumscribed over the course of the century.

In attempting to demonstrate the continuing potency of the rhetoric of the Puritan in the Gilded Age, Conforti parallels the importance of the 1840 centennial of the First Great Awakening[29] with the 250th anniversary of Plymouth Colony in 1870,[30] cultural and historical events that, like the early Calvinist/ Unitarian debates, occasioned a frenetic outpouring of writings and speeches. Indeed, in opposition to what Dawson titles America's "unusable past," Conforti asserts that as the century aged "the Puritan past became usable precisely because it was now distant [in the 1870s and 1880s]." He points to the Gilded Age's wave of Puritan scholarship, monument building, and ritualizing of anniversaries of the Puritan past, all of which "provided occasions for lay and religious elites to perorate on America's glorious Anglo-Puritan past and to invoke religious tradition against such Victorian era symptoms of moral degeneration as political machines, labor strife, saloons, and consumerism."[31] In the late nineteenth century, the place and meaning of *Puritan* were evoked in order to determine what America means, here in elitist terms that carry on the Romantic exhortation to moral purity, especially as that call is refracted through a critique of America's unstoppable capitalist economy. In this conceptual economy, Puritanism became the imaginary space through which American pragmatism was constructed.

Puritanism in the Gilded Age

After the Civil War, Puritanism became employed less as a political category and more as a religious category of social critique. The concept's rhetorical capacity to galvanize antebellum social and political movements was considered too threatening and divisive in the years of Reconstruction and thus, according to Dawson, the term's meaning began to acquire more personal connotations.[32] The shift resonated with antebellum Calvinists—Christian social conservatives who stressed personal reformation—but was now inflected less with the discourses of justice and morality than with those of psychology (consciousness and will) and phrenology (character).[33] For example, one of the prominent social debates of the early 1880s (hauntingly being replayed today) centered on public education and its perceived inability to inculcate proper values in children. Advocates for teaching values in public schools pointed directly to the Puritans as paradigmatic pedagogues who refused to separate the value of education from the values being taught. From the opposite side of the political pendulum, Dawson notes that early Social Gospelers drew upon Puritan names, images, and words in promulgating their particular theocratic vision. The Social gospel movement, rather than using theology to strengthen the state and tame its citizens, subordinated the state to theology and depicted citizenship in terms of a narrative of personal sin and redemption.[34] In addition, mainline liberal Christians used the rhetoric of Puritanism to construct a moral vision of the self that was principally characterized by sobriety and trustworthiness. According to Dawson's account, in short, the 1880s demonstrated a delinking of Puritan "ideals" from the "traditional theological core of Puritanism."[35]

Overall, Dawson's history is committed to a vertical tale of glory and decline: the glorious Puritan days of the seventeenth century yielded to a steady, slow decline of the "use" of Puritanism. Conforti's narrative, on the other hand, is much more multifarious. He argues that interest in Puritans and Puritanism occurs in waves and spurts throughout the nineteenth century, the Puritan imaginary becoming, if anything, *more* usable during the Gilded Age, not because of a steady increase in Puritanism but, somewhat paradoxically, because its very doctrinal or institutional rarity made it more ideologically potent. I agree with Conforti. The delinking of Puritan ideals from theology (or rhetoric from realism) has no beginning but is intrinsic to the very notion and use of the terms *Puritan* and *Puritanism* and constitutes the power and persistence of the Puritan imaginary.

Dawson's and Conforti's accounts of the 1890s overlap considerably. Both maintain that appeals to Puritanism were divorced almost completely from collective political interventions and increasingly involved proposals to improve personal character. A Puritan character in the 1890s implied a "tough-minded" person who acted with propriety and integrity.[36] Both authors evoke an image for this era of a new social discipline being constituted from the ground up, from the individual to the collective. In other words, appeals were made to Puritanism not to encourage a theocratic collective politics but rather to motivate personal, individual conversions, in the hope that individuals of strenuous character would choose to undergo private reform for the (eventual, but always deferred) sake of the public good. Dawson's reference to such a tough-minded character appears in her rendition of the 1897 Plymouth Church tribute to Henry Ward Beecher, in which he was called "a Puritan of the Puritans." Dawson notes that the media response to this phrase was thoroughly critical: some reporters continued to link Puritanism with divisive political movements, and others argued that Beecher was too secular a character to hold that honorific. To Dawson, both critics missed the point of "The New Puritanism" (as Lyman Abbott's keynote speech for the ceremony was titled). "Puritanism" fit Beecher not because of his theological or political commitments but because of his personal character, his principled stance for self-discipline, which included a strong critique of the Gilded Age's crass materialism.

Conforti also refers to the tough-minded character of the New Puritan, and although his argument points in a decidedly more academic direction, it does suggest a direct connection between the pragmatists and the cultural use of the term Puritanism. John Fiske was a Harvard historian who regularly attended the Cambridge Metaphysical Club, which, by Peirce's account, functioned as the seedbed for pragmatism. According to Conforti, one of Fiske's students, Brooks Adams, composed a book, *The Emancipation of Massachusetts* (1886), which Fiske critiqued "for failing 'to define the elements of wholesome strength' in the Massachusetts theocracy." As Fiske's subsequent book, *The Beginnings of New England* (1889) explains, the Puritan was, in Conforti's paraphrase, "in every fiber a practical Englishman with a full share of common sense." Fiske exhorted Americans to remember this religious image, to "reaffirm the 'Puritan's ethical conception of society.'"[37] To me, Fiske's critique of Adams encapsulates the Puritan imaginary of the Gilded Age and hence of the cultural space that bred American pragmatism: the Puritan was above all an individual of strenuous and practical character who envisioned society as an ethical commonwealth and who sought to incarnate that vision through his or her own personal conduct. Here again we can see the Puritan imaginary as that through which concepts of self (strenuous and practical), society (ethical commonwealth), and ethics (personal character refined through conduct) were filtered and negotiated.

I have given only a brief conspectus of nineteenth-century culture; it serves primarily to elaborate the dual claim that (1) the term *Puritan* was prevalent and potent in the nineteenth century, and (2) that it diverged considerably from its seventeenth-century semantic antecedents. It is necessary to say, albeit briefly, how this cultural sketch correlates to Peirce and James, viewed here less as individuals with unique biographies than as persons symbolic of positions within a cultural field.

The class elitism of pragmatism's founding thinkers (raised in the introduction) supports Dawson's account of the Romantic revaluation of Puritanism, for though the revival fires of the Second Great Awakening affected a wide spectrum of people, the Romantic reinterpretation of Puritanism was generated for and by an educated, reading elite. Henry James, Sr., passed to his son William his romantic impulses, his love of philosophy, and his insistent vision that science and religion may be reconciled, despite their growing separation in the nineteenth century. I understand this putative reconciliation as part of America's Puritan imaginary, which views both faith and knowledge as unifying gifts from God, along with the ethical mandates to act well and to believe in the face of a disbelieving world. The latter are familiar themes in William James's writings and I hope they now can be interpreted within the cultural framework of the post–Civil War reworking of the concept of Puritanism to model an inwardly directed, moral person exemplifying discipline, fortitude, and integrity. To the degree that these traits connote a "strenuous" personality, Benjamin Peirce, too, passed on to his son Charles what can be viewed as 'Puritan' commitments to community, discipline, and truth. For C. S. Peirce, however, discipline yields not an individual self but the ability to lose the self for the sake of the community and its truth.

These legacies from father to pragmatist son can be read as Puritan by analyzing understandings of self, science, and religion and by comparing them to nineteenth-century social and political debates about industrialization, consumerism, secularization, and disintegrating morality. I will argue for the Puritan roots of American pragmatism by suggesting that there is a conceptual overlap among philosophical concepts, cultural debates, and the cultural deployments of Puritanism, a set of connections this chapter has attempted to clarify. It remains for me to establish the thesis that the American character of American pragmatism lies in America's Puritan imaginary.

Conclusions

One extraordinarily common account of Puritanism posits a marked and steady falling away from the faith of the seventeenth-century "fathers." Mark A. Peterson has analyzed this account, known as the declension narrative, in his book *The Price of Redemption*. Peterson notes that no matter what criticisms, counterevidence, or alternative perspectives are used to challenge the declension narrative, it is still the case that "the ship won't sink."[38] According to Peterson, the dogged persistence of the declension narrative is due to three specific myths, which reflect and refract particular stories of America: the myth of the first settlers (a myth of origin: where did we come from?), the myth of the exemplary life (a myth of ethics: who are we [supposed to be]?), and the myth of community (a myth of politics: what are our goals?). Though Peterson comments on Puritan scholarship and not the semiotics of its key term, the parallel to my argument is fitting. I have sought in this chapter to demonstrate how the persistence of the concept of Puritanism resides in the ability of the term to link, rhetorically and ideologically, conceptions about America's past, present, and future and to distill and deploy questions of identity, ethics, and politics succinctly and efficaciously.

The next two chapters will deal with the texts of two German thinkers who were widely read by Peirce and James. They will clarify the connections and differences that obtain between America and Europe and specify the connections between science and philosophy in ways that intersect with these Puritan questions of identity, ethics, and politics. The work of Hermann von Helmholtz evinces an understanding of science and natural law that was only partially accepted by the pragmatists, their criticism pivoting on a refusal to understand scientific inquiry as being constitutively devoid of purposiveness (final causality). The work of Wilhelm Wundt is the outcome of the professionalization of psychology, a process that challenged the radical individualism and commitment to liberal democracy that was inherent in the pragmatists' American cultural and political lineages and backgrounds. I will focus on particular concepts employed by both pragmatism and its continental interlocutors before going on to consider how the Americans transformed them. Of particular importance will be the concepts of causality (Helmholtz) and will and consciousness (Wundt).

I

EVOLUTION OF
GERMAN PSYCHOLOGY

Hermann von Helmholtz

"Have Trust and Act!": A Real Physics of Sign Theory

To delineate the development of German psychology in the nineteenth century, I have chosen thinkers whose work exemplifies larger cultural debates about the status of psychology (is it a philosophy or a science?), the relation of psychology to other sciences, and the possibilities of scientifically studying "the human."[1] The social and intellectual prominence of Hermann von Helmholtz aptly fulfills this requirement. The physicist's life work functions superbly as shorthand for the changes in nineteenth-century German natural science, especially as his life and career demonstrate the growing dominance of physiology and other sciences tuned to the human subject. My treatment of Helmholtz draws out only those filaments of his works that were appropriated and transformed by Peirce and James, that is, I wish only to show how particular concepts or themes (for example, causality, signification, and law) function in Helmholtz's texts according to general and sometimes vaguely articulated questions about scientific inquiry and human being. Ultimately, it is the transmutation of those questions on American soil that guides my work.[2]

The life of Hermann Ludwig von Helmholtz spans the nineteenth century (1821–1894) and stands as an example of the social and intellectual changes wrought by the increasing professionalization of the natural sciences. Although he was most famous for his invention of the ophthalmoscope and his formulation of the law of the conservation of energy (*die Erhaltung der Kraft*), Helmholtz's scientific investigations and popular lectures covered an immense intellectual territory and established him as *the* representative of German science.[3] Helmholtz had been interested in physics and mathematics from an early age, but in the 1830s physics and physiology were just beginning to separate into university disciplines that could promise economically viable jobs, so his father urged him to choose a more practical career.

Helmholtz conceded to attend a military medical institution, whose terms of admission required him to serve eight years in the Prussian army as a medical officer. Despite this extended tour of duty, Helmholtz managed to publish a number of papers in the field of physics. The fame he garnered through these papers—especially the excitement and critique surrounding his 1847 essay on the conservation of energy—won him an early discharge. Through this fame and the patronage of his mentor, Johannes Müller, Helmholtz gained entrance to Germany's university system, first as an instructor and assistant at small institutes in Berlin and then, in 1849, as an associate professor of physiology at the University of Königsberg. From there, his scientific skill, popular charm, and administrative aplomb served as keys to a series of academic posts, including positions at the University of Bonn, the University of Heidelberg, and, finally, the University of Berlin. His successful career and scientific contributions have led a recent commentator to claim that to study Helmholtz is to embrace "one of the most important visions of nineteenth-century science," both with regard to results and theories and with respect to the very nature of the concept of science and its relations to society.[4]

It is important to establish that Helmholtz's work was available to and influential on American thinkers. As spokesman for the success and potential social benefits of science and as the premier physiological theorist of his time, Helmholtz's reach extended far beyond his native country. France, Great Britain, and the United States all honored him with various titles and awards.[5] His popular lectures (including that on the conservation of energy) first appeared in English in 1873; further essays were published and translated through the 1880s and 1890s. His American admirers gathered these essays into a two-volume collection published the year after his death (1895); it continued to be reissued at least through 1908.[6] Convenient for my argument, the years 1873–1908 frame the time of the most active writing and thinking for both Peirce and James. If the origin of classical pragmatism can be set in the informal philosophical colloquium that Peirce and James attended in Cambridge, and if its end can be set with Peirce's death in 1914, then the period in which Helmholtz's fame was at its height was also the period in which the pragmatists solidified their distinctive philosophical and psychological positions.[7] Indeed, Peirce and James both cite Helmholtz. References to the German scientist appear in most of Peirce's *Collected Papers* and throughout James's *Principles of Psychology*.[8] Predictably, the two Americans appropriate Helmholtz quite differently. Peirce categorizes him strictly as a physicist and physiologist, while James labels him a psychologist, even when the pragmatist culls quotations from the *Handbuch der physiologischen Optik* and *Die Lehre von den Tonempfindungen als physiologisch Grundlage für die Theorie der Musik*, which are texts structurally oriented to the physiology of sensation. James's psychological interpretations of Helmholtz run counter to the German's own 1891 "Autobiographical Sketch," which never mentions the term *psychology*.[9]

Indeed, the ambiguous intellectual position of psychology underscores the importance of Helmholtz for my argument. Through the efforts of men like Helmholtz the discipline of psychology begins to separate from those of physiology and philosophy. Thus the gradual movement within psychology from the figural dominance of Helmholtz to that of Wundt (discussed in the next chapter) marks the change in cultural value from philosophical to experimental psychology. Even though today Helmholtz is regarded primarily as a physicist, his appropriation by the pragmatists shows his philosophical formation and his concern for issues that later scientists would investigate under the disciplinary rubric of psychology.[10]

Two themes of Helmholtz's writings convey his proximity to psychology and make up the central focus of this chapter. Both themes explore the status of "the human" and especially the status of human knowing. First, I analyze Helmholtz's theory of causation and his conviction that this theory reconciles German transcendentalism and British empiricism. Second, I demonstrate how what I call Helmholtz's physical sign theory (*Zeichentheorie*) places his reflections on causality in a semiotic frame. Throughout my discussions of Helmholtz, the goal remains to understand the American character of pragmatism. I suggest that different understandings of causality form the crucial difference between European and American pragmatic understandings of science. Reminiscent of the use of the term *Puritanism* in the Gilded Age to evoke a strict personal ethics that inflects all action with purpose, the pragmatists stress purposiveness as inherently human and as a crucial facet of the science of studying human thought and being. Helmholtz, however, like the majority of European natural scientists, elides purpose from his scientific inquiries and presumes only the efficient causality advocated by a Baconian scientific method. The assumption of causal efficacy structures his philosophic and semiotic commitments. The pragmatists share this commitment but express it differently as a result of their allegiance to purpose or final causality. Despite this basic disagreement about the condition and ramifications of causality, both Helmholtz and the pragmatists use the concept of *causality* to explore how the relation between the human mind and nonhuman world can be asserted without skepticism and without naive dogmatism.

I contend that it is useful and informative to demonstrate a theoretical resonance between Helmholtz and Peirce. The contention has a number of theoretical obstacles, however, for although Peirce does share theoretical proclivities with Helmholtz, he also maintains a sharp distance from his German interlocutor. It would be more expected to argue a resonance between Helmholtz and James since James embraces Helmholtz as an authoritative colleague. James relies on the German physicist's experiments and conclusions, and he recognizes their differences as ones within a common psychological enterprise. Moreover, both James and Helmholtz attained wide popularity in their lifetimes and have become mythic figures in intellectual history. Nonetheless, I find it more noteworthy to clarify the links between Helmholtz and Peirce as men who theorize across many discourses and who attempt to construct syntheses or generalizations among them. Moreover, both men meditate extensively not only on the changing meaning of *science* but also on the communal character of a "good" scientist and the transcommunal duties that science can perform in society and in history. Finally, Helmholtz and Peirce both advocate non-practical theoretical endeavors and a realist semiotics that attempts to constellate and reconcile Kantian idealism with British empiricism. Peirce consistently scorns Helmholtz as a "nominalist" proponent of mechanistic philosophy, however, and his "semeiotic" (Peirce's spelling, which I retain to distinguish his system from Saussure's semiotic) differs strongly from Helmholtz's sign theory (*Zeichentheorie*).

In Germany, Helmholtz's efforts to reconcile Kantian and empiricist philosophical legacies form part of the philosophical movement of *Idealrealismus*, through which German intellectuals attempt to harmonize their philosophical legacy (Kantian idealism) with the current scientific and technological exigencies of empirical research (realism). Since Helmholtz worked primarily as a physicist, an interest in the continued success of the empirical method affects his return to and rethinking of Kant. Indeed, Peirce names Helmholtz the one "who has done more than any other man to bring the empiricist theory into favor."[11] Helmholtz's reinterpretation of Kant produces a sign theory (*Zeichentheorie*) that presents a physiological interpretation of the theory of perception laid out in Kant's *Critique of Pure Reason*. What Kant attributes to the synthesizing powers of the faculties of imagination, understanding, and reason, Helmholtz explains through nerve impulses and sense organs. By this reinterpretation, Helmholtz uses a theory of signs to reconcile idealism and realism, a task Peirce also undertakes through his unique semeiotic.[12]

The latter is Peirce's primary claim to philosophic fame; more generally, pragmatism can be viewed as negotiating how meaning is represented and conveyed through signs.[13] As chapter 5 will demonstrate, Peirce's semeiotic does not simply construct theories about human consciousness, but provides an account of how consciousness becomes human. Since it presents the universe as composed of signs the way a poem is composed of words, Peirce's semeiotic asserts that meaning is everywhere. Meaning remains virtual, however; it remains vague and useless until narrowed and focused by an act of interpretation (a human or other "interpretant") according to particular purposes. Peirce directs this purpose-laden semeiotic toward the goal of reconciling idealism and realism through heated arguments against what he termed "nominalism" and through a "scholastic" or "evolutionary" realism that insists on the "reality" of possibles.[14] Peirce's rejection of nominalism results in his conviction that the philosophical and scientific position of skepticism requires a prior assumption of the possibility of certainty. By denying this possibility, Peirce critiques the sufficiency of efficient causation and bolsters his claim for the personal and cosmic scope of purposiveness.

The (Ir)reversibility of Energy

Helmholtz guaranteed his fame, and the pragmatists' knowledge of his work, through his 1847 formulation of the law of the conservation of energy in an essay by the same title (*"Über die Erhaltung der Kraft"*). The introduction to the essay sets forth the respective tasks of the physical and theoretical sciences:

The task of the physical sciences is to discover laws so that individual natural processes can be traced back to, and deduced from, general principles. These principles, such as the laws of refraction and reflection of light . . . are obviously nothing but generic concepts through which the phenomena falling under them are collectively understood. The search for such laws is the task of the experimental part of our sciences. *The theoretical part, on the other hand, seeks to ascertain* from their visible effects *the unknown causes of natural processes*; it seeks to comprehend them according to the law of causality.[15]

In this passage the physicist immediately belies his debt to Kant by subsuming the practice of science under its theory. The physical sciences concentrate on the practical task of articulating heuristic principles by which to organize the results of observation and experimentation, while the theoretical sciences push to discover the truth about nature that supports those heuristic principles. That truth, according to Helmholtz, is necessarily articulated in terms of causality. For instance, the "laws of refraction and reflection of light" correctly predict the behavior of light *because* that behavior relies essentially on "unknown causes of natural processes." Helmholtz continues to delineate the tasks of theoretical science in the next paragraph:

Thus the final goal of the theoretical natural sciences is to discover *the ultimate invariable causes of natural phenomena*. Whether all processes may actually be traced back to such causes, in which case nature is completely comprehensible, or whether on the contrary there are changes which lie outside the law of necessary causality and thus fall within the region of spontaneity or freedom, will not be considered here. In any case it is clear that science, the goal of which is the comprehension of nature, must begin with the presupposition of its comprehensibility and proceed in accordance with this assumption until, perhaps, it is forced by irrefutable facts to recognize limits beyond which it may not go.[16]

Causality, as both necessary and invariable, provides the "comprehension of nature" that defines science's ultimate (and theoretical) goal. Such an overarching role of causality, however, neither mandates a determinism (what Peirce will call "necessaritarianism") nor denies it. Whether or not causal explanations encompass all that can be said about nature, they certainly stand as the teloi of all putatively scientific inquiries inasmuch as the theoretical sciences form the telos of the practical sciences. Helmholtz thus views the universal law of causality as the condition of possibility for the law of the conservation of energy; the former is the theoretical and causal explanation for the latter. The task for practicing scientists is to expound how the various forces in and between material objects relate and to articulate the changing direction and degree of force within those relations.[17] Helmholtz's theoretical innovation asserts that the empirical delineation of these forces is only possible because the total amount of force in the universe is constant; it merely changes position according to the effects of the law of causality.[18]

Helmholtz put forth his new law as a physicist, but it had immediate ramifications for psychologists. Before the widespread acceptance of the conservation of energy, theories concerning the relation of mind and brain were restricted to arguments of association. Associationist psychology held that mind and brain communicate with each other through a so-called exchange of energy, a flux in the quantity of energy present in the mind (brain) at any one time. This position achieved a fragile compromise between empiricists focused on the brain and Cartesian rationalists interested only in the mind. Helmholtz upset this compromise by theorizing that energy does not change quantity, but merely position. As a consequence, the exchange of energy gave way to laws of physics and catalyzed the modern debate on how to relate the insights of physiology to the insights of philosophy. By the second half of the nineteenth century, the implosion of these two lines of thought formed the discursive terrain of psychology.

Causality remained at the center of this debate. Physicists subsequent to Helmholtz (such as Peirce)[19] declared that the law of the conservation of energy implied the possibility of a strict reversibility of physical events. Such a notion is familiar to those of us bred on the cultural ramifications of twentieth-century quantum theory, but it was incumbent on Peirce to support the notion with a complex mathematical proof.[20] The conundrum yielded by this proof is that the nature of physical events is theoretically conservative or reversible (energy is conserved) and as such starkly contradicts the obviously nonconservative (irreversible) quality of psychical events (energy is not conserved; energy is not involved in the same, physical way). Peirce's treatment of this issue exemplifies the sort of mutation of concepts that guides this book. Helmholtz's formulation of the conservation law popularized a notion of causality that fed intense reflection on the character and roles of science, but he never directly discusses the consequences of the law for the way *humans* experience causality.[21] Peirce takes up the reflection on causality and applies it to the character of human knowing and being, specifically, to the relation of mind and nature discussed in the context of teleology (whether events really and/or actually have definitive ends, that is, are irreversible).

Helmholtz's concern lies more with the nature of *Wissenschaft* than with the nature of *Geist* (or the place of *Geist* in nature). His laboratory's attempts to verify theories like the conservation of energy and the specific energies of nerves explore the role of *Naturwissenschaft* in formulating laws or general principles according to the logic of cause and effect.[22] In this sense, the conservation law exemplifies the temporal linearity of strict efficient causality that is characteristic of all events worthy of being tagged *naturwissenschaftlich*. Understanding causal relations thus becomes the medium for all human understanding; according to Helmholtz, the law of causality itself causes humanity's evolutionary ascent to global dominance:

> We are particles of dust on the surface of our planet, which is itself scarcely a grain of sand in the infinite space of the universe. We are the youngest species among the living things of the earth, hardly out of the cradle according to the time reckoning of geology, still in the learning stage, hardly half-grown, said to be mature only through mutual agreement. *Nevertheless, because of the*

mighty stimulus of the law of causality, we have already grown beyond our fellow creatures and are overcoming them in the struggle for existence.[23]

In the essay from which this quotation is drawn, "The Facts of Perception" (1879), Helmholtz does not clarify how the law of causality stimulates humanity's success in the struggle for survival. But the epistemological issues raised in the essay suggest that Helmholtz attributes the species' success both to the inexorable working out of that law and to humanity's ability to perceive and describe it. Consider his discussion of how we come to know the laws of nature:

> The law of causality actually is an *a priori* given, a transcendental law. A proof of it from experience is not possible, since the first steps of experience, as we have seen, are not possible without employing inductive inferences, i.e., without the law of causality. . . . Here the only advice is: have trust and act! The inadequate/It then takes place [*Das Unzulängliche/Dann wird's Ereignis*].[24]

Helmholtz here proposes that laws formulated according to efficient causation are merely regulative (as opposed to determinative); humans can never trust the capacity of law fully to explain future events. His earlier essay from 1847 sidesteps the question of determinism versus spontaneity, but in this essay Helmholtz demonstrates the epistemological impossibility of making that judgment. The law of causality is universal; it so completely conditions events that it cannot itself be proven without a regressive circularity, since to prove the law of causality would require employing it. Helmholtz thus advises readers to believe in the reality of the law of causality without presuming that any single instance or effect of the law fully represents it or explains it. "Have trust and act," he enjoins; the law of causality regulates our behavior but does not necessarily define or determine it.

By this advice, Helmholtz touches on the paradoxical relation between a general law and individual instances of that law, namely, that individual instances display and yet inadequately represent the general formulation. Just such a realization prompts Peirce's stringent antinominalism, his insistence on the necessary reality of generals. The position can be explained in terms of causality by considering that each experience of cause and effect exemplifies the law of causality, but does not completely instantiate it. For example, I can let go of a rock and it will fall down, but this does not completely instantiate the law of causality. Each instance of the law is an adequate example or approximation of it, but each remains inadequate for purposes of definition or completion. "The inadequate . . . takes place," however, for the law really does fragment into individual and approximate expressions. Laws for Helmholtz thus function as what Peirce calls a general concept. The reality of generals, for Peirce, is strictly virtual; each instance of a law is simultaneously its actualization and its becoming partial.[25]

Helmholtz describes the law of causality as "an a priori given, a transcendental law." In this capacity, it is by definition a law of thought (*ein Denkgesetz*). In addition Helmholtz posits the law of causality as a law of nature, as was shown in the quotation from "The Conservation of Force." For Helmholtz, *die Naturgesetze* do not exist merely in the mind (*der Verstand*), as Kant supposed, but are real generals that exist and operate in nature.[26] In short, the law of causality (*das Kausalgesetz*) is both a law of nature and a category of mind. An example will help clarify the effect of this claim. For Helmholtz, the law of causality functions as the condition of possibility for "unconscious inferences" (*die unbewußt Schlüsse*). Unconscious inferences derive from the immediate perceptions of the sensory apparatus and subsequently assemble to construct conscious thought. The derivation process works by strict causal efficacy, thus exemplifying the law of causality as a natural law. But the associative process by which unconscious inferences build up to conscious thought is not determined by the law of causality, and that is the law's flexibility as a category of mind.[27] To repeat, *das Kausalgesetz* regulates human behavior but does not define or determine it.[28]

The regulative character of causality (the most general natural law) is demonstrated in Helmholtz's assertion that humans must presume a nature operating according to cause and effect, for "without that causal nature, there is no intellectual action, no human *praxis*."[29] Human action depends on and proceeds from a certain level of predictability. Thus the human assumption gained from multiple inductive inferences is that nature operates according to efficient causation. This fact encourages humans to rely on perceived patterns in their environments and to assume further that those patterns will remain stable. The more someone's actions in and with the world validate these assumptions, the more stable and coherent are her subsequent actions. If a particular pattern proves unpredictable, humans tend to subdivide the pattern to a level of cause and effect that does lend itself to prediction (for example, the weather is famously unpredictable, but everyone knows that thunder follows lightning, that certain types of clouds bring rain, and so on). In short, presuming the predominance of causal efficacy in nature lends human beings greater control over their environments, a control that, Helmholtz argues, has enabled humans to evolve into the world's dominant species.

The thematics of Helmholtz's writings resonate deeply with Peirce's brand of pragmatism called pragmaticism. Both philosophers embrace the basic tenet of British empiricism—that truth relies on induction from experience—without, however, accepting its atomism and consequent mechanism. Quite the contrary, they presume the continuity and relatedness of experience and seek to explain it in terms of nature and not, as Kant did, in terms of the mind's ability to synthesize nature. Specifically, Helmholtz explains the continuity of experience through the overarching law of causality and the way that law expounds the truth behind the heuristic empirical results of the practical sciences. Peirce, on the other hand, incorporates efficient causality into a complex logical and ontological theory of continuity called "synechism" and asserts its importance only in tandem with a theory of chance ("tychism") that makes room for final causality.[30] Through these manipulations of the notion of causality, Helmholtz and Peirce both assert an exquisite dovetailing of Kantian transcendentalism with practical empiricism, and as such they reject their cultures' more recent engagements with Hegelian idealism. Helmholtz succinctly articulates this attempt to conjoin science and philosophy at the end of "The Endeavor to Popularize Science." After bemoaning Germany's suspicion of John Tyndall's work, he attributes it to a "philosophical opposition to the inductive method of science, which was first formulated by Bacon and which was followed earliest and has been followed most seriously by his fellow Englishmen." He calls this difference between deductive and inductive reasoning "an old point of contention" between Germany and Britain, and he suggests it could be healed by the natural sciences:

> The natural sciences have made extensive and rapid progress precisely to the degree in which they have freed themselves from the influence of so-called a priori deductions. We in this country have been the last to break away but at the same time the most resolute, and German physiology in particular bears witness to the range and significance of this freedom. The break occurred, however, in opposition to the last great systems of metaphysical speculation, which have harnessed and fettered the expectations and interest of the educated part of the nation. It occurred in a fight against the belief that only pure thought involves important, intelligent work, while the collection of empirical facts is, on the contrary, low and common.[31]

Helmholtz's reworking of Kant is symptomatic of broad and complex cultural interactions. Helmholtz stands as a social type, as part of the vanguard of a generational movement in Germany to abandon the idealism of Hegel and Schelling for the more pragmatic idealism of Kant.[32] In this respect, Helmholtz employs Kant only to the extent that the philosopher illuminates better approaches to science. As he writes, "The sole purpose of Kant's critical philosophy was to examine the sources and the validity of our knowledge and to establish standards or criteria for the other sciences."[33] Helmholtz thinks science desperately needs these criteria, but the cultural dominance of Hegel problematizes the place of philosophy in science, because the scorn heaped upon Hegel's philosophy of nature by the physical sciences incites suspicion of all philosophical reflection (and thus all theoretical investigations) within scientific endeavors. According to Helmholtz, science, to its detriment, thus rejects "the legitimate aims of philosophy: the critical analysis of the sources of knowledge, and the establishment of standards for intellectual endeavors."[34] Reestablishing this "legitimate aim of philosophy" inside the battlements of science requires more than simply reasserting Kant's three *Critiques*. Helmholtz's return to Kant signals the difference of posing Kantian questions in the nineteenth century, a century marked by ambitious industrialization, technological innovation, and shifts both in political organizations and in the divisions of knowledge in the universities.[35] Helmholtz's focused examination of the law of causality signals his culture's growing reliance on the efficient causation of industrial machines. His insistence that apperception of efficient causation is humanity's evolutionary stepladder to global dominance indicates both the increasing mechanization of *Naturwissenschaft* and its reflexive inclusion of the human subject.

In short, then, the figure of Helmholtz and his philosophical and scientific promotion of the law of causality encapsulate his culture's desire for and excitement about technological progress. Into this boisterous celebration of causal efficacy, however, Helmholtz also inserts a tremor of confusion about the relation of mind and brain. By his assertion that the law of causality merely regulates our behavior without determining it, Helmholtz implies that the associative processes of mind that produce the "unconscious inferences" supersede the mechanistic functions of the brain's sensory motor system. Helmholtz himself never fully articulates this paradox, but Wilhelm Wundt does, and he rises to meet the challenge the paradox raises for the "scientific" study of human beings.

That is the story of the next chapter, however. For now, I need only stress that Helmholtz's confusion about human consciousness can be read, in part, as a consequence of his sole concern for the success of the natural sciences (practical or theoretical) to the exclusion of whatever social and cultural ramifications that success yields for a culture's concepts and treatments of human beings. As the next chapter shows, Wundt's challenges to Helmholtz's epistemology and cognitive theory poignantly display the impossibility of ignoring how connotations of mind and self change as persons try to cope with changing connotations of science. Helmholtz built his career reflecting on causality; indeed, his theories about law deploy the notion of causality as a lens or tool for comprehending his culture's changing dispositions toward the concept of science. Accordingly, his lectures and research lead to questions about the meaning and scope of nature, law, and history; but his analyses only tangentially affected analyses of human thought and being. Wundt's defense of a scientific psychology shifts Helmholtz's focus on causality to consciousness and will, and thereby articulates his culture's struggles to name and reconcile the natural (psychology) and the technological (science). Where Helmholtz uses his law of the conservation of energy to reposition Kant's transcendental aesthetic onto the more empirical and technological plane of the nineteenth century laboratory and its industrial capitalist society,[36] Wundt forges novel understandings of empiricism and objectivity, and applies them to the non-Kantian realms of psychology and sociology. Before turning more fully to Wundt, I need first to expound Helmholtz's semiotic (*Zeichentheorie*), in order to explicate its realist and relational assumptions.

A Physical Sign Theory

Helmholtz is *pragmatisch* in a Kantian sense: his use of signs is not intended to sustain a gap between mind and world but to bridge mind and world by minimizing incorrect assumptions that hinder thought and action.[37] Since the physicist views all human sensations as signs of the external world that must be further interpreted by the mind, Helmholtz might not seem to differ at all from Kant's philosophical system.[38] As argued in Kant's *Critique of Pure Reason*, the manifold of sensations that bombard the sense organs are synthesized by the imagination and then subsumed under the pure concepts of the understanding.[39] Physical sensations are real signs of an object (*Ding*),

the actual nature of which is in itself (*an sich*) noumenal. Helmholtz agrees
with this basic Kantian account. He also agrees with the first *Critique*'s assumption that the specific qualities of experience are completely subjective
since they inhere neither in the objects themselves nor in the nervous system.[40] For example, the red color of an apple is neither *in* the apple nor *in* my
retinal nerves. Helmholtz differs from Kant in stressing the role of the sensory motor system in sign interpretation, which is why I term his semiotic
physical. Thus "red" is an experience constructed from the signs given off by
the object, processed in and by my retinal nerves and brain, and related to
expectation and memory. All of these factors coalesce in the brain's subjective interpretation of a conscious experience as "a red apple." Though the
process is subjective, it also is lawful and this lawfulness relates both to the
categorial schema and to material, somatic processes.

Physical sensations are signs, but these signs consist of true signals about
the world:

> Although our sensations, as regard their quality, are only *signs* whose particu-
> lar character depends wholly upon our own makeup, they are still not to be
> dismissed as a mere semblance, but they are precisely signs of *something*, be
> it something existing or happening, and—what is most important—they can
> form for us an image of the *law* of this thing which is happening.[41]

The subjective decoding of physical signs does not imply their "mere sem-
blance." As the red apple example demonstrates, signs are always "signs of
something." The physicalist tenor of this quotation accentuates Helmholtz's
repositioning of Kant. By focusing on nerve action and memory, Helmholtz's
work ties the transcendentalist project to empiricist research methods, which
were gaining wide acceptance in his culture. More particularly, Helmholtz
joins his Kantian allegiances to what was known as the "specific energies of
nerves,"[42] which explored how singular objects and events are sensed by
human sense organs. The sun, for example, is sensed as both light and heat,
and a rock is perceived as both cold and heavy. These plural sensations result
from the different capacities of nerves, not simply from alternate intuitive
routes for synthesizing the sensory manifold. This physical interpretation of
Kant's transcendental aesthetic coalesces in Helmholtz's physical account of
signs.

The primary consequence of Helmholtz's transmutation of Kant lies in
the status of the law of causality. As argued in the last section, *das
Kausalgesetz* is both a law of nature and a category of mind. The dual status implies that, unlike Kant, Helmholtz accepts the process of perception
itself as a justifiable part of transcendental philosophy, in addition to its more
obvious status as an empirical process. Where "Kant investigates the conditions of possibility of perception, not perception itself," Helmholtz does
not hesitate to examine both.[43] Viewing perception as subjective, lawful, *and*
physical, Helmholtz seeks to close the gap between the phenomenal and
noumenal realms, though, like Kant, he never does fully heal the break. The
semiotic character of physical sensations and the dual status of the law of

causality function in three specific ways for Helmholtz. They acknowledge that a gap exists between a sign and its object, even if that gap is structural, or epistemological. They insist that the gap in no way lessens the reality of the sign but rather confirms the reality of generals or laws. And they posit that the object of a sign can be a process as well as a material object ("something existing or happening").

The connection between signs and their objects is pragmatic, in the Kantian sense of bridging mind and world by minimizing incorrect assumptions. For Helmholtz, this actual pragmatic link guarantees the reality of laws and can best be seen in his account of language acquisition and use. For example, consider the comparison Helmholtz makes between physical signs and a person's native language:

> Its [our mother tongue's] words are arbitrarily or accidentally chosen signs— every different language has different ones. Understanding of it is not inherited, since for a German child who was brought up amongst Frenchmen and has never heard German spoken, German is a foreign language. The child becomes acquainted with the meaning of the words and sentences only through examples of their use. In this process one cannot even make understandable to the child—until it understands the language—that the sounds it hears are supposed to be signs having a sense.[44]

The language a person speaks is arbitrary, Helmholtz asserts, dependent on place and circumstance. Not only is language acquisition arbitrary, but the internal functioning of language is also largely conventional, dependent upon "examples" of a word's "use." Why does "cow" mean cow and not horse? There is no reason; language just happened to evolve in this way, and it could have developed in many other, equally useful ways. Indeed, it is precisely the *usefulness* of language that constrains and propels its applications and migrations. Language is arbitrary and conventional yet regulated by real laws. These laws are merely regulative, not determinative. A similar pragmatic perspective applies to Helmholtz's theories of physical sensations. Both the laws of the language of society and the laws of the language of the body must be learned, and the guideposts for that learning are whether or not a particular signal enables effective navigation through life.

In insisting on the relative conventionality of both physical and linguistic signs, Helmholtz denies the necessary iconicity (or image quality) of these signs. Helmholtz sees no reason why the impulses we receive through our nerves should actually resemble at all the object or event signified by the stimulus:

> For from an image one requires some kind of alikeness with the object of which it is an image—from a statue alikeness of form, from a drawing alikeness of perspective projection in the visual field, from a painting alikeness of colours as well. But a sign need not have any kind of similarity at all with what it is a sign of. The relation between the two of them is restricted to the fact that like objects exerting an influence under like circumstances evoke like signs, and that therefore unlike signs always correspond to unlike influences.[45]

If sensory signs do not operate through iconicity or correspondence, then how do they function? Helmholtz argues that signs work through relations, either through the repeatable relation of an object's signs to the sense organs, or through the relations between the signs of an object, that is, through the association of signs as, for example, in a conversation or a gesture.[46] Such a stance opposes a Lockean view of simple, atomistic ideas. Physical sensations are relational and are known through their relationality. From this physicalist position, Helmholtz transposes Kantian questions to a wider field of investigation by asking how objects relate to human nervous systems, how nervous systems relate to memory and reflections, and how these construct conscious experiences. Helmholtz describes this entire process as unconscious inferences becoming conscious thought.

Though Helmholtz's essays and lectures never directly engage the Peircean nominalist/realist debate and though, indeed, his writings rarely contain the terms *realism* or *idealism*, I find Helmholtz's works surprisingly resonant with the pragmatist's. Both thinkers walk with one foot grounded in idealist a priori assumptions about the real lawfulness of the universe and the other foot grounded in a realist stress on the conjunction of past memories with present experience toward the formation of particular—and thus contingent—intuitions, perceptions, and thoughts. Helmholtz suggests this balance of idealism and realism both in his theory of unconscious inferences as the means of processing physical signs and in his formulation of the law of causality as both a fact of nature and a category of mind.

The Nature of *Naturwissenschaft*

Helmholtz's work on causality and signs forms part of his more general attempt to turn an epistemological lens on the nature of science and the social function of scientists. In his 1879 essay, "The Facts of Perception," Helmholtz notes that the preceding scientific generation had asked, "What is true in our intuition and thought? In what sense do our representations correspond to actuality?"[47] His own written work attempts to answer these questions both philosophically (mentally, as he termed it) and scientifically (physically). Taking inspiration from the way he frames these questions, I would expand the questions for Helmholtz's generation of *Naturwissenschaftler* to include: How can we know what is true? How do we proceed to discover and record this truth? By what methods do we experiment? By what criteria do we accept others' experiments? As Michel Foucault shows in *The Order of Things*, the classical grid of the West breaks up and rearranges in the nineteenth century, forming new assumptions for how to organize data into knowledge.[48] Specifically, discourses congeal around the contested category of science as the center of authorized knowledge. The absent organizer of the classical grid, the human, quickly becomes the central object of the modern grid. Such coalescing attention on the human as object boomerangs back on the human as subject, experimenter, and scientist: What is it that enables me to know? How do I see? feel? smell? hear? What is "normal"? What is abnormal or deviant? Why is the body this way and not another way?

Anatomy and the relatively new field of physiology were the first avenues for exploring these questions. Helmholtz and other older investigators remain loyal to physiology's rules of discourse, but a younger set of scientists begins to break away from those rules and establish a new sort of psychology, one with a shape and methodology different from its traditional roots in philosophy and physiology. Through their work, traditional questions about the relations of mind and body gradually fuel a concentrated debate over the purview of physiology versus that of psychology and over the very possibility of studying the human "scientifically." Psychologists thus began the battle (still waged today) over how or whether the status and procedures of their investigations are scientific. Helmholtz does not push his investigations into that fray, but Wilhelm Wundt, the "father of psychology," makes it his life's work.

Helmholtz does not altogether shy away from debate, however. His lectures and addresses indicate that his concern lies less with the bickering within and between developing disciplines than with the role and duty of a scientist, regardless of the object of inquiry. To him, the position of scientist is justified as a social type with moral responsibilities. For example, in "The Relation of the Natural Sciences to Science in General," he stresses three qualities that the age demands of scientists, qualities that Peirce also embraces. First, scientists recognize the importance of taking the long-term view and seeing their work as a small part of a larger, global project ("fellow laborer[s] on one great common work").[49] The work of science is inherently and necessarily communal. Second, good scientists acknowledge the need to avoid hubris and recognize their intellectual limitations by engaging those faculties that are not their specialty (be it math, music, literature, or astronomy). To the degree it is humble, science can act as a transcommunal force within and between societies. Third, good scientists know that "action alone gives a man a life worth living. He must aim either at the practical application of his knowledge or at the extension of the limits of science itself."[50] Helmholtz, in other words, believes that scientists should not necessarily expect immediate practical results from their investigations. His lectures reference Newton, Galileo, and Galvino as examples of scientists whose theoretical results lay fallow—sometimes for centuries—before applications of them were implemented. Nevertheless, Helmholtz also believes that scientists are constantly involved and as such contribute responsibly to social and national progress.[51] In sum, Helmholtz views a scientist as an "expert" whose practical responsibilities to society stem from a more general duty to truth.

Pragmatic Consequences

In this chapter I have shown how Helmholtz's understandings of the law of causality lead to his rethinking of Kantian idealism, especially with respect to his theorization of the operation of natural laws and his physicalizing of the sign theory of perception. I have suggested that his transmutation of Kant mirrors Peirce's nominalist/realist debate in arguing for both the reality of laws and the importance of discrete experiences. Let me now briefly delineate the contours of this debate, to which we will return in chapter 5.

Peirce draws his understanding of nominalism from the scholastic debates but turns them to his own purposes. He declares three primary aspects of nominalism. First, nominalism denies that laws or general principles are "really operative in nature."[52] Second, nominalists "block the road of inquiry" by supposing that some things are absolutely inexplicable, "since in nominalism experience is discrete and the laws joining experiences—laws which function to explain the discrete events—are mere abstractions."[53] Third, nominalism assumes an original definiteness and a consequent degenerative quality of all indefiniteness, assumptions that lead to an incessant and unsuccessful pursuit of certainty.[54] Peirce rejects each of these philosophical positions. He argues for a realism in which laws are really operative in nature; he asserts that no event is absolutely inexplicable since at least its context is partially understandable (real laws create real relations between events); and he posits that the primary indefiniteness or vagueness of things is not only the source of all novelty and growth, but also the universal site of mind or thought.[55] As I have argued, Helmholtz also asserts the reality of natural laws, at least as regarding the task and goal of the theoretical sciences, which seek the causal truths behind the heuristic principles of the physical sciences. In addition, Helmholtz's positions on the operation of both natural laws and physical signs advocate a basic trustworthiness and continuity of experience and thus assert a confident ability of humans to explain the objects and events of their world. Helmholtz, however, does not share the third aspect listed by Peirce, that of the logical priority of indefiniteness. He instead upholds the search for certainty. Nonetheless, I have indicated in this chapter how Helmholtz's understanding of natural law does suggest a pragmatic fallibilism. In that sense, though Helmholtz assumes the theoretical possibility of certainty, in practice that certainty is always deferred (hence the need to "have trust and act").

Helmholtz articulates his theories about the real operation of natural laws through the law of causality. His assumptions about causality lead to his formulation of the law of the conservation of energy, which itself instigates debates about the conservative (reversible) nature of physical events and the apparently nonconservative (irreversible) character of psychical events. Wundt and James take up this issue in decidedly psychological terms, but in line with Helmholtz, Peirce tackles the apparent aporia through his categorization of the sciences. In his 1902 *Syllabus of Certain Topics of Logic*, Peirce places the "sciences of discovery" at the most general level of investigation. These sciences include mathematics, logic, and philosophy, with mathematics and logic given the tasks of studying the reversible quality of physical events, while philosophy (including phenomenology and metaphysics) treat the irreversible quality of psychical events.[56]

Another point of congruence between Peirce and Helmholtz resides in the relation between a general law and individual instances of that law. For both men individual instances of a law display and yet inadequately represent the general formulation. The realization of this character of laws or generals prompts Peirce's stringent antinominalism. The reality of generals is, for Peirce, strictly virtual; each instance of a law is simultaneously its actualization and its becoming partial. In my reading, Helmholtz characterizes laws as regulative, a fact that resonates well with the empiricist and action-oriented interests of the American pragmatists, though Peirce and James differ from Helmholtz in insisting on either teleology (James) or purposiveness (Peirce) as endemic to "intellectual action" and "human *praxis.*" The pragmatists' commitment to final causality stems less from prioritizing the language of causality (like Helmholtz) and more from their theories of habit (Peirce) and will (James). Habits and willed actions are predictable and conducive of self-control, both of which are important factors for Helmholtz, who stresses that control is a leading evolutionary trait. Something the German physicist does not discuss, however, is that habits and willed actions also have reasons or ends. By stressing habit or will, the pragmatists effectively shift the plane of inquiry from Helmholtz's focus on single objects or events (wherein a cause yields an effect) to networks of events. The reason or purpose of a habit or act of will can only be explicated in terms of other habits or acts of will. Herein lies the Americans' mutation of Helmholtz's causality and hence of his questions about science, nature, law, and event. From the German's perspective, the only processes of pragmatic note are the apperception of efficient causality and the eventual growth of humans' control over the earth by amassing a sort of database of such apperceptions; an individual event has a cause but no purpose. For the pragmatists, however, notions of causality inherently entail issues of purpose and, more specifically, issues of self-control and self-formation. Causality is not simply applicable to nature in general, but also to the ascesis incumbent upon every human being. It is both, and equally, scientific and ethical.

My discussion of Helmholtz's physical sign theory emphasized its empiricism and pragmatism and stressed that Helmholtz rejects an iconic understanding of signs in favor of a relational account. The three semiotic issues of iconicity, relationality, and effective navigation of thought and action are also important for Peirce and James, especially by virtue of the nominalism/realism debate. First, as a facet of his realism, Peirce insists on iconicity as a phenomenological not a metaphysical character of signs.[57] James restricts the notion of sign to language and is consistently nominalist regarding its use and development. Second, in terms of relationality, the keystone of Peirce's whole philosophy is his logic of relatives, which posits relations as more fundamental than substance and which draws upon his antinominalist assertion of the reality of possibles to construct his theory of continuity, or synechism. While such a notion (and surely the complex logic) is never so thoroughly or mathematically discussed by James, he too draws on the central importance of relationality in many respects, most dramatically through his concept of "fringe." Introduced in *The Principles of Psychology*, the fringe indicates the welter of conditions, affectations, and contingencies that swirl around any one particular perception.[58] Third, the relation of semiotics to issues of effective navigation of thought and action might be a reductionistic summary of pragmatic philosophy. But though Peirce does insist on the gospel tenet "by their fruits ye shall know them," he also claims that action is not the necessary end of all thought, or of every sign. Explicating this dual claim will effectively distinguish Peirce from both James *and* Helmholtz and show why Peirce's semeiotic is both a more radical repositioning of Kantian tenets and better suited to treat the changing understandings of subjectivity and of the self's social and ethical obligations.

Those social and ethical obligations matter immensely to Helmholtz, as indicated by his vision of the good scientist. Peirce agrees with Helmholtz's call for the communal focus and personal humility of practicing scientists, though he never directly advocates state support of science. Peirce often berates James and Dewey for foregrounding the practical sciences to the denigration of theoretical inquiries that are free from the exigencies of government or the desires of business. Peirce, like Helmholtz, perceives such utilitarianism as tragically shortsighted, for while he believes in the ultimate practicality of all scientific endeavors, he insists that such success can be won only by immolating present desires, including the desire for success itself.

This chapter has discussed the emergence of German psychology as part of the story of how nineteenth-century cultural, intellectual, political and religious interactions enabled the only indigenous American philosophy to develop out of questions formed within and by European scientific enterprises. Specifically, I have articulated Helmholtz's discussions of causality (one of a number of competing understandings of the concept) as part of my larger analysis of how continental concerns became repositioned on American soil. The scientific and technological developments of the twentieth century muted the voices of Helmholtz and Peirce, upstaging their contributions and commitments through the excitement and easy accessibility of Wundt and James. Their versions of pragmatism, however, mandate a theoretical thickness and moral consequence that offer an alternate vision of the meaning and interactions of self and nation.

Wilhelm Wundt

Relational Processes: Physiological Psychology and Its Social Consequences

Like Helmholtz, Wilhelm M. Wundt (1832–1920) evinced early interest in physiology and experimental science, but he left those fields for the more practical and lucrative career of medicine. Like his compatriot, Wundt used his medical training as a means of exploring questions of physiology, and he too was drawn to the seminal work of Johannes Müller in Berlin. Wundt studied under Müller for one academic term, after which he returned to the University of Heidelberg and entered a program in physiology (degree received in 1856). He remained at Heidelberg, giving lectures in physiology and working as an assistant in Helmholtz's laboratory until 1864, at which time he was promoted to the official position of lecturer. He retained that post for a decade. After one year (1875) in Zurich as a professor of inductive philosophy, Wundt settled into a forty-year tenure at the University of Leipzig as professor of philosophy.[1] At Leipzig Wundt worked out what his generation titled the "new psychology," an approach to questions of human knowing and being that stressed rigorous and empirical experimentation. In 1879 he opened at Leipzig the first laboratory dedicated to psychological research.

Wilhelm Wundt's research demonstrates an application and broadening of the questions that structured the work of Helmholtz. The latter studied the character of natural law and the social duties incumbent on a scientist. Wundt absorbed the results of those investigations and applied them to an experimental psychology that he hoped would adequately explore the nature of being human and assist scientists in curing social ills. The central axis of their research was the relatively new field of physiology, perhaps an unsurprising framework for scientists attempting to take questions about human nature out of the domain of philosophy. Helmholtz grounded his physiological work firmly within the broader territory of physics, but Wundt wavered between his commitments to physiology and to what we might today call the humanities, namely *Geisteswissenschaft*.[2] Thus, though historians appropriately call Wundt the father of scientific psychology in deference to his carving out an institutional space for that discourse, his later work and institutional affiliations within philosophy indicate his enduring affinity to *Geisteswissenschaft*.

To me, Wundt's methodological pluralism justifies constellating and comparing his work with that of William James, whose writings persistently oscillate between a scientific and a humanistic temper. Indeed, the pluralism shapes even James's most apparently scientific treatise, *The Principles of Psychology* (1890), of which Wundt reportedly said, "It is literature, it is beautiful, but it is not psychology!"[3] Moreover, James and Wundt share a similar public demeanor and portfolio. Both spearheaded public lobbies for the support of scientific research, but even as they struggled to advance scientific endeavors, they displayed doubt and confusion about what "science" meant. This conceptual struggle helps explain why James, like Wundt, relinquished an early training in physiology and medicine, first for psychology and then for philosophy and ethics.

In this chapter, I continue my discussion of the development of German psychology. I argue that Wundt's career portrays how psychology becomes accepted as a science, albeit always with accompanying ambivalence and debate. I contend that examining Wundt's writings on consciousness and will clarifies how questions about the body that were initially framed within anatomy and physiology (as during Helmholtz's career) gradually shift into a psychological frame more familiar to James and other twentieth-century investigators. The historical links between Wundt and Helmholtz are clear. Wundt's writings adopt the gains made by Helmholtz's research in defining and defending an empirical *Naturwissenschaft*, but Wundt also insists that these gains apply to the human as subject, that is, to the human as both body *and* mind. His lectures and essays exhibit a desire to extend the authority held by the natural sciences to psychology, that is, to legitimize psychology in its own right as an empirical science. Wundt thus advocates a methodological pluralism that diverges from Helmholtz's strict loyalty to the single empirical method of *Naturwissenschaft* (first articulated in Bacon's *Novum Organum*) and Wundt delineates new interpretations of empiricism and consciousness. Two lines of inquiry within Wundt's corpus best exemplify the difference between the German peers: physiological psychology, which solidifies a *naturwissenschaftlich* approach to consciousness, and linguistics, gestures and ethnography, which acknowledge the necessary social and volitional components to any psychological science. Each line of inquiry merits a brief explication.

The term *physiological psychology* "suggests . . . that psychology, in adopting the experimental methods of physiology, does not by any means take them over as they are, and apply them without change to a new material. The methods of experimental physiology have been transformed—in some instances, actually remodelled [*sic*]—by psychology itself, to meet the specific requirements of psychological investigation.[4] Wundt here emphasizes psychology's simultaneous reliance on and independence from physiology. He enjoins his scientific peers to regard psychology as a science (as opposed to a philosophy) since it relies as much as does physiology upon the experimental method. Nonetheless, Wundt does not apply "science" wholesale, but adjusts the term to the particular exigencies of studying human minds. These "specific requirements" demarcate a new sphere within science and within psychology, a hybrid space that leads Wundt to declare that physiological psychology, "seeks to accomplish a reform in psychological investigation comparable with the revolution brought about in the natural sciences by the introduction of the experimental method."[5] Wundt notes the consequences of adopting but not capitulating to physiology:

> Physiological psychology thus *ends* with those questions with which the philosophical psychology of an older day was wont to begin,—the questions of the nature of the mind, and of the relation of consciousness to an external world; and with a characterization of the general attitude which psychology is to take up, when it seeks to trace the laws of the mental life as manifested in history and in society.[6]

Through physiology, psychology gains empirical grounding for what was traditionally explored under the aegis of philosophy. Wundt thus legitimizes psychology both by granting it the same intellectual status as *Naturwissenschaft* and by stressing the scientificness, that is, the empiricity, of *Geisteswissenschaft*.

For Wundt the philosophical deductions about psychology (its inheritance from *Geisteswissenschaft*) indicate a decidedly social component of the science; as he puts it, psychology "trace[s] the laws of the mental life as manifested in history and society." These philosophical *Gedankenexperimenten* include elements that eventually will coalesce in discourses such as sociology, ethnography, ethics, and religious studies. Sociality thus forms the second branch of Wundt's work, that which concentrates on the nature of language, the nature of society, and the volitional relations between the individual sense of self and the social sense of self. These lines of inquiry stem directly from what Wundt perceives as limitations of the physiological part of psychology. He writes, "There are other sources of *objective* psychological knowledge, which become accessible at the very point where the experimental method fails us. These are certain products of the common mental life, in which we may trace the operation of determinate psychical motives: chief among them are language, myth and custom."[7] Wundt asserts the strict objectivity of these alternate sources of psychological knowledge, a feat he accomplishes by changing the very meaning of *objectivity* in order to claim a different and "objective" understanding of consciousness. Volition is the keystone of this conceptual mutation.

Volition ("psychical motives") forms the conceptual link between Wundt's linguistic and ethnographic work and his research in physiological psychology. Wundt writes in his *Ethics*:

The outward signs of this transition from individual to social consciousness [or will; the German phrase is *der Individualwille und Gesamtwille*], and the corresponding social will, are all those elements of culture and morals which express the common feeling and thought of a society. Speech, religious views, like habits of life and standards of action, point to the existence of a common intellectual possession, which far exceeds in scope anything that the individual can obtain.[8]

Later in the same passage, Wundt asserts that the volitional bridge between the individual and the social justifies the objectivity of language, religious views, and other communal habits. The passage thus displays the two facets of Wundt's work that concern me in this chapter: the strict objectivity of nonphysiological sources and the function of motive or will as the bridge between physiology (or *Naturwissenschaft*) and philosophy (*Geisteswissenschaft*). These two facets merge in what I call Wundt's theory of parallel causalities, which emphasizes the empirical fact but existential separation of physical and psychical causality. The effect of this parallelism is to rework "consciousness" and "causality" to fit the "specific requirements" of a scientific psychology. The theory of parallel causality thus exemplifies the change from Helmholtz to Wundt insofar as each thinker typifies nineteenth-century understandings of science, objectivity, and empiricism. Wundt asserts the scientific status of psychology (though his theories change the very meaning of science), while he also acknowledges that experiments designed to probe the mind do not yield the same kind of certainty as that gained from physiological or chemical experiments. The concession troubles Wundt's claim that psychology is objective and empirical, and he attempts to resolve the apparent contradiction through the theory of parallel causality

In the following pages I delineate Wundt's attempt to adhere to the empiricism of the natural sciences while also asserting the difference and social relevance of the mental sciences. In his desire to study the human mind, Wundt extracts psychology from both philosophy and physiology and creates a disciplinary space that he asserts is both empirical and social. To the extent that he succeeds in this venture, he does so only by redefining concepts presumed to be *naturwissenschaftlich* (for example, *objectivity, empiricity, causality*) and by positing mind and will as simultaneously individual and social processes.

Similar to Wundt's attempts to mediate the methodological claims of physiology and philosophy, William James wavers throughout his professional life between what he perceives to be the contrasting demands of science and religion (or sentiment). His inability to resolve this tension propels the pragmatist out of science and fully into philosophical and ethical reflections. Like Wundt, James redefines concepts presumed to be the sovereign property of the natural sciences, and like Wundt he concentrates on the will as the aspect of human being that might resolve his opposing commitments. However, while Wundt's third space of physiological psychology makes room for social inquiry, James's attempts to reconcile matters of the head (science) with matters of the heart (religion) center on the individual.

In short, this chapter analyzes Wundt's understanding of science (physiological psychology), his redefinition of traditionally scientific terms (objectivity, empiricity, causality, the actuality of mind, attention, and feeling), and his theories on how will informs the social consequences of a scientific psychology. Together, these discussions continue the delineation of German psychology that I began in chapter I. Throughout, my focus remains the clarification of concepts and questions that Peirce and James take up and that are thus inherent to a genealogy of American pragmatism. If causality formed the focus of the previous chapter, the foci here are consciousness and will.

Two Empiricisms and Parallel Causalities

As previously indicated, Wundt redefines his notion of objectivity in its relation to science in order to encompass pursuits traditionally opposed to *Naturwissenschaft*. Wundt generally equates objectivity with empiricism (*Empirismus*), and he uses that term to guide both his theories of physiological psychology and his work in linguistics, ethnography, and ethics. Indeed, one might say that Wundt reformulates Helmholtz's work by theorizing a bridge between the empiricism of natural science and the empiricism of mental science and thereby reinterpreting consciousness as actual and objective. Wundt acknowledges that only recent theoretical developments allow psychology to be treated as an empirical science. This new, experimental approach to psychology was roundly rejected by most natural scientists, who strongly rejected its claims to scientific stature. As one reads Wundt's work, it becomes clear that Wundt speaks to the skepticism of other scientists not simply by insisting on the empirical character of psychology but by "remodeling" the very concept of empiricism so as to make it more suitable for psychological enterprises.[9] In his *Outlines of Psychology*, for example, he writes that an empirical science "deals, not with a limited group of specific contents of experience, but with the immediate contents of all experience."[10] He continues: "While natural science and psychology are both empirical sciences in the sense that they aim to explain the contents of experience, though from different points of view, still it is obvious that, in consequence of the character of its problem, psychology is the *more strictly empirical*."[11] Wundt can claim the "more strictly empirical" character of psychology because he has defined *empirical* as that which treats "the immediate contents of all experience." Psychology does examine experience in its immediacy and hence in its entirety. The natural sciences, on the other hand, divide experience into discrete quantities and analyze it by parts.

Wundt's broadening of the conception of empiricism typifies his concern both to make use of physiology and to distinguish it from psychology. Wundt's compromise between *Naturwissenschaft* and *Geisteswissenschaft* has particular consequences for "consciousness," namely, he theorizes a parallel between physical sensation and what he terms "actuality of mind," which he explains as follows:

It has been shown that the experience dealt with in the natural sciences and in psychology are nothing but components of *one* experience regarded from different points of view: in the natural sciences as an interconnection of objective phenomena and, in consequence of the abstraction from the knowing subject, as *mediate experience*; in psychology as *immediate and underived experience*. When this relation is once understood, the *concept of a mind-substance* immediately gives place to the *concept of the actuality of mind* as a basis for the comprehension of psychological processes.[12]

Wundt asserts a monism of experience that can be examined from multiple "points of view." The concept of "mind-substance" might be appropriate for some points of view (the physiologist's inquiries into the placebo effect, for instance), but to him the "actuality of mind" defines the proper methodological perspective for psychological investigations. As he writes just following the previous quotation, the actuality of mind "defin[es] the nature of mind as the immediate reality of the processes [of the mind] themselves."[13] By this, Wundt posits his psychological point of view as processual, and this focus on the *process* of human cognition has important implications for psychology's scientific status:

When the concept of actuality is adopted, a question upon which metaphysical systems of psychology have been long divided is immediately disposed of. This is the question of the *relation of body and mind*. So long as body and mind are both regarded as substances, this relation must remain an enigma. . . . If we start with the theory of the actuality of mind, we recognize the immediate reality of the phenomena in psychological experience. Our physiological concept of the bodily organism, on the other hand, is nothing but a part of this experience, which we gain, just as we do all the other empirical contents of the natural sciences, by assuming the existence of an object independent of the knowing subject.[14]

Whereas in the prior quotation, Wundt denominates physiology and psychology as two "points of view" for studying the monism of experience, this quotation slips a hierarchy into this perspectivalism by claiming that physiological knowledge "is nothing but a part" of our psychological experience. This purported hierarchy might simply function to indicate that even the most crassly materialist approach to natural science requires human cognition for its operations, and hence depends on psychology. Such an interpretation is supported by the fact that with respect to which type of knowledge is more real or more accurate, Wundt asserts a strict parallelism: both physiological and psychological knowledge are real and accurate; they simply examine the same data according to two distinct methodologies. On the other hand, asserting the cognitive priority of psychology counters those natural scientists who would denigrate psychology for not being sufficiently objective. If knowledge of physical entities depends on abstracting from a "knowing subject," then that knowledge is only as objective as our knowledge of that subject.

Wundt sustains this sleight of hand in his discussion of causality. The parallelism he asserts between physical sensation and actuality of mind mirrors that between physical causality and psychical causality. Wundt never adequately argues for psychical causality; instead he draws upon presumed common human experience that assumes that many mental processes cannot be subjected to experimental procedures. Thus he argues from lack; he suggests that psychical causation must exist since physical causation does not sufficiently explain all aspects of human experience.[15]

Wundt argues for parallel causality on the basis of an inability to analyze certain psychological phenomena as simply epiphenomena of physical phenomena. As we saw in the last chapter, Helmholtz inches toward a similar position in his demarcation between the process of unconscious inferences becoming conscious thoughts and the process of the sensory motor system generating (through physical semiosis) the raw data of felt experience. Helmholtz, however, merely implies that the associative processes of synthesizing unconscious inferences cannot be explained by physical causality. He does not take Wundt's step of asserting a full-fledged psychical causality. In this sense, Wundt demonstrates greater sensitivity to the complexities and contradictions broached by making the asssumptions and methods of *Naturwissenschaft* self-reflexive.

The Process of Actual Mind

The effect of Wundt's causal parallelism is twofold. First, it asserts that consciousness is a reality and not an epiphenomenon of material causality. Second, in prioritizing process over substance, the parallelism mandates that consciousness be studied through experiments that measure the relations of sensations to one another instead of measuring individual sense impressions.[16]

According to *Outlines of Psychology*, experimental psychology distinguishes psychical and physical objects only with respect to the level of abstraction required to examine them. Where the natural sciences abstract from the subject under investigation by making it an object that has qualities in common with other objects, psychology, being a mental as well as a natural science, examines its object in immediate relation to a (knowing) subject. Thereby, psychology focuses less on the object's uniqueness and more on the capacity of mind to perceive it.[17] Both methods seek to explain an object and to grasp its truth, but each charts a different path toward that truth. In terms of causality, Wundt notes that in sensation (physical causation) the "perceiving organ and the perceived object are two different things"; for example, the constitution of a particular rock acts in conjunction with light rays to cause the eye to sense a gray rock. But psychical causality operates within a unified field for "consciousness and conscious process" are not two different things; conscious process does not cause consciousness, nor is consciousness the cause of conscious process. The mental process itself is all there is: "we must think of the range of consciousness as denoting simply the sum of mental processes existing at a given moment."[18]

Another way of formulating this point draws again upon the reality of consciousness or the actuality of mind. Physical causality and psychical causality explain the singleness of experience, but they cannot be collapsed, since they inform experience in different ways. If scientists could reduce psychical causality and psychical events to physical explanations, Wundt would have to concede the latter's superiority and thus fail in his attempt to scientize psychology. Since the two causalities stand as parallel but separate modes of processing the world, Wundt concludes that consciousness is a real process— that mind is actual. Moreover, our concept of consciousness itself arises through an abstraction from that real process. As he writes in his *Ethics,* "When we abstract from the particular processes of our inner experience, which are its only real elements, and reflect upon the bare fact that we do perceive activities and processes in ourselves, we call this abstraction Consciousness. The term thus expresses merely the fact that we have an inner life; it no more represents anything different from the individual processes of this life than physical life is a special force over and above the sum of physiological processes."[19] This quotation evinces a fundamental consequence of Wundt's parallelism, namely, that consciousness must be studied processually via relations between sensations. The necessity of a processual point of view is merely a corollary of the process of abstraction. Both psychical and physical causality operate by efficient causation, but the causal efficacy of psychical causality is nonmechanical: mental events flow out of and enter into the single, continual, and actual process of mind. Hence Wundt argues that one can describe the causal efficacy of mental events only retrospectively and by abstraction from that flow.[20]

As a novel intervention into the concept of science and thus a novel argument for the scientific status of psychology, Wundt grants process the same status claimed by the empirical method of *Naturwissenschaft.* He justifies this move by defining process as simply another form of empiricism. By Wundt's definition, psychical empiricism is at least as valid as physical empiricism (and perhaps more so), but it is a different type of empiricism and thus submits to different criteria. For example, empiricism limits scientific experimentation to observation of the effects of mental processes; Wundt cannot include traditional modes of introspection without introducing methods he considers philosophical and hence damaging to his attempts to scientize psychology. Moreover, psychical empiricism must be applied not to analyze discrete data but to focus instead on cognitive relations that indicate the unified process of mind. Therefore the application of psychical empiricism confronts the ephemeral nature of mental phenomena.[21] Wundt negotiates these limitations through his theories about the will that conjoin the individual to the social and therefore bridge the psychological events being studied (mind as individual object) to the psychological events performing the study (mind as social subject).

Willing Sociality

For Wundt, *process* is not an ontological category, but strictly psychological.[22] Prioritizing process and the relations between sensations legitimizes psychology as an empirical science and circumvents what Wundt considers to be the metaphysical mistakes of faculty psychology. In response to the contemporary dominance of Schopenhauerian philosophies, Wundt strives to avoid any hint of the commonly presumed existence of a will.[23] Nevertheless, he is pointedly interested in the human capacity to produce intentional actions, so much so that he views intentional acts as both the grounding of experimental psychology and the direct or indirect end of all mental processes.[24] On the basis of this commitment, Wundt categorizes himself a "psychological voluntarist," which he describes as a "position that looks upon empirical volitional processes with their constituent feelings, sensations, and ideas, as the types of all conscious processes."[25] If not synonymous, volition and consciousness are for Wundt strictly concomitant.[26] As a consequence, willed action becomes the facet of mental life most experimentally accessible. Though much more occurs in mind and body, only intentional action is suitable for psychological research for only intentional actions can be controlled effectively and varied purposefully according to the dictates of scientific experimentation. By stressing the processual character of all mental life and the virtual congruence of volition and consciousness, Wundt argues that willing forms the end or product of mental processes, just like a meal forms the end or product of cooking—and, importantly, both are equally purposeful.

To recapitulate: "Physiological psychology is primarily psychology, and therefore has for its subject *the manifold of conscious process*, whether as directly experienced by ourselves, or as inferred on the analogy of our own experiences from objective observation."[27] This conscious process proceeds according to psychical causality, an associative process of abstraction that is just as empirical but not as predictable as physical causality. Mind and consciousness are synonymous in Wundt's writings, and consciousness and volition are at least concomitant. Through experiments that draw upon and manipulate human volition, Wundt supposes he is indirectly—but empirically and objectively—accessing the process of mind. Methodologically, his experiments freeze points of the mind's process by taking time measurements that can be compared (related) to each other.

How do the experimental emphases on the actuality of mind and the process of mental events affect Wundt's understanding of selfhood? Helmholtz never frames such a question. For him the self remains an object of physics and physiology. Wundt posits a self-reflexive transformation of the empirical methods of *Naturwissenschaft* and thereby redefines and expands the scope of concepts like empiricism, objectivity, and causality. For him, the self is an object-subject. This epistemological transformation models the change in the scientific approach to the self and to human being generally that was occurring throughout the knowledge networks of Wundt's culture. To answer how Wundt's research priorities affect an understanding of selfhood requires a look at his theories of feeling and attention as processes constitutive of personality and character.

Willing a Social Self

Attention, according to Wundt, is a compression of consciousness that occurs as an effect of willing.[28] He explains in his *Lectures on Human and Animal Psychology*: "The whole circle of subjective processes connected with apperception we call *attention*. Attention contains three essential constituents: an increased clearness of ideas; muscle-sensations, which generally belong to the same modality as the ideas; and feelings, which accompany and precede the ideational change."[29] Feelings are both the condition of possibility of attention and its companion element. Essentially Wundt is arguing that affect grounds human behavior and human consciousness. Affect focuses the part of the world selected for apperception, guides memory and the sensory motor system in enabling apperception to become perception, and steers mental and physical responses to perception. Since Wundt wishes both to avoid the language of faculty psychology and to hierarchize some mental processes over others, he stresses that attention is not a "special activity" but is "simply the name of the complex process which includes those three constituents."[30]

Wundt's laboratories were well known for their work on attention, work that centered on response times and memory capabilities.[31] More pertinent to this discussion, Wundt studied attention as a bringing to the surface of the potential that delimits the contours of consciousness. As Wundt describes it, "We imagine [attention] as the central region that surrounds the subjective fixation-point, and it is cut off by a more or less clearly defined boundary-line from the larger and darker field that surrounds it."[32] Wundt views consciousness as a series of imbricating collages, not as a static state or stage upon which thought acts. In his words, consciousness is not a thing or a state, but simply the constant and constantly changing "interconnection of psychical processes."[33] These imbricating collages are formed continually and from many levels of sensation and perception. Such an image of consciousness aids his critique of British associationist psychologists, whom Wundt considers too limited in their conception of association. According to Wundt, the British limit their discussion of association to the "combinations of ideas," "thereby excluding non-ideational facets of the process of consciousness, as, for example, feelings, moods and emotions."[34]

Wundt's parallel causality effectively redefines the concept of consciousness (the "actuality of mind") and stresses process as the principal datum of psychological research. Since psychology examines objects in their immediate relation to the subject, the datum of psychology is not a series of discrete facts but the *process* of perception itself, as measured by comparing points of perception at different points of time. These points are not the discrete, substantial points of fact employed by the natural sciences, but are heuristic abstractions extracted from the continual flow of mind. Since psychical causality operates within and through the moving process of mental events, it can never transmit the same level of certainty about the world as that conveyed by physical causality. Psychical causality is swathed in "tendency"

(*Richtung*) and potentiality: "In the case of psychical events the most we can do is to indicate the general direction [*Richtung*], not the specific form, of the result."[35] In fact Wundt posits this "general tendency" (*allgemein Richtung*) as the most unequivocal aspect of psychical causality, thereby grounding psychical causality in feeling and volition. He speculates that the unified and internal character of feeling creates a dearth of terms for expressing simple feelings (especially relative to the comparative abundance of terms for colors and sounds). Put differently, since the unified field of feeling is internal, "all the motives of practical life which give rise to the names of objects and their attributes are here wanting."[36] The subtlety of language is generated on the effective end of the process of mental life, not on the conditioning end. Feelings are crucially important to human existence generally, but not for the actions of everyday life. These actions entail interactions with other persons and hence propel the intricate differentiation of and within specific words. Feelings, on the other hand, are only the inner preface to external action. Feelings help determine a band of attention and motivate intentional action. As he wrote in his *Outlines of Psychology*, "There is no feeling or emotion that does not in some way prepare for a volitional act, or at least have some part in such a preparation."[37]

Two consequences result from conceiving action as the end of most feelings (and hence of most willings and most thoughts). First, action marks the self's *inter*action with others and hence implies the social realm; and second, the feeling and volition that condition action mark the self's uniqueness and form what Wundt calls the "stamp of individuality."[38] The self is thus not a substance or entity, but rather a useful concept composed by abstraction from the process of mental life. The "'self,'" he writes, "is not an entity, but the coalescing of all concurrent mental processes. To reveal 'self' more exactly requires probing the causes of our volitional acts."[39] The preceding discussion functions as just such a probing, determining that "the causes of volitional acts" are feelings, and that feelings steer volition toward a unified tendency or disposition that focuses consciousness into a band of attention and actualizes itself in action. In less technical language, feelings embrace, enable, and express the *purpose* of human behavior.

As actions are repeated, purposes are solidified. Thus Wundt asserts that actions determine the character of the self, and he sometimes refers to the process of forming character in terms of control over the self: "What we call our 'self' is simply this unity of volition *plus* the univocal control of our mental life which it renders possible."[40] Wundt divides character into two branches of volition—ego and personality—which are distinguished according to whether volition is being considered in its conscious or in its self-conscious role. He writes, "As the Ego is the will in its distinction from the rest of conscious content, so personality is the Ego reunited to the manifold of this content and thereby raised to the stage of self-consciousness."[41] To Wundt, reflection on personality constitutes the field of ethics and best informs the way humans develop character. As he describes in his *Ethics*, "To reflect concerning oneself means to be conscious of one's personality as determined by previous volitional development; and to act with reflection is to act with a consciousness of the significance which the motives and purposes of the action have for the character of the agent."[42] Here Wundt argues not only that character is the expression of personality through action—and hence that character is the expression of the social self—but also that volitional acts (the only acts psychologically, that is, scientifically and ethically, worth considering) always indicate motives and ends or purposes (*Zwecke*). For Wundt, however, the purposes of action remain something that can only be indicated. Purpose itself is not scientific or open to scientific investigation. Only when purposes solidify into repeatable (and hence observable and quantifiable) actions can they be granted a place within scientific explanation.

Wundt's insistence that willing is always accompanied by conation and feeling illuminates the process and function of psychical causality, which constitutes the empirical character of physiological psychology. Psychical causality is itself a volitional process.[43] As Wundt notes, "Psychical causality is the immediate form, given directly as that of motives and purposes in thought; it involves no hypothesis beyond the immediate fact as it exists in thought."[44] In short, psychical causality not only legitimizes psychology by suggesting different understandings of empiricity and objectivity, it also carves out a unique disciplinary space by insisting on a direct linkage between physical action and ethical formation, reflection, and inspiration. Later in his *Ethics,* Wundt continues to explicate the connection of character (an ethical "class-concept")[45] to psychical causality (a scientific "class-concept"): "What we understand by character is thus the total result of past psychical causality, itself forming part of the cause of each new effect."[46] The social effect of this narration of character is a level of predictability about one's neighbors and hence a level of regularity in society that might generally only be expected of *Naturwissenschaft*:

> As the conditions that determine character become more constant, and crystallize into the fixed moral tendencies of the individual's disposition, we are able not only to deduce actions from character after the fact, but to predict from our knowledge of a man's character the way in which he will react to given motives. *Thus we see that in this highest form psychical causality approaches the invariable regularity of the mechanism of nature.*[47]

Earlier I claimed that Wundt acknowledges that psychological phenomena yield less certainty than physiological phenomena and I suggested that Wundt solves this limitation of psychology through his theories of the will, which link the individual to the social. The preceding quotation aptly summarizes this position. Psychical causality produces its own certainty, not about the causal relations of material objects, but about the way human action solidifies into a predictable character. This is a certainty of processes (actions) and intuited feelings, not of objects and tangible qualities. This quotation also ably indicates the place of purpose in Wundt's psychology. His emphasis on volition and feeling gives a central role to purpose, but Wundt is interested in *Zwecke* only to the degree that their influence on psychical causality lends the

latter an "invariable regularity" like efficient (physical) causation ("the mechanism of nature"). This nearly "invariable regularity" of psychical causality is
not of concern to Wundt because of an interest in self-control or self-discipline (*ascesis*), but rather because of an interest in social control and social
discipline.

Despite his sociological view of human psychology, Wundt agrees with
natural scientists that psychical causes are never fully determinable. Psychical causes "lie outside consciousness, and belong to an inaccessible series of
past experiences." Psychical causality depends on the association of factors
such as memory, hope, and anticipation and thus can only be accessed through
abstraction from a continual flow of mental process. On the other hand, psychical causes "form part of a more general conscious nexus, of which the
individual mind constitutes only one link."[48] The abstractions performed by
a single mind never remove simply one strand or layer of the process of actual mind, but always involve memories and aspirations that exceed the concerns of the moment by plugging into surrounding concerns. Abstraction
removes one filament of thought from the larger, moving process within the
individual subject, which flows into ever-larger networks of sociality. Put differently, psychical causality is never fully determinable because it relies upon
abstraction, both from the individual's actual mind and *as* the individual mind
(that is, the individual's actual mind is itself abstracted from the social mind).

It is thus no wonder that Wundt's texts usually proceed to discussions of
social consciousness and will. The self is an abstraction from mental process
and that mental process is conditioned by sensations derived from the external world. Language also is conditioned by the need and desire to commingle
with other humans. Hence Wundt states that the "isolated individual man . . .
does not exist and undoubtedly never has existed as a fact of experience."[49]
The individual will (a processual network of individual consciousness, feeling, and conation) is derived from the social will (a larger processual network
of social consciousness, feeling, and conation). Derivation is not, however,
determination. Assimilation and reactions to external stimuli differ for each
person and guarantee what Wundt calls the "stamp of individuality."

Wundt analyzes the conjunction of consciousness, feeling, and conation
through another concept: altruism. Since the individual arises out of the social, altruism is both concretely real and evolutionarily important. In his *Ethics*, Wundt gives two grounds for the successful persistence of altruistic actions, one objective and the other subjective:

> The objective reason is the fact that an altruistic tendency on the part of ac-
> tions makes possible a more extended functioning of the moral will, and thus
> serves the common ends of society and humanity at large. The subjective rea-
> son, which is perhaps the more important, is that every unselfish action serves
> as a test of character, by which we can measure the general worth of the indi-
> vidual personality.[50]

Wundt prioritizes the subjective argument for altruism because of its importance in developing character. Though he asserts that character arises out of

and through a person's larger social context, he stresses the subjective way in which a person assimilates and responds to that context. James shares this priority, though he utilizes the will not as a bridge between the individual and the social, but as precisely that aspect of being human that protects the sanctity of the individual. The religious overtones of "sanctity" aptly pinpoint what is absent in Wundt and clearly demarcates the German from the pragmatists. Peirce and James both assume some sense of mystery and purpose in life, assumptions narrated in America within the language of religion. As I see it, James is a becoming-ethicist, while Wundt remains a becoming-sociologist. Wundt's focus remains mundane, tuned to the changing tides of society and scientific discourse. One strain of his work does raise ethical concerns, but Wundt never connects these ethical questions to the larger frame of the meaning of and possibilities within life in general. The larger frame is a metaphysical, cosmological, or religious question, spheres embraced by Peirce and James, but shed by Wundt in order to secure psychology within the coveted space of "science."

To Know Thyself

This chapter has argued that Wundt retains the important advances of a *naturwissenschaftlich* physicalism in an effort to ensure psychology's place within scientific discourse. In asserting this physicalism, Wundt agrees with Helmholtz's realism, at least to a point. Wundt's theories of the actuality of mind and the processual nature of consciousness, attention, and the self posit that the rules and concepts of psychology are really bounded by—embedded in—the rules of *Naturwissenschaft*. Though they also supersede those rules, they are neither heuristic abstractions from real particulars nor real entities separate from bodily (physical) processes. On the other hand, Wundt's realism remains on a theoretical level; it abandons discussion of embodiment almost as soon as it is asserted. That is, Wundt's discussions of consciousness and the self center on the concept of process, which is real, Wundt asserts, because humans experience it as real. True as this may be, his "mental process" does not rely for its explication on the physiological processes of the brain or sensory motor system.

Wundt's conviction that mental process is grounded in but also supersedes physiological process forms the basis of his theory of parallel causality. Wundt extrapolates the reality of psychical causality from the brute experience of having a mental life, but the wider context for his reworking of causality is the philosophical claim that physics does not and cannot assess all levels of human being. Physics cannot analyze myths or languages or religions. To Wundt, these facets of human thinking and being are true and effective, and this conviction guides his reworking of the concepts of empiricism and objectivity in addition to causality. Empiricism, according to Wundt, pertains to the whole content of experience (not just the aspects analyzable by *Naturwissenschaft*), and objectivity signifies any repeatable method of analysis, regardless of the level of certainty guaranteed by that method. Wundt requires these conceptual permutations in order to argue successfully for his most radical conceptual transformation, that of consciousness as an actual, objective, and empirically accessible process.

As stated at the outset of this chapter, Wundt's success lies in widening the discursive boundary of *Naturwissenschaft* to include psychology, while simultaneously revaluing the concepts of *Naturwissenschaft* in order to broaden their scope for exploring the mysteries of human thinking and being. It is in this latter mode that Wundt is considered so influential in the development of twentieth-century psychology and is thus often called the "father of psychology." Yet what can it mean, really, to credit Wundt with such a momentous siring? William James—whose excitement about traveling to Germany in 1868 was due in part to the possibility of hearing Helmholtz and Wundt lecture at Heidelberg—caricatured Wundt as a typical German pedant, a man who was more interested in gathering together the knowledge of other men than in developing his own, unique intellectual contribution.[51] Supporting this description, one commentator has noted that the numerous Americans who studied with Wundt took back to the United States "not a fresh set of ideas but rather *a new liturgy*."[52] Wundt offered nothing new conceptually, as others of his culture were also developing their efforts to scientize psychology. What Wundt did offer was his academic standing and his unflagging institutional warfare to establish the legitimacy and integrity of psychological research. Perhaps it was the aura of authority and respect that made Wundt so important and effective, for others could draw upon his reputation in the fighting of their own institutional battles.

The institutional success of Wundt was particularly important for American intellectuals in the late nineteenth century, for it allowed them to stand under the aegis of his psychology and declare it an ambassador of the truths of *Naturwissenschaft*. Doing so proved immeasurably fruitful in fighting the challenges brought to American intellectuals by sciences (like evolution) less charitable to *Geisteswissenschaft*,[53] for it permitted intellectuals to claim the mantle and power of "science" in defense of the religious and ethical truths that formed their personal and national identities. Wundt's more strictly physiological work was thus taken up in America by theorists specifically interested in ethical, philosophical, and theological questions.[54] Considering these institutional and discursive exigencies, it seems unsurprising that Wundt's name and work faded from intense discussion with his retirement from the academy and the loss of institutional authority that had accompanied his treatises. By the 1930s the questions and issues surrounding the roles of science and religion in American society had simply changed; they no longer required the mediating figure that Wundt had provided so beautifully.

Pragmatic Consequences

I wish now to suggest a theoretical link between Wundt and James that includes four primary themes: (1) the relation of psychical events to physical (efficient) causation, (2) the repositioning of empiricism, (3) the purposiveness of consciousness, and (4) the role of will or volition.

James's *Principles of Psychology* presents a parallelism of causality within a monism of experience reminiscent of Wundt's writings. In the chapter entitled "The Mind-Stuff Theory," James wonders whether "the ascertainment of a blank unmediated correspondence, term for term, of the succession of states of consciousness with the succession of total brain-processes, be not the simplest psycho-physic formula, and the last word of a psychology which contents itself with verifiable laws, and seeks only to be clear, and to avoid unsafe hypotheses. Such a mere admission of the empirical parallelism will there appear the wisest course."[55] James does here propose an "empirical parallelism," but it is directly opposite that of Wundt. Where the German argues for a parallel causality that interprets psychological events as neither reducible nor epiphenomenal to physical events, James concedes that psychical processes lack scientific qualities and suggests that for "a psychology which contents itself with verifiable laws, and seeks only to be clear" it should suffice to presume only physical causality. This allegiance to physical or efficient causality, however, oscillates with James's conviction that studying human cognition requires negotiating the final causality or purposiveness of consciousness. James describes consciousness as "at all times primarily *a selecting agency*,"[56] a function and activity of consciousness that differs fundamentally from Wundt, who places purpose solely in will. Chapter 6 will discuss how James's philosophical writings attribute human purpose both to will and to consciousness. Either way, James accepts Wundt's lesson but refuses the moral; he understands that psychology cannot easily engage *Naturwissenschaft* on its own terms, but he does not redefine the notion of causality to include purpose. In the end the tension between the claims of efficient and final causation marks James's departure from psychology and positions his launch into philosophy as an attempt to find a disciplinary space that will accommodate his commitment to purpose as integral to studying human thought and being.[57]

The link between Wundt and James appears more clearly in their descriptions of consciousness as processual. James's famous depiction of "the stream of consciousness" functions much like Wundt's image of consciousness as a series of imbricating collages. The difference between the two psychologists lies again in the role of purpose. James calls purpose the function of consciousness; consciousness transmits experience into practical (purposeful) knowledge. In his later writings on radical empiricism, James constructs consciousness as the "external relation" connecting experiences to one another, a relation that is real, actual, and inherently purposive. James also calls consciousness a "fighter for ends" and avers that every consciousness is personal, just as every thought is personally owned.[58] Wundt, on the other hand, perceives consciousness as the product of abstracting from "the particular processes of our immediate inner experience."[59] The actuality of mind as immediate process gives way to the abstraction of consciousness as reflected knowledge.

Since consciousness is an abstraction, Wundt theorizes the will as immediate knowledge (grounded in feeling), which clears theoretical ground for his theory of the social construction of the self, and he theorizes purpose as the unobservable but indicated form of this immediate knowledge, which clears the ground for his theories of social character and social control.

Finally, Wundt and James share a theoretical focus on the will. For Wundt, psychology is the space that combines the empiricism of the natural sciences with the ethical and social import of the mental sciences. His theory of parallel causality results in a nonnominalist, though disembodied, theory of mind and consciousness. Helmholtz's realism attempts to bridge the concerns of both empiricism and transcendentalism. Wundt's realist theories can be seen to effect a similar balancing act, though he does not engage this debate directly since his theories specifically address the relation of individual to society instead of analyzing Kant and Hume. Through his discussion of volition, Wundt's theories about the social construction of the individual become the central axis for his theories of mind. James too is a voluntarist, though the pragmatist does not explore the volitional connection of the individual to society so much as he delineates the freedoms and obligations of the individual with regard to society. In language I employed earlier, Wundt is a becoming-sociologist—asking questions that are taken up by ethnography, phenomenology, and sociology—while James is a becoming-ethicist, whose efforts center on questions of freedom, choice, and value.

For both men, redefining empiricism furthers their scientific and philosophic goals. Wundt changes empiricism to mean that which examines all of experience and then declares that psychology is a line of inquiry that encompasses a greater portion of experience than physiology. James develops his radical empiricism as both a critique of the atomism of the British empiricists and as a means of arguing for a monism of experience that legitimizes metaphysical (and religious) inquiries.[60] In a sense, James extracts the impact of Wundt's theory of physiological psychology and articulates a general proposition about relationality and empiricism that has far-reaching effects for how humans understand truth and reality. James reads the work of men like Helmholtz and Wundt and shares their desire to reconcile the legacy of Kant with the empirical tenets shared by British philosophers and industrialists, but unlike the Germans, James grounds the concepts of causality, consciousness, and will in his strong allegiance to purpose. Like Wundt he wishes to clear a discursive space, not for a scientific psychology but for the sanctity of the individual and for the inescapable mystery of life.

This chapter concludes my discussion of German psychology, a field that developed in parallel with and response to larger nineteenth-century commitments to empiricism, technological progress, and the intensification of capitalist modes of production. Wundt stands as a figure for how these commitments came to function reflexively, that is, how they came to affect nineteenth-century understandings and analyses of human thought and being. Culturally, Wundt's theories gained immense support. But transposed to American sites, they were found lacking in attention to what Peirce and James would call religious concerns.

II

EVOLUTION OF
SCOTTISH PSYCHOLOGY

William Hamilton

The Philosopher of the Conditioned

During his career as professor of logic and metaphysics at the University of Edinburgh, Sir William Hamilton (1788–1856) won the intense admiration of both students and colleagues. John Veitch, his principal contemporary biographer, went so far as to assert that Hamilton was "a name that will not be forgotten in the history of philosophy."[1] History having relegated Hamilton to obscurity, it may be surprising that the eminent philosopher J. S. Mill agrees with Veitch: "Among the philosophical writers of the present century in these islands, no one occupies a higher position than Sir William Hamilton. He alone, of our metaphysicians of this and the preceding generation, has acquired, merely as such, an European celebrity: while, in our own country, he has not only had power to produce a revival of interest in a study which had ceased to be popular, but has made himself, in some sense, the founder of a school of thought."[2] Mill, who today sits securely in the philosophical canon, considered his now uncelebrated Scottish colleague worthy of a 650-page detailed examination and point-by-point refutation, of which the preceding sentences form the opening lines.

The stir caused by Hamilton was not lost on nineteenth-century American thought. In an appendix to his massive *Memoir* entitled "On the Influence of Sir W. Hamilton's Writings in America," John Veitch reprints a letter about Hamilton from the Yale moral philosopher and metaphysician Noah Porter.[3] Porter praises Hamilton's erudition and courage in introducing considered reflections on German and French philosophers and in reawakening an interest in logic and the history of philosophy. Particularly, Porter writes, Hamilton was instrumental in advancing and reforming the thought of Kant, Victor Cousin, and Archbishop Whatley.[4] Though Hamilton's early and widely read essay, "The Philosophy of the Unconditioned," had a delayed influence because of Americans' unfamiliarity with Cousin, nevertheless "the astounding erudition, the vigorous thought, the masterly analysis, the acute criticism, and the self-relying independence by which they were distinguished, made a profound impression upon the many readers whom they at once excited and astonished."[5] Porter attributes the strong appreciation of Hamilton to Americans' relative ignorance of European philosophy, in essence suggesting that Hamilton introduced Americans to continental thought. Before Hamilton, Porter asserts, most American philosophers had relied almost exclusively on the British thought of T. H. Reid, Dugald Stewart, and Thomas Brown, the only exceptions being a scant knowledge of European names and a perusal of the classical philosophers "chiefly for purely linguistic or philological purposes."[6]

Porter explains Hamilton's American reception relative to the current intellectual climate. The period from about 1820 to 1850, he notes, dates "a very active and earnest controversy" within "the entire New England school of theology, which turned entirely upon the application of certain mooted psychological and philosophical principles to the received evangelical doctrines."[7] Porter here refers to the controversies discussed in the prologue between the Old Calvinists of Princeton and the New Divinity theologians of Yale and Andover seminaries, debates that were spurred in part by the growing "Methodization" of Protestant revivals in New England (the so-called Second Great Awakening of the 1820s).[8] As previously indicated, these controversies revolved around the legacy of Jonathan Edwards, both as a Calvinist and as an American. Porter, however, does not inform his readers that before the debates of the Second Great Awakening, there was a distinct *lack* of attention to Edwards. Indeed, Edwards's works were so seldom read in America in the latter half of the eighteenth century that his relatives and intellectual devotees had to appeal to overseas publishers to maintain circulation of his texts. Their pleas were answered primarily in Scotland, where Edwards was republished steadily and read widely.[9] The return of Edwards to the American scene, then, was accompanied by the new Scottish voice of William Hamilton, who pointed Americans' philosophical compass toward Europe.

The theological controversy in New England and Hamilton's maieutic reflections on current European thought catalyze a general academic interest in continental philosophy. Porter writes to Veitch, "It was just beginning to be the fashion with us to study the German language, and many an ardent youth looked forward with eagerness to the time when he should be able to read Kant in the original, or penetrate the secret of Schelling and Hegel, by hearing these writers interpreted through a German professor." As a result, Porter continues, "There was probably never a time in our history which could more truly or appropriately be termed a period of fermentation and almost of revolutionary anarchy in our philosophical thinking, than the time when the articles of Sir William Hamilton began to be read among us."[10] Who exactly Porter includes in "our history" and "among us" is unclear. For my purposes I wish Veitch had consulted a Harvard theologian, since I cannot be certain that what Porter writes of Hamilton held as strongly for Boston's Unitarians as he asserts it did for New Haven's New Divinity.[11] But I do presume that Hamilton was well known and read in Peirce's and James's intellectual environments (if, perhaps, toward different ends) for the simple reason that their writings assume a knowledge of him. Hamilton is referenced in every volume of Peirce's *Collected Papers*, usually as an aside in the wearied tone of this line from a letter to William James: "Hamilton's hammering on the *ego* and *non-ego*, we'll take for granted."[12] On his part, James's *Principles of Psychology* references Hamilton eight times, in an equally familiar manner, and his opening to *The Varieties of Religious Experience* claims, "Hamilton's own lectures were the first philosophic writings I ever forced myself to study."[13]

Hamilton's widespread influence did not last long, despite the legion of students required to push through his dense *Lectures* and articles. Perhaps J. S. Mill's searing critique is apt: Hamilton spent his erudition on collating quotations from sources rarely read and too long overlooked (hence his reputation in the history of philosophy) and had too little stamina left over for real thought. His writings, Mill gripes, quickly devolve into bitter polemic, as if destruction of another's position could substitute adequately for the construction of one's own.[14] But the reason also could revolve around more social factors, including the increasing economic and discursive dominance of the natural sciences, which favored a blunt naturalism and a critique of metaphysics that Hamilton found philosophically and theologically offensive.[15] Merited or not, and however short-lived his fame, Hamilton was widely studied and quoted as authoritative during his active years of teaching and writing, and it is this fact that sustains the following examination of his philosophy as one of the generating conditions of American pragmatism.

By training and profession Hamilton was a philosopher, though his early studies were in medicine, anatomy, and botany (at both Glasgow and Oxford universities). Both his father and grandfather had held the chair of anatomy and botany at the University of Glasgow, and his family assumed that Sir William would follow suit. As a consequence, excursions through his *Lectures* are met with occasional detours into contemporary or self-made physiological experiments, for example, on attention, phrenology, or the weight of the brain.[16] Nonetheless, most of his time and energy were spent on philosophical inquiries, and his reputation for the prompt recall of classical and medieval philosophers was evidently not misplaced. Veitch characterizes Hamilton's Oxford years as a constant scrutiny of every philosophical manuscript he could access, and he reportedly impressed the examination committee with his unusually broad knowledge.[17]

In terms of the evolution of British psychology, then, Hamilton stands as a thinker more than mildly interested in the natural sciences and yet who still fully encompasses psychology under the rubric of philosophy. In his *Lectures on Metaphysics*, he defines psychology as "the Philosophy of the Human Mind, strictly so denominated . . . the science conversant about the *phoenomena* [*sic*], or *modifications*, or *states* of the *Mind*, or *Conscious*-

Subject, or *Soul*, or *Spirit*, or *Self*, or *Ego*."[18] The elements of his system most influential on the pragmatists include the relativity of knowledge, the philosophy of the conditioned, and the doctrine of free will; each of these will be examined separately.

In this chapter I will demonstrate the resonance between Peirce and Hamilton, which can be outlined in three ways. First, both men present a philosophy that balances Kant's idealism with Reid's naturalism (Peirce calls this task a "critical common-sensism"). Second, they both discuss questions of faith in a manner that implies a transcendent or cosmological perspective. Third, they exhibit a focused interest in logic. The pragmatist always evinces slightly different priorities, however. While Hamilton remains a committed nominalist throughout his writings, Peirce attempts to reconcile Kant and British empiricism as part of his larger argument against nominalism. While Hamilton maintains a Calvinist trinitarianism, Peirce's musings on questions of faith direct him closer to Spinoza's panentheism. Finally, while Hamilton's logic remains an important but separate line of philosophical inquiry, Peirce develops a logic of relations that conjoins his interest in logic to his semeiotic and phenomenology and thus becomes a pervasive part of his philosophy.

After giving a brief exposition of the main points of his philosophy, the discussion of Hamilton will examine how relativity, conditionality, and free will inform his statements about causality, consciousness, belief, and action. Of greatest interest is how the concept of consciousness relates to the concept of belief, such that the former acts as the guarantor of the latter.

The Relativity of Knowledge

Hamilton's interlocutors include Locke, T. H. Reid, Dugald Stewart, and Thomas Brown on his side of the channel, and Kant and Victor Cousin on the other side. Much of his writings are taken up with defending Reid's commonsense philosophy against Brown's "hypothetical realism,"[19] and with defending Kant against Cousin's interpretations. This dual and seemingly contradictory allegiance can be explained through his doctrine of the relativity of knowledge.

From one perspective, the relativity of knowledge replicates Kant's split between the phenomenal and the noumenal. Hamilton asserts the basic tenet of phenomenology: that we perceive not the objects and events of the world, but those objects and events in their phenomenal aspect, that is, as they are taken up and interpreted by our faculties. "The existence of an unknown substance is only an inference we are compelled to make, from the existence of known phaenomena," he asserts without comment, an obvious allusion to Kant's noumenal object.[20] Statements like this seemed to baffle J. S. Mill, who did not know how to reconcile their idealistic bent with Hamilton's insistence that natural realism is "the one legitimate doctrine."[21] Natural realism (Hamilton's term for Reid's philosophical position) holds that though all of our perceptions are phenomena, they are reliable phenomena of the objects we perceive. This understanding of realism requires a basic dualism between the ego and the world; indeed, Hamilton staunchly supports the necessity of this dualism. Consciousness, he says, testifies that phenomena transmit immediate knowledge of actual objects, and "by the very act of refusing any one datum of consciousness, philosophy invalidates the whole credibility of consciousness, and consciousness ruined as an instrument, philosophy is extinct."[22] Reworking the concept of consciousness to mean "testimony" has direct consequences for the concept of belief. As he writes, "Consciousness is to the philosopher what the Bible is to the theologian. Both are revelations of the truth,—and both afford the truth to those who are content to receive it, as it ought to be received, with reverence and submission."[23] I will return to the connection of consciousness and belief after I conclude this discussion of Hamilton's realism.

Hamilton accommodates his commonsense realism to his acceptance of Kant's relativity of knowledge by adjusting Locke's theory of primary and secondary qualities. He begins by introducing a new subdivision, that of the secundo-primary qualities, and by translating these numerical designations into relations of subject and object. In consequence, the primary qualities are termed the objective qualities, the secondary are named the subjective qualities, and the secundo-primary are called the subjectivo-objective qualities. Hamilton stresses that these denominations are not "physical" but "psychological."[24] By this he invokes Locke's separation of sense from understanding, or sensation from perception. As such, primary qualities are strictly percepts, secundo-primary are both percepts and sensations, and secondary are strictly sensations.[25] Hamilton's footnote at this point is worth quoting:

> *All* knowledge, in one respect, is *subjective*; for all knowledge is an energy of the Ego. But when I perceive a quality of the Non-Ego, of the object-object, as in immediate relation to my mind, I am said to have of it an *objective* knowledge; in contrast to the *subjective* knowledge, I am said to have of it when supposing it only as the hypothetical or occult cause of an affection of which I am conscious, or thinking it only mediately through a subject-object or representation in, and of, the mind.[26]

Hamilton agrees that absolute knowledge of the physical world is ultimately impossible since all knowledge is phenomenal or "an energy of the Ego." Psychologically, however, he claims to be able to distinguish ego and non-ego through a perception of the non-ego in an "immediate relation to my mind." This claim derives from Reid's and Stewart's commonsense philosophies, which find no plausible objection to the everyday belief that humans really perceive a world filled with objects and that human percepts are really of that world and those objects. What must be kept in mind throughout this discussion is that Hamilton makes no arguments about the physical world itself, but only about psychology, about the world of consciousness, the testimony of which he declares is indubitable.

Throughout his categorization of primary, secondary, and secundo-primary qualities, Hamilton aims to present as obvious and irrefutable the two facts that all human knowledge is relative to the operations of consciousness and that, nevertheless, this knowledge is reliable. He asserts the commonsense heritage of Reid and Stewart, to which he adds Kant's sophisticated phenomenological analyses. In this way, Hamilton expresses a concern shared by Peirce and James to accede to Kant's characterization of the mind (*Verstand*) as constitutive, without relinquishing the British legacy of commonsense realism.

The Philosophy of the Conditioned

Hamilton thus develops "the philosophy of the conditioned," a position that directly counters Victor Cousin's philosophy of the unconditioned and proceeds logically from the doctrine of the relativity of all knowledge. He delineates the position in his widely read article, "The Philosophy of the Unconditioned," in which he purports to differentiate himself from Kant, Cousin, and Schelling:

> In our opinion, the mind can conceive, and, consequently, can know, only the *limited, and the conditionally limited*. The unconditionally unlimited, or the *Infinite*, the unconditionally limited, or the *Absolute*, can not positively be construed to the mind; they can be conceived, only by a thinking away from, or abstraction of, those very conditions under which thought itself is realized; consequently, the notion of the Unconditioned is only negative—negative of the conceivable itself.[27]
>
> As the conditionally limited (which we may briefly call the *conditioned*) is thus the only possible object of knowledge and of positive thought—thought necessarily supposes conditions. *To think* is *to condition*; and conditional limitation is the fundamental law of the possibility of thought. For, as the greyhound can not outstrip his shadow . . . so the mind can not transcend that sphere of limitation within and through which exclusively the possibility of thought is realized.[28]

The resemblance of this description to Kant's antinomies will be apparent to those familiar with *The Critique of Pure Reason*. Yet unlike Kant, who declares the unconditioned a regulative principle of thought, Hamilton asserts that it is merely a negation of what is positively possible to think, namely, a negation of the conditioned. In a circular logic, Hamilton surmises that since only "conditionally limited" thought is possible, "thought necessarily supposes conditions." This philosophy of the conditioned restates Hamilton's doctrine of the relativity of knowledge from the perspective of concepts instead of percepts, or from the process of drawing conclusions or progressing in thought instead of the logically prior process of coming to know something. Whereas the relativity of knowledge argues that knowledge is always relative to our faculties, the philosophy of the conditioned claims that "to think is to condition." The process of thought itself is one of a progressive limiting.

Hamilton does not define *condition* in his famous article, where one might most expect it, but he does discuss the concept in his *Lectures on Metaphysics and Logic*. There he quotes Krug's *Logik*: "A condition is a thing which determines (negatively at least) the existence of another; the conditioned is a thing whose existence is determined in and by another."[29] From the doctrine of the relativity of knowledge, Hamilton concludes that thought is itself both condition and conditioned, for the secundo-primary and secondary qualities subjectively condition thought, while thought is conditioned by the primary qualities, that is, by the objects of thought themselves. Hamilton's philosophy of the conditioned states these relations in other terms. Thinking, according to this doctrine, is either predicative on existence or not. If it is predicative, then it must fulfill either the principle of non-contradiction (which includes the laws of identity, the excluded middle, and sufficient reason) or the principle of relativity.[30] The principle of noncontradiction is a law of things (an "insuperable" law), but the principle of relativity is only a law of thought (and therefore not insuperable). Though there are many nonnecessary, contingent relations under this principle of relativity, there are but three necessary ones: the relations of knowledge, which divide self from nonself; the intrinsic relations of existence, which include substance and quality (analogous to the secondary and secundo-primary qualities); and the extrinsic relations of existence, which include time, space, and intensity or degree (analogous to the primary qualities).[31] Again, this way of formulating the philosophy of the conditioned in terms of the principles of thought and objects restates the doctrine of relativity from the perspective of logic instead of psychology.

The heart of the philosophy of the conditioned is the claim that the conditionally relative character of knowledge is a law of thought. We know that relativity is only a law of thought (as opposed to a natural law) because it is perfectly possible for us to think of two opposite situations but not be able to resolve which one of the two is true. Importantly for Hamilton's philosophy, however, even though we cannot decide between the two situations, one of them "must" be true.[32] He argues the necessity of one of the two sides of any antinomy being true by appealing to the law of the excluded middle. Though this law is part of the principle of noncontradiction, and hence a statement about things and not thoughts, still Hamilton claims it is always necessary and applicable.[33] Some compromise position must be reached, and for this position Hamilton turns to the testimonies of consciousness, which he, along with Reid and Stewart, deem incontrovertible and which operate under known limitations (conditions). Hence the label "the philosophy of the conditioned."

The consequences of this philosophical position are threefold. First, it shows Hamilton's Kantian leanings in stating that human knowledge of the world is limited in principle as well as in fact. The mind's limitations are not fully explained by experience, ignorance, or inclination, but are part of its essential nature. Second, the philosophy of the conditioned differentiates his and Reid's natural realism from Mill's realism by asserting that the natural sciences do not yield the only truths about the universe, since a realm of the unconditioned must be presumed. Third, "reason is shown to be weak but not deceitful"; belief in the unconditioned is justified (since either side of an antinomy is in itself unconditioned), even if that belief cannot be filled in with positive content.[34] From these consequences it is clear that the philosophy of the conditioned relies on Hamilton's Christian presuppositions of a transcendent world (the supernatural or God) in which humans can justifiably believe, even though nothing positive can be known about it. The next section will demonstrate how Hamilton uses the philosophy of the conditioned to specify philosophical and theological claims about the world.

Freedom of the Will

The way Hamilton applies the philosophy of the conditioned to the law of causality clarifies his position on the will. Since the law of the conditioned posits that the mind thinks only under certain forms, Hamilton describes the mind as imminently engaging the antinomy of time and eternity. Thus, the mind thinks under the condition of existence and under the condition that existence is relative over time (at different points in time, different qualities manifest themselves), but the mind can imagine neither an absolute commencement or termination of an object or situation nor an absolute noncommencement or nontermination. Though Hamilton argues from the law of the excluded middle that one of these two options "must" be true, he recognizes that the mind cannot decide between them. Hence, he concludes, humans "infer" the notion of causality from the testimony of consciousness; causality is a familiar explanation for the expected association of events, or for their brute existence. By this description, the law of causality is not a positive law of thought, "but only an incapacity of thinking the opposite."[35] Even when we do not know *the* cause of something, it is still necessary to presuppose *a* cause.

The relation of this account of causality to free will is not hard to specify. The options delineated in most discussions of the will are either the absolutely uncaused (spontaneous) creation of a volition or willed act, or the willed act absolutely determined by a prior series of causes. Hamilton rejects the former position in that it asserts as true one of the two sides of the antinomy of causality, namely, the absolute commencement of an object or situation. The latter position seems just as unlikely to him in that it is equivalent to asserting a positive law of causation that effectively argues against theism:

> To suppose a positive and special principle of causality, is to suppose, that there is expressly revealed to us, through intelligence, the fact that there is no free causation, that is, that there is no cause which is not itself merely an effect; existence being only a series of determined antecedents and determined consequents. But this is an assertion of Fatalism. . . . The assertion of absolute necessity . . . is virtually the negation of a moral universe, consequently of the Moral Governor of a moral universe; in a word, Atheism.[36]

At first this quotation seems more appeal than argument, but its argument lies in the fact that the philosophy of the conditioned is grounded in the testimony of consciousness, which, Hamilton claims, assures us of humanity's moral freedom. Since we feel ourselves to be free and hold ourselves to be morally accountable, we must be. Any resolution of the conundrums of the will must not contradict this simple witness of consciousness. Therefore, though we cannot prove or even conceive that voluntary acts are uncaused, we must believe that human freedom somehow exists.

Hamilton's depiction of free will is driven by his theological motives:

> The only valid arguments for the existence of a God, and for the immortality of the soul, rest on the ground of man's moral nature; consequently, if that moral nature be annihilated, which in any scheme of necessity it is, every conclusion, established on such a nature, is annihilated also.[37]

By this statement Hamilton shows himself participating fully in Calvinist arguments that debate the connection between free will and the origin of sin. If God did not will sin, then humans must be able freely to will it; if, however, human will is not free, then God is directly or indirectly responsible for sin. The former option threatens Calvinist doctrines of providence and predestination, while the latter attributes a malevolent intent to God. Hamilton views his resolution of the conundrum through his philosophy of the conditioned as the most logically simple and the most theologically sound. By stating that we must act as if we have free will because we cannot imagine our lives or God without it, he does not claim that we are certain of free will. On the contrary, we are certain only that the will is either spontaneously motivated or motivated by an infinite series of causes. Since our limited (conditioned) minds cannot choose between these options, we must use our common sense and live under the assumption of moral freedom and moral accountability. God in God's unconditioned realm may still be affecting or causing our actions; in our conditioned realm, we remain free and, therefore, liable to blame.

The Testimony of Consciousness

I have outlined the consequences of the relativity of knowledge and philosophy of the conditioned for Hamilton's positions on causality and the will. Those discussions indicate the importance Hamilton gives to the testimony of consciousness, and so I turn to that testimony more directly in this section. J. S. Mill correctly identifies two of the most common descriptions Hamilton gives to consciousness:

> Consciousness is . . . the recognition by the mind or ego of its acts and affections. Consciousness is an actual and not a potential knowledge . . . [and it] is an immediate, not a mediate knowledge.[38]

Mill views these two statements as contradictory, but Hamilton reconciles them by invoking the tenets of relativity and conditionality. The first statement, for example, stems directly from the doctrine of relativity and basically asserts that consciousness manifests a dual relation between the mind and its object. The object may affect consciousness externally (a thing) or internally (a memory), or it may be an action of consciousness (a volition or judgment). Regardless, consciousness arises among, and is one with, the processes of mind. With Kant and against the British empiricists, then, Hamilton asserts the mind's active, constitutive disposition: consciousness is a process of over-lapping, necessary, and contingent relations that mutually conform and that conform to that which is not consciousness. This depiction of consciousness also indicates how Mill's first quotation above can be explained through Hamilton's philosophy of the conditioned. That philosophy presupposes three necessary relations of knowledge that constrain thinking, foremost of which is the relation of ego and non-ego. Consciousness thus arises out of the rec-ognition of Otherness that might be an internal act or an external affection.

Mill's second quotation describing consciousness can likewise be ex-plained via Hamilton's philosophy of the conditioned, especially through his use of that philosophy as the platform of his (and Reid's) natural real-ism. Hamilton's revision of Locke's categories into the tripartite schema of primary, secundo-primary, and secondary qualities demonstrates the ways in which the world we perceive both modifies and is modified by conscious-ness. Though all three types of quality denominate limitations (conditions) of the mind, he views the primary qualities as the least subjective, that is, as exhibiting conditions of consciousness set by the objects of conscious-ness themselves. Similarly, he views the secundo-primary qualities as an effective bridge between the conditions of consciousness (primary quali-ties) and the idiosyncrasies of consciousness (secondary qualities). By vir-tue of this phenomenological schema Hamilton claims that the knowledge attained by consciousness is immediate and actual: perceptions do not have to be mediated through ideas but are inherently and immediately connected to sensations, and these sensation perceptions deliver actual knowledge about the objects of consciousness.

Through this equation of consciousness and immediate knowledge, Hamilton thinks he has effectively critiqued Reid's faculty psychology.[39] His articulation of consciousness as mind manifesting itself processually through acts and affections directly counters Reid's faculty psychology. Consequently, consciousness for Hamilton is known through its own pro-cesses, and the propositions "I know" and "I know that I know" are iden-tical; there is no need to assign them to different mental spheres.[40] Hamilton likewise refutes Reid's claim that one "can be conscious of an act of knowl-edge, without being conscious of its object." Hamilton's doctrine of rela-tivity formally prohibits this conclusion. "A mental operation is only what it is, by relation to its object; the object at once determining its existence, and specifying the character of its existence."[41] It is this relation of con-sciousness and object, guaranteed by the processual character of con-sciousness, to which Hamilton points as the positive proof that conscious-ness is immediate knowledge.

Unexpectedly, it is the processual understanding of consciousness that acts as the stable foundation for the workings of the mind:

> Consciousness is not contained under either knowledge or belief, but, on the contrary, knowledge and belief are both contained under consciousness. In short, the notion of consciousness is so elementary, that it cannot possibly be resolved into others more simple. It cannot, therefore, be brought under any genus,—any more general conception; and, consequently, it cannot be defined.[42]

Since consciousness must be accepted as given, its testimony speaks to fundamental or indubitable beliefs. Other than the primary qualities, Hamilton does not assert any standard content to these fundamental beliefs. He argues more generally that though we can doubt the truth of any moment of consciousness, we cannot doubt the fact of it.[43] By this fairly mundane distinction, Hamilton purports to vindicate commonsense notions of the trustworthiness of consciousness. Further, he presumes that his philosophy of the conditioned and the doctrine of relativity already have proven that the testimony of consciousness is correct.[44] Indeed, humans learn skepticism only because the assumption that consciousness normally delivers authoritative testimony is correct. For Hamilton, then, the concept of consciousness directly implies the concept of belief. What we are conscious of is what we believe to be true. The subsequent distinctions that the philosopher makes between knowledge and belief are in my reading much less important than this basic confession that all knowledge rests on the belief in the trustworthiness of consciousness.[45] As a point in favor of this conclusion, Hamilton defines *psychology* around the clear revelation of consciousness: "Psychology is only a developed consciousness, that is, a scientific evolution of the facts of which consciousness is the guarantee and revelation."[46]

Process and Action

Hamilton prefers process to fixed categories on more issues than the nature of consciousness. His introductory lecture on the goals and characters of philosophy, for instance, stresses that philosophy is not the promulgation or attainment of truth, but primarily the "search" for truth. He even declares that were God to give him a choice between having and searching for truth, he would choose the latter, for the process of seeking truth gives life its meaning and depth.[47] The process of seeking truth is not an end in itself, however. Hamilton does claim that humans are always restless to seek for further truth, but he also suggests that the end of truth is practical application. In both the search for and application of truth, Hamilton insists that knowledge should be useful, either in awakening the "nobler" capacities of the mind or in guiding persons into a life of service and contribution to society. This balancing of the utility of the pursuit of truth with the utility of that truth for a happy and productive life leads Hamilton to consider himself a utilitarian.[48]

Though Hamilton himself does not connect his interest in process and utility to his doctrine of relativity or philosophy of the conditioned, it may be possible to suggest some linkage. Much if not most of his writing aims simultaneously to support and counter Reid's natural realism. Considering this, his refutation of Reid's faculty psychology is no minor point. By replacing that faculty psychology with a processual account of consciousness that depends for its cogency on the essential duality of consciousness (the relation of ego and non-ego) and the limitation of the human mind, Hamilton indicates his priorities of process and application. If knowledge only arises through the actions of consciousness, and if consciousness is manifested only through the actions (effects) and affects of mind, then a person must continually inspire those actions and affects and, through this process, continually strive to understand the ever-changing network of relations in which she or he lives (by applying knowledge to life).

The priorities of process and utility appear more overtly in Hamilton's nonmetaphysical writings, such as those on the university curricula in mathematics and on the preferred structures of universities. In such essays Hamilton questions the ways in which various disciplines are useful, the best way to teach them, and with what other curricula they should be taught. "On the Study of Mathematics," for example, offers five points that should guide university administrators in prioritizing fields of study. Surprisingly, the essay argues against placing too much emphasis on mathematics since, he claims, math only engages the lower capacities of imagination.[49] A preferred field of study, he notes, will first of all "cultivate a greater number of the nobler faculties on a higher degree." Second, it will affect a majority of the students enrolled in the university (this applies to a situation in which the students have no required courses). Third, it will offer "greater general utility for the conduct of the business or for the enjoyment of the leisure of after life." Fourth, it most easily will act as grounding for other fields of study. Fifth, its importance will require an "external stimulus" to be studied as it ought. Each of these points either inspires the pursuit of knowledge as a continual process or usefully applies to the betterment of life. The third point draws particular attention because of its reference to "after life," which can be read as either one's avocational hours, or one's life after death. Again, it must be recalled that Hamilton's social and professional context is best defined as orthodox Calvinism, and, as such, his philosophical focus is always embedded in his theological one. Indeed, his introductory lecture in metaphysics immediately links the pursuit of truth to seeking after God, and the end of truth (as a practical application to life) to one's calling or vocation, the chief purpose of which is, in all cases, to glorify God. Further, this introductory lecture moves from the purposes of philosophy to two psychological proofs of God, both of which entail an assertion of human freedom in balance with divine omnipotence. This cosmological scope is not highly imaginative, and certainly not novel, yet it is always assumed, and its presence smooths Hamilton's introduction of German philosophy to an American readership steeped in Calvinism and suspicious of metaphysics.

Pragmatic Consequences

I stated at the outset that Hamilton shares with Peirce a love of logic, a concern for a cosmological scope, and a motivation to reconcile Kant's idealism with Reid's commonsense philosophy. These are not unconnected with the pragmatists' most common reference to Hamilton, that of his insistence that natural realism requires a necessary dualism between ego and non-ego. Peirce and James both reject this claim, though James does so with more ambiguity and hesitation since his conception of natural science still requires that dualism, and for much of his writing career he is concerned to heed the dictates of the natural sciences. Peirce rejects dualisms absolutely, replacing them with schemas of Thirds. Indeed, Peirce does not accept Hamilton's claim that human perceptions are no more than phenomenal, albeit trustworthy, presentations of an actual, external world. In effect the pragmatist rejects Hamilton's doctrine of relativity as it is embedded in his natural realism and replaces it with a realism grounded in his logic of relatives and a theory of continuity (synechism) grounded in semeiotics. Though Peirce and Hamilton both take issue with Kant's notion of the noumenal realm, Peirce seeks a logical and ontological explanation for how perceptions are partial, fallible, and yet fully actual. Again he develops an answer through semeiotics and the logic of relatives. Where Hamilton's logic is much more classically structured, Peirce's mirrors his commitments to cosmology and commonsense phenomenology.

James also accepts the relativity of human knowledge, and his account more closely parallels Hamilton's. Indeed, James's early writings accept a noumenal realm and seem to proffer a presentationalism quite reminiscent of the Scottish philosopher. According to both thinkers humans gain knowledge of the external world only through psychological relations, namely, the faculties of perception, sensation, and, for James, memory. James sometimes refers to this limitation as the difference between truths and facts, with facts being the indisputable items and conditions of the world and truths being the relative ways in which humans access and appropriate the facts. Just as Hamilton's doctrine of relativity and philosophy of the conditioned mutually explain one another, James's understanding of the relativity of knowledge is part and parcel of his conviction of the mutability and practicality (or expediency) of truth. Since truth is human interpretation of facts, and since the facts can never be accessed absolutely, what one acknowledges as truth changes as one's life situation and experiences change. Hamilton, of course, would reject the notion that humans judge truth; for him, truth is God's and something humans can access only with God's aid. Hamilton does, however, overlap the meanings of consciousness and belief; James carries that imbrication out of the logical realm of commonsense philosophy and applies it to a more relativistic pragmatism.

Peirce retains an understanding of truth that is singular and universal, a point that might be unexpected since he does refuse the notion of a noumenal or factual realm beyond human perception. Ultimate truth, however, is lodged in the future and its attainment "in the long run" is infinitely delayed. In the short run, Peirce avers, human understanding of truth is fallible.[50] Peirce's fallibilism differs from James's theories of a mutable truth in that Peirce emphasizes communities of inquiry that embrace standards of accountability, while James remains focused on individual experience and judgment. As such, Peirce's theories of truth resonate more closely to those of Hamilton in the sense that both place final authority on the objects of consciousness themselves, and not on an individual's interpretation of them.

Both pragmatists accept from Kant what Hamilton accepts: the assumption that the mind does not passively receive sensations from the world, but actively appropriates information from the external world and synthesizes it through and with the mind's own capacities. Parallel with this commitment is the shared description of consciousness as processual, though the three men differ profoundly in the details of this claim. Further, all three philosophers recognize belief, not knowledge, as foundational both to consciousness and to human being. Finally, the thinkers' prioritizing of belief, process, and mental action effects a strong commitment to the practicality of knowledge, that is, to the ways humans use knowledge (beliefs) for the betterment of themselves and their world.

In beginning to delineate the professionalization of Scottish psychology, this chapter upholds William Hamilton as a figure for his culture's assumptions about God and about human nature. Like Helmholtz, Hamilton levels a keen eye on the increasing influence of the natural sciences and on the rising power of crass empiricism. To me, it is telling that the American pragmatists embrace the commonsense realism of their Scottish interlocutor, but reject his orthodox justifications for it. As I argue in the prologue, the Puritan imaginary persists in the nineteenth century not as a doctrine but as a cultural idea, habit, and mandate. My chapters on Peirce and James will establish that the Americans reject the orthodoxy of thinkers like Hamilton because they transmute concepts like relativity, logic, and belief into concepts that function religiously.

4 〰

Alexander Bain

The Practical Psychology of Belief

In the line of Scottish philosophers that begins with Hartley and Hume and proceeds through his own day, Alexander Bain (1818–1903) stands out as the only man not of aristocratic lineage.[1] The changing structure of universities in Europe and Britain in the nineteenth century made surprising room for Bain, a self-taught man from a working-class family: not only did he manage to attend college, he was named chair of logic and english at Aberdeen University in 1860. Unlike Hamilton, whose appointment at Edinburgh was facilitated by personal and political connections, Bain won his academic post by distinguishing himself in the expanding sphere of professional publications. His academic appointment came after widely acclaimed response to his two large volumes on psychology, *The Senses and the Intellect* (1855) and *The Emotions and the Will* (1859). Thereafter, Bain worked solely within the university system and remained acutely interested in its institutional changes during the latter half of the nineteenth century. Like Hamilton, Bain responded in writing to debates on university reform, curricula decisions, and the ethics of teaching.[2] Being a generation younger than Hamilton, however, Bain had to face squarely the growing dominance of the natural sciences.[3] Convinced of the efficacy of those sciences over metaphysics, Bain asserted that physiology grounded the study of psychology and argued that above all else psychologists needed to attend to the scientization of their chosen field.

Bain works hard to support the separation of psychology from both philosophy and physics, and he establishes viable and satisfactory methods for this work. His two major texts conveniently display the growing professionalization and scientization of psychology in that each was revised every few years in order to update fully the sections on physiology and neurology. The trajectory of these revisions can thus be read as a genealogy of physiology and neurology. Ironically, Bain completely lacked the medical training to which Hamilton and other philosophical psychologists were exposed. Least qualified for the effort but most convinced of its importance, he forges the parameters of a "scientific" psychology that agrees with Wilhelm Wundt's approach in numerous respects.[4]

The two basic differences between Wundt and Bain speak to their cultural differences. First, true to his Scottish commonsense heritage, Bain rejects much of the idealism of Wundt's system, especially what he calls the division of the psychological powers of association into lower (material) and upper (mental) levels.[5] Second, Bain's theoretical empiricism does not match Wundt's practical empiricism. Though theoretically more idealistic than Bain, Wundt carries the scientization of psychology to an empirical conclusion by inaugurating the first psychological laboratory in 1879 and lobbying to require laboratory training for all students of psychology. Bain never insists on this move, perhaps because he lacked specific training in the sciences and, more importantly, because he lacked the institutional power of Wundt. Bain's inability or unwillingness to develop his empirical theorizing into an empirical practice also accounts for Bain's inability to draw the disciples who flocked to Wundt. Nevertheless, Bain's texts were read widely and were successful in moving psychological questions and practices from the metaphysical realm of classical Scottish philosophical psychology toward the more quantitative approaches suggested by Wundt and his followers.[6]

Within the narrative I am giving for the cultural evolution of psychology, Bain stands to Hamilton, as does Wundt to Helmholtz. In both cases the younger thinkers reacted to the professionalization of the academy in general, and to the growing dominance of the natural sciences in particular, by striving to legitimize psychology as a full-fledged science. Lining up the four men chronologically (Hamilton, Helmholtz, Bain, Wundt) clearly shows the movement of psychology out of the spheres of philosophy and physics and into a still-existing struggle to establish itself as a hard science that yet addresses the mysteries of human existence.

Bain's indebtedness to his Scottish philosophical predecessors is readily evident. Two points characterize the loyalty to this heritage. First, Bain continues to combine ethics, aesthetics, and political commentary in a single, comprehensive volume. This classical and philosophical arrangement of topics typifies nineteenth-century treatises, including those of the pragmatists, though the pragmatists' writings are rarely organized as comprehensively and systematically as are Bain's. Second, Bain wavers between an understanding of consciousness that is processual and relational and one that is stable and intuitive. Viewing consciousness relationally, Bain avoids faculty psychology by naming consciousness as the effect of the reciprocal workings of the mind's various aspects (feeling, intellect, and volition). As stable and intuitive, consciousness instantiates the indubitable testimony of personal experience. The relational model is measured quantitatively or objectively; the intuitive model can be assessed only qualitatively or subjectively. To me, Bain's straddling the classical and modern expressions of psychology mirrors the way his work straddles the commitments of Peirce and James. Before turning to a more detailed examination of Bain's system, I will indicate schematically its position relative to pragmatism. In general Peirce's work resonates with the classical angle of Bain's work, while James appropriates those aspects of the Scot's system that have been embraced by twentieth-century behaviorists. As is well known, Bain is honored by the pragmatists as the "grandfather of pragmatism" in light of his articulation of the intersection of belief and action. For Bain "what we believe we act upon," either directly or potentially (in preparing to act).[7] In this chapter my first goal is to present Bain's phenomenology of belief in order to delineate the relations he asserts among belief, consciousness, and action; these are the most direct ways in which Bain becomes an interlocutor of the pragmatists. Of special emphasis in this regard is action, which the pragmatists mutate into concepts of behavior (Peirce) and willed effects (James). The relations of belief, consciousness, and action can be interpreted in many ways, some of which emphasize the importance of a person's character (developed dispositions) and others of which do not. The distinction displays itself in Bain's theory of causality, a term he divides into a psychological concept and a scientific concept. On the one hand, in insisting on the importance of character, Bain shares Peirce's desire to focus on conduct rather than on individual acts. On the other hand, his confusing resolution of the complexities of causality into a dual scheme that separates psychology from science foreshadows the way James attempts to secure a proper realm for scientific inquiry in *The Principles of Psychology* with a similar use of dualities. Thus my second concern in the following discussion is to expound on the relations of will, causality, and action.

Bain substantiates his accounts of belief, will, and causality through his theories of psychological association and the law of relativity. I discussed Hamilton's law of relativity in the previous chapter and want to stress here the way in which Bain changes Hamilton's meaning from a fundamental epistemological duality to the necessary processual character of knowledge, something the pragmatists both share. As for associationism, Bain shares the psychological legacy of Hartley and Hume, but rather than simply asserting the association of ideas—which he depicts as proceeding by laws of contiguity and similarity—he stresses the "association" of mind and brain. He describes this relationship as "concomitant" and tries but fails to verify it through empirical experimentation. Bain thus asserts that the connection of mind and body is fundamental, but concedes it cannot be explained in any satisfactory detail. In the end, Bain asserts a psychological parallelism much like that of James and Wundt.

Both pragmatists share with Bain the priority of process in the constitution of knowledge and the influence of belief (as opposed to knowledge) on human action. Peirce inserts these commitments within a metaphysics of purpose and chance and an anthropology that stresses dispositions and habits; James turns to questions more oriented to event and behavior. Since both pragmatists esteem Bain as the grandfather of pragmatism, it behooves us to ponder what they borrow from Bain as well as what they mutate in the process. The last section of this chapter will address the transformations more directly, but of immediate note is that the Calvinism so prevalent in Hamilton's writings all but disappears in Bain's system. By the time Bain was composing his two major volumes on psychology in the 1850s, it was no longer tenable in the general academy to view scientific endeavors as extending or corroborating theological investigations. The growing dominance of the natural sciences entailed a parallel shrinking of theological dominance, at least as far as the academic pursuit of these domains was concerned. The pragmatists, however, never conceded this point. Their religious views were hardly orthodox, but they were also hardly ever far beneath the surface of their writings. Indeed I argue that their embracing of "belief"—or, for James's late writing, the "expediency" of truth—as more determinative for human knowledge and action than "truth" in any absolute sense, has everything to do with their refusal to subordinate matters of the heart to the matter of laboratory investigation.

The Basics of Psychology: The Alliance of Mind and Body and the Law of Relativity

As indicated earlier, Bain exerts considerable effort to update his psychological tomes with the latest physiological and neurological discoveries. In the 1894 preface to *The Senses and the Intellect*, he states the reason for this effort as the need to "disburden" psychology from metaphysics. In a later essay in the journal *Mind*, he clarifies why psychology should supersede metaphysics:

> I believe that, in strictness, a disinterested Psychology should come first in order, and that, after going on a little way in amassing facts, it should revise its fundamental assumptions, and improve its language and definitions: and, when so revised, should resume consideration of the wide field of mental facts of the neutral or disinterested kind—those that deal with practical applications rather than with the metaphysical groundwork.[8]

This description encapsulates Bain's understanding of science as a process of observation, definition, induction, and deduction.[9] Psychologists "amass facts" by observation and induction, and then use them to amend their working definitions; finally, through induction and deduction they "resume consideration of the wide field of mental facts." To Bain, this last step, which is an assimilation of logic to the tasks of psychology, does not invite metaphysical speculation. Logic for Bain—both deductive and inductive—is eminently practical.[10] The processes of observation and redefinition lead toward the "final ends of the study in the *economy of life*" or the systematization of human activity and conduct.[11]

By advocating the methods of science for psychology, Bain does not abandon completely more classical and more subjective approaches. For instance, in the essay just quoted, Bain acknowledges the usefulness of introspection, of a search for the origins of psychological phenomena, and of a qualitative or classificatory analysis of the psychological "powers." These powers he especially praises as yielding information that bears more immediately upon general human conduct than do the other methods. Quantitative or "psycho-physical" analysis adds to these traditional approaches by offering reliable methods whereby human behavior can become more predictable to observers. Bain's efforts to move the methodology of psychology into the domain of science lead him to define "the Science of Mind" as the study of both "Mind proper" and "its alliance with Matter, in the animal body."[12] Bain exerts considerable effort during his professional career in articulating exactly what the obvious but strange alliance of mind and matter (or body) entails. Though he never himself terms the relation a parallelism, it seems the best description of the "concomitance" of an insubstantial mind and a nerve- and electricity-driven body. He rejects the notion that mind and body "act on" one another, since the phrase assumes they exist separately prior to their relation. Rather, he notes that mind and body define one another. Their "union" is constant and stands as "the very law of our mental being," albeit a law that remains essentially mysterious.[13]

Though unable to demystify the relation, Bain does suggest the problem can be appeased through the laws of association ("connexion"):

> The mystery will be still further reduced if we can resolve the connexion as stated in gross, to separate and specific laws of connexion. . . . Let us resolve into the highest possible generalities, the connexion of pleasures and pains with all the physical stimulants of the senses, with all the suggestions of thought, with all the external manifestations in feature, gesture, movement, and secretion; and when this is done we shall have resolved one part of the mystery by the only mode of resolution that the case admits of. Let us go farther if we can: let us generalize the connexions of thought or intellect with nervous and other processes; find out what physical basis specifically belongs to memory, to reason, to imagination, and what are the most general statements of the relationship: we shall then fully, sufficiently, finally explain the alliance of mind and body in the sphere of intellect.[14]

The program Bain here advocates combines what we can know about mind through external observation and categorization of the senses—"the only mode of resolution that the case admits of"—with what we can know about brain or body through physiological analyses. With these two techniques the psychologist must be satisfied. Bain ends this discussion of the mysterious relation of mind and body by suggesting its analogy to the Athanasian Creed. He notes that humans are "one substance, with two sets of properties, two sides, the physical and the mental—a *double-faced unity*," which we accept as we do the language of the creed, that is, without "confounding the persons nor dividing the substance."[15] Notably, this is one of only two references to theology I came across in Bain, and he employs it here to express the only mystery he admits into the domain of psychology.[16] Instead of enlisting science to bolster theology, as per Hamilton, Bain compartmentalizes theology as the arena of mystery, as that which defines the limit of scientific inquiry.

In Bain's long excursus on the senses and emotions, he refers frequently to two methods. One relies on both the testimony of feelings and the observation of behavior (use of mind); the other employs controlled experimentation in order to prove a reproducible, causal relationship between phenomena (use of matter). Both methods articulate the law of relativity, which Bain calls the most basic law of mind after the law of concomitance of mind and body. His version of this law differs from Hamilton's, however. Bain does echo Hamilton's law of relativity in asserting that all knowledge is mental and that "the *summa genera* of things must be at least two: say mind and not-mind, subject and object."[17] But neither of these assertions falls under Bain's law of relativity. Bain categorizes relativity as a subset of one of the laws of association, that of succession. Within this categorization he defines the law as "the dependence of each state upon the state or states preceding."[18] Unfortunately, Bain does not here explain what he means by "dependence," and so I must take us to other discussions of relativity in order to clarify Bain's repositioning of Hamilton.

In most references to the law of relativity, Bain asserts transitions or changes of impression as "necessary to our being conscious."[19] Keeping tangential to Hamilton's epistemological duality and true to his own mind/body parallelism, Bain divides the meaning of this assertion into a mental and a physical side. He then explains why change is "necessary" through what psychologists today term *accommodation*, the fact that humans are mentally inured to aspects of the environment that remain constant, and yet are readily aware of features that introduce a change. The most familiar example of this is the tendency not to notice a bland and constant hum (such as a heating system) until it suddenly stops. In the new sensation of quiet, we retroject the presence of noise. Bain calls such accommodations the "mental" side of relativity. The physical side applies the principle of accommodation to the activity of nerves: when a sensation is new and fresh, or unexpected, the nerves respond more quickly and with greater vigor than after the nerves have been barraged. For both the mental and physical aspects of relativity, what is relative is the state of consciousness to the intensity or "degree of transition" of that which affects consciousness.[20] For the law of relativity to function as Bain desires, life and the world must be orderly. Indeed, he assumes the basic uniformity of nature as one of the necessary conditions of empiricism and for this reason considers the law of relativity the foundational law of psychology.[21] Though the assumption might stand more as a conviction of Bain's generation and Scottish culture than of psychology itself, Bain depends upon it as one of the conditions for predicting human action. As we shall see, his assumption of an ordered connection between nature and human character was taken up directly by Peirce and James.

Consciousness to Action: A Phenomenology of Belief

Bain divides the Mind into three functions: feeling (emotion), volition (will), and thought (intellect), but consciousness is omitted from this classification. Oddly, Bain does not give a systematic answer to this most obvious psychological issue, one that engaged the efforts and ink of many of his contemporaries. Bain offers only two extended discussions of consciousness, one in a section of *The Emotions and the Will* and one in a later essay, "Definition and Problems of Consciousness," but even these two excursuses offer mainly lists of various views on consciousness arranged in an expanded outline form. Bain fails to examine in any depth his own assessment of the contending views. Instead he supplies a general depiction of consciousness as that which is "coextensive with mental life, and is expressed more or less strongly as that life is considered to rise or fall in degrees."[22] The lack of a fully developed position on consciousness seems remiss considering Bain at one place states the goal of psychology as "a systematic and precise account of the states of human consciousness—a Natural History of the Feelings."[23] Bain hesitates to define consciousness in fear of falling into the traps of metaphysics that he thinks inherent to the debates surrounding consciousness. Nonetheless, his writings do suggest certain definite understandings of consciousness. At times Bain seems to view consciousness as an umbrella term that envelops the operations of feeling, volition, and thought (as in the general depiction quoted earlier). At other points, Bain maintains a notion of consciousness as a tool of introspection, as the means by which persons probe "the varieties of human feeling."[24] Introspective consciousness, he asserts, provides a certain indisputable testimony about human nature and personal experience. Bain tries to distinguish his acceptance of such personal testimony from that of Hamilton and other intuitionists. As he describes it, whereas Hamilton allows the testimony of consciousness to stand as the ground of truth and experience, and hence as foundational to human knowledge and universal in application, Bain stresses the singularity of such testimony: "Be it observed . . . that this knowledge which, if not infallible, is at least final and unanswerable, is to the last degree special and confined. Being applicable in strictness only to my individual mind, at some one single instant, it contains the very minimum of information, the smallest portion of fact that it is possible to express."[25] As a consequence of the posited singularity of such testimony, Bain recognizes that even the most private assessment of a feeling or sensation requires repetition in order that its testimony be held warranted. Bain thus differentiates himself from Hamilton in recognizing that even one's own private assessment of a sensation or feeling is open to further interpretation. Where Hamilton states that although the truth of a conscious assessment may be doubted, one cannot deny the simple fact of its existence, Bain assumes that illusion can seep into even a seemingly simple fact. Thus the best description of consciousness for Bain is that of a "mode" of "consistency after many repetitions." As this mode, consciousness is "the final court of appeal."[26]

Finally, whereas Hamilton relies on the testimony of consciousness as the basis for human knowledge, Bain sets up an inverse relation between the knowledge of consciousness and knowledge "in the larger and more applicable sense." The issue revolves again around fallibility and this time centers on the use or practicality of knowledge. As a private testimony, consciousness can offer indisputable knowledge, but can be useful only to the experiencer:

"A statement so limited, therefore, is but the minimum of knowledge." Knowledge must somehow move beyond the singular event and incorporate personal memory or the testimony of others into the assessment. "But," remarks Bain, "by the very act of extending the affirmation [the experiencer] trenches upon the region of fallibility," for memory fades and the testimony of others lacks the felt immediacy of personal experience.[27] Thus knowledge is more useful to more situations and more persons, but it is fallible. Testimony of consciousness is more likely to be infallible, but is much less practical.

Clearly, Bain's understanding of consciousness does not fully escape metaphysical tenets about perceptual immediacy, despite his insistence that repetition is necessary even for conviction about sensation or feeling. Partly one can attribute this to a quite classical metaphor he makes to distinguish between consciousness and mind. Consciousness includes only the present (immediate) train of thoughts, whereas mind includes factors that may be brought to consciousness but are not currently present. Thus consciousness "resembles the scenery of a theatre actually on the stage, at any one moment; which scenery is a mere selection from the stores in reserve for the many pieces that have been, or may be, performed." Mind, in other words, is like the backstage and storage room areas in which old or newly purchased items will be stored while the current play is running.[28] Bain imports all of these various assumptions about consciousness into his treatments of perception. In general, Bain follows Hamilton in combining an empirical approach to knowledge with a Kantian theory of the noumenal. Again, he contributes to the field of psychology a physiological hypothesis.[29] Bain, even more than Hamilton, resists accounts of human perception that portray the mind (or consciousness) as passively receiving stimuli and only then actively assimilating or formatting it. For him, the mind is singularly restless, proactively reaching out into its environment, and hungry for reaction. For evidence he points to the spontaneous activity of infants, movements that do not have the controlled purposiveness of will and yet do indicate the welter of activity that is the human being before—or despite—received sensations from the external world.

Bain in effect suggests that our proactive movements help form our notions of what is other to the self. More, Bain avers that one of the quintessential questions of psychology seeks "the genesis of our notion of externality, considered as part of our conscious being." In his words, "the sense of the external is the consciousness of particular energies and activities of our own." In other words, we believe in the external world because we experience our bodies moving through it, resisting it, and reacting to it.[30] This picture of human activity seeding human perception is central to understanding Bain's treatment of belief. Perception of the external world entails changes and transitions through space and time—this is the law of relativity—and experiencing such changes produces consciousness. Beliefs arise through the repetition of certain moments of consciousness and are supported by further experience, further moments of consciousness. Just as consciousness, as the by-product of the experience of transition, relies upon the order of the natural world, so belief too, as the state of expecting sameness, depends upon that order. Consciousness is produced from the experience of change, and belief from the experience of sameness, but the meanings of *change* and *sameness* are relative to the basic (predictable and expected) order of the world.[31] Bain argues this position through an anthropological assertion: humans all "naturally" believe more than we have experienced directly, as when children believe that all families are like their family or all cultures are like their culture. Only experiences that disrupt our beliefs move us to change them. The uniformity of nature leads us to expect and believe in consistency unless otherwise informed. From such premises Bain concludes that only experience (action) can be the standard of truth, while belief must always be held as provisional until experience (including the empirical experiments of science) bears them out.[32] Bain carries his insight one step further by developing what might be called an empiricism of belief. Whereas truth is universal and infallible, beliefs must be fallible since they are always particular and always embodied in specific individuals. To adhere to a notion of indubitable or inherent beliefs would be to assert a universality of the particular, an assertion that Bain judges an obvious logical fallacy.

Peirce opposes Bain's theory of belief as nominalistic; to him, Bain would insist that real generals could not exist, since existence is a character only of individuals. His empiricism of belief also foregrounds the tension within Bain's system between a classical psychology of indubitable beliefs with its attendant infallible (or at least indisputable) testimony of consciousness and a modern psychology of experimentally tested beliefs and a consciousness that can yield private convictions but not truth. It is contradictory to assert both that humans "naturally" believe more than they experience and that indubitable beliefs are a logical fallacy. It is also contradictory to point to the indisputable testimony of consciousness and (yet) to the fallible nature of belief—or, spoken from the reverse side, to the fallible character of experiential knowledge and yet to the fact that truth originates from precisely that experience. Bain does not resolve this tension, and though it becomes something taken up by both William James and C. S. Peirce, only Peirce offers a system that puts forth a logically coherent solution.

That phase of the story will be told in the next part of this book. Of more relevance here is Bain's theory of belief and its relationship to consciousness and action. Distilling what has been stated, Bain depicts belief as the form or disposition of our consciousness; it is an aptitude with which humans are born. The naturally active nature of human being puts this aptitude to work molding expectations and, thereby, steering our attention and motivating our feelings in ways that directly affect our thinking, acting, and willing.[33] By this depiction, beliefs function somewhat like habits that can connect the moments of consciousness. After all, consciousness is only the present moment, the "scenery on the stage" of the mind; the other contents of mind remain "off stage" until something in consciousness spurs their entrance. Beliefs are stable but mutable. They guide what is perceived, but they are not those perceptions. To extend Bain's metaphor, one could say that beliefs form the stage itself, the size and shape of which affect the way the scenery is arranged.

Predictably, Bain does not end his thoughts on belief with such an intellectual depiction. He states emphatically, "Belief has no meaning, except in reference to our actions; the essence, or import of it is such as to place it under the region of the will."[34] In a move that foreshadows his appropriation by behaviorists, Bain suggests that belief links this tightly to action because humans live as if we adhere to a theology of works: "In the practice of every day life, we are accustomed to test men's belief by action, 'faith by works.'"[35] This assertion paves the way for Bain's formulation, made famous by the pragmatists, that "belief is preparedness to act, for a given end, in a given way."[36] If belief is the form of consciousness, molding our expectations, then belief is the form of action: humans do not *act* their beliefs, but act *on* them. At the same time, belief is the expression or "manifestation" of human action. Actions express the actual beliefs of a person, with or against her verbal professions, and a person's beliefs explain or manifest her actions.[37] With this phenomenology of belief in place, we can turn our focus to Bain's accounts of action and its relationship to will and causality.

Will and Causality: A Phenomenology of Action

Bain defines *will* quite classically as the seeking after pleasure and avoidance of pain.[38] Will is the guiding effect of feeling (usually pleasure and pain) that results in human action: "Will or Volition comprises all the actions of human beings in so far as impelled or guided by Feelings."[39] Emphasizing the link between will and action right at the outset, and concerned that human volition might be read too idealistically or spiritually, Bain emphasizes that the will "can operate only upon the muscular system." Of course he is unable to provide a causal explanation of how feelings act on the will or how the will affects the muscular system. These desired but merely suggested relations return him to the indubitable but mysterious concomitance of mind and body, a relation that can be asserted—and even strongly suggested by empirical investigation—but cannot be proved.[40]

Not all human action stems from the will; some actions are spontaneous, others are reflex, and still others are habitual. Willful actions are best characterized as linking "a present action and a present feeling, whereby the one comes under the control of the other." Feeling thus spurs the will toward actions that are both voluntary and controlled and by this process, the particular feeling involved itself gains direction and meaning.[41] Will, in short, supplies control to an action and purpose to feeling.

As the mediating factor between the desire to act (the attraction and repulsion of pleasure and pain) and the act itself, will is intimately connected to knowledge. "The final end of all knowledge," Bain writes, "is Practice, or the guidance of conduct."[42] Clearly, the mode of consciousness that enacts this "final end" is the will. For the scientist this insight is crucial, since it implies that by analyzing human conduct one has the key to human feelings and hence to the motivations that steer their wills.[43] Bain's anticipations of later behaviorism are evident in this position. Yet, for this behaviorism to work, he must posit knowledge as something public and fallible, that is, something that reaches beyond the individual testimony of consciousness, that explains an individual's past or a group's present collective experience, and that remains fluid enough to adapt to changing circumstances. Such a scientific position assumes the order or uniformity of nature. Uniformity engenders the regularity of human action as well as of natural rhythms and encourages the scientist to hypothesize laws for both realms. Like the concomitance of mind and body, the uniformity of nature cannot be proved, only assumed, and yet if it were an invalid hypothesis, we would expect experience to contradict it. Since experience apparently corroborates the hypothesis, Bain feels confident in basing his theories of causality and free will upon it.[44] Indeed, Bain calls the notion of causality the chief example of the uniformity of nature, and he asserts not only that belief and volition depend upon it, but that the logical processes of induction and deduction do as well.[45]

Bain asserts the link between causality and the uniformity of nature without clarifying what he means by causality. He fleshes out his position in *Induction*, beginning with the qualification that nature is not one uniformity but rather a web of interconnected uniformities.[46] The systematician then divides the plethora of uniformities into three basic areas of scientific investigation: uniformities of co-existence, uniformities of equality and inequality, and uniformity of succession, under which causation belongs.[47] In a more detailed examination, Bain first rejects the formulation that "every effect has a cause, and every cause an effect" and rephrases the phenomenon in line with his law of relativity: "In every change, there is a uniformity of connexion between the antecedents and the consequents."[48] He continues:

> A law is more sharply stated by help of its denials. Causation denies two things. First, it denies pure spontaneity of commencement. . . . Secondly. The law denies that events follow one another irregularly, indiscriminately, or capriciously. . . . In short, the law is the statement of *uniformity* in the Succession of events.[49]

Bain's first denial follows Hamilton, who lists the absolute commencement of events as one of the two extreme positions to which the law of the excluded middle must apply. In general, Bain accepts Hamilton's theory of causality. He pushs beyond Hamilton, however, in his assumption of the uniformity of nature. To deny that events are either purely spontaneous or capricious is less to press a logical proposition than it is to argue for the regularity or predictability of both natural processes and human action.

So far I have been delineating what Bain terms in *The Senses and the Intellect* the scientific understanding of causality, "those successions where the consequent depends on its antecedent, and is always produced by it."[50] In this text Bain has an extensive discussion of his understanding of causality relative to the scientific process of observation, investigation, and discovery. He wants to make it clear that though the order of nature and human action is evident, causality or the repetition of one causal pattern in different circumstances may well remain veiled for generations. By this account, Bain joins other nineteenth-century advocates of the natural sciences in offering a history of science that tries to explain why it took so many generations of humankind to develop methods for studying such a logical, regular, and predictable world.

In a later text, *Logic of Induction*, Bain offers a familiar definition of scientific causality: "In scientific investigations, the Cause must be regarded as the entire aggregate of conditions or circumstances requisite to the effect."[51] In his essay "The Empiricist Position," however, Bain attributes this definition to James S. Mill and dismisses it by claiming that too many objections have been raised against it, primarily that it makes the determination of causality nearly impossible.[52] Thus Bain turns back to a related discussion in *Induction*, that of the "advance" made by physicists through the doctrine of the conservation of energy.[53]

Bain labels this doctrine "the highest expression of Cause and Effect" and summarizes its ability to address questions of causation:

> In every instance of causation, there is a putting forth of force in given circumstances, and the law in question states exactly what becomes of the force, and is often the sufficing explanation of the special phenomena, as well as the embodiment of nature's uniformity in successions.[54]

To Bain it is important to note that traditional theories of causation employed by "intuitionists" and the principle of conservation developed by physicists employ the same evidence. Both theories recognize and attempt to explain the order and predictability of the succession of natural events and human action. In light of my use of Helmholtz, it is interesting that Bain describes Hamilton's law of causation as "almost exactly co-incident with the principle of Conservation, which he may be said to have anticipated."[55] I am tempted to discount this statement as merely expressing loyalty to his Scottish philosophical heritage since his next paragraph launches a critique of Herbert Spencer's account of causality as inappropriately arguing from "the inconceivability of the opposite" (the primary characteristic of Hamilton's theory of causality). Perhaps what Bain approves of in Hamilton is the notion that causes and effects do not stand separate from their contexts, that webs of interconnecting uniformities or regularities of succession are necessary for the pinpointing of any one occasion of causal connection. Just such an antimechanical argument opens for Hamilton a way to argue for the freedom of human action, and hence to assert the moral culpability of humanity as intimately related to the basic moral character of the universe. Bain, too, desires to ground "scientific" causality in the larger system of the uniformity of nature. He, too, extrapolates from this grounding to argue against a deterministic or mechanistic account of human action.

Bain rejects the familiar framing of the debate surrounding human action in terms of free will versus necessity. That debate, he states emphatically, is merely one of semantics.[56] Once again, he resorts to the uniformity of nature to explain himself. The notion of cause is not innate (as the intuitionists, such as Hamilton, assume) but arises inductively out of human experience, from which humans deductively form expectations and beliefs about the world that prove reliable upon further experience. The reliability stems, of course, from the uniformity of nature.[57] For Bain, resistance or effort is the means by which inductive experience produces a notion of causality. As humans move through the world, willed actions run up against limitations and obstacles. Repeated experience with similar obstacles eventually leads to an inductive understanding of the relation of cause and effect.[58] Since the notion of causality is learned, it rests upon habits or dispositions of belief and expectation about the world and about humans' ability to act in the world. Thus to Bain it simply makes no semantic sense to ask whether the will is "free," as if any human volition were purely uncaused. The very concept is impossible.[59] Human will is habitual, predictable, and produces chosen behavior of the self in the world.[60] As such, causation as applied to human action is, for Bain, simply the fact that "under a certain motive I act in a certain way."[61] He admits that this is not a scientific notion of causality: though it does entail a noticeable change of self or environment that is repeatable (predictable), in this human context the important aspect is the concomitance of succeeding events, without any necessary generalization to a principle of causal efficacy.[62]

To summarize Bain's stated relation between action and belief: human action stems from embodied beliefs through the mediation of the will. Beliefs are molded out of an inductive experience of the uniformity of nature, and actions proceed according to the same reliable uniformity. In consequence, humans are able to predict one another's behavior by becoming accustomed to and anticipating their particular dispositions and habits. For Bain this does not imply that humans are not free, that they are somehow deterministically "bound" to their developed habits. In the domain of human action (as opposed to nature, which Bain treats solely along lines of efficient causation) the central issue is the choice of state of mind (that is, the beliefs in operation). A person can act within a range that remains consistent with her beliefs, without necessitating mechanical responses or the inability to change her beliefs or reactions. The importance of this for Bain is not to assert that human will mirrors the moral order of the universe, as it does for Hamilton, but to turn the discussion immediately to issues of legal culpability and the effectiveness of discipline (especially in the schools) and punishment (through the justice system). As noted in the introduction to this chapter, questions of religion and theology are almost completely absent from his texts. A weak echo is his tendency to separate ethics from morality, designating the former as part of a public system of controlling conduct and the latter as the private sense of conscience. Conduct is open to public scrutiny, but one's relationship to the God who judges one's heart is not, hence his acute interest in forms of public punishment and reform and almost complete silence about religion, the sector of human life that is most unscientific.

Pragmatic Consequences

To Bain's definition of belief as "that upon which a man is prepared to act," Peirce writes, "Pragmatism is scarce more than a corollary; so that I am disposed to think of him as the grandfather of pragmatism."[63] This famous quip does much to encapsulate an enduring distinction between Peirce and James. For Peirce, Bain's phenomenology of belief supports his own theories about the nature of human conduct and its relation to the habits that constitute human subjectivity. For both Peirce and Bain, belief takes on a public identity in the sense that belief is formed inductively (through experience) and acted upon deductively (by forming hypotheses, for Peirce, and by proactively reaching out to the world, for Bain). Peirce develops this public character of belief into a subtle theory of community and carries his thoughts in directions that somewhat divide science and morality. Yet for both Peirce and Bain, the public character of belief is also its scientific character; it is that which allows collaboration of inquiry as well as corroboration of data.

For James, the relation of belief to action remains both centered on the individual and focused on particular acts (as opposed to general conduct). Still, in the shared desire to legitimize psychology as a natural science, James and Bain both resort to sets of dualisms that enable them to employ methods of causal efficacy without abandoning more classical—and more metaphysical— insights into human consciousness and behavior. As such, James and Bain appear in their texts as more mainstream scientists than does Peirce, despite Peirce's broader scientific training and deeper scientific commitments.

I have mentioned the tension in Bain between the indisputability of consciousness and the fallibility of knowledge, as well as the tension between rejecting innate beliefs and yet appealing to humanity's "natural" tendency to believe. As the next two chapters will show, James is caught in a quite similar set of tensions and, like Bain, resorts again to sets of dualities to try to resolve them. The attempt founders, however, because examining subjectivity by the methods of the natural sciences surrenders the terms of debate to those forces enabling the growing dominance of those sciences and leaves no room for the more metaphysical perspectives from which they are unable to extricate themselves. I contend that Peirce offers a coherent (albeit perhaps not convincing) solution to this problem, and the next chapter will outline the elaborate cosmology that subtends this solution.

The concept of the uniformity of nature stands as an intriguing connection between Bain and the pragmatists. If the assumption of uniformity is expressed in terms of habit, it correlates well with the pragmatists' emphasis on habits, which engender character and predictability in things and events. Peirce, especially, recognizes habit as a cosmological category, such that rocks and stars and rainfall all are habits. Moreover, Bain's uniformity of nature, which makes scientific investigation possible, is mirrored in the pragmatists' epistemological or anthropological insistence that the nature of nature and the nature of mind cannot be incommensurable. James simply posits this harmony of human and nature as a condition of science and assumes it proved by the results of science. Peirce argues for the correlation through both cosmology and theories of evolution but always tempers the claim with an equally strong argument against determinism.

Bain's statement that the end of all knowledge is practice or conduct is prototypical of pragmatism. So also is the process by which humans move from fallible beliefs that are held simply because they work to a fallible knowledge that is retained on the basis of one's experience of and in the world. Noteworthy for both belief and knowledge is how a particular understanding will enable a more trouble-free and productive life. In other words, the goal for Peirce and James is not to move from belief, as some tenuous state, to knowledge, as a state of greater certainty. Rather the pragmatists stress the movement from doubt to less doubt, whether the latter be termed belief or knowledge. For Bain, too, knowledge and belief are equally fallible, and the questions for him are how beliefs are embedded in a person's mind or how knowledge of the world enables a person to move reliably and confidently through it. The striking difference, as we shall see, is that while Bain's theories remain on the level of ease and convenience, the pragmatists gravitate toward strong ethical—and religious—accounts of being in the world.

The purpose of the previous four chapters on the evolutions of German and Scottish psychology has been to obviate one simple story of the origin of American pragmatism, namely, the reconciliation of German idealism and British empiricism. I have argued that the intellectual constellation of these geographic terrains elicited less a reconciliation than a mutation. Peirce and James learned from their German interlocutors how to articulate theories of realism and objectivity that do not succumb to crass empiricism and how to incorporate into their philosophies such non-Kantian themes as will, belief, and community. From the Scottish philosophers, the pragmatists took not Hamilton's religious orthodoxy and not simply Bain's focus on belief and action, but more important, the need to theorize and reconcile to one another the concepts of truth and consciousness. Importantly, Peirce and James took up this mandate with and through the cultural inclination to frame thought by reflections on a palpable sense of the "more" or "all," an inclination in America that is both religious and part of the nation's Puritan imaginary.

III

PRAGMATIC RECEPTION OF
EUROPEAN PSYCHOLOGY

Charles Sanders Peirce

The Impossible Necessity of Community

The writings of Charles Sanders Peirce (1839–1914) are remarkable. His work includes significant contributions to the physical sciences ("chemistry, geodesy, metrology, and astronomy") and demonstrates his skill as a "mathematical economist, a master of logic and mathematics, an inventor of the field of semeiotics [*sic*], a dramatist, actor and book reviewer." That Peirce is known widely only as the pragmatist who developed a complex semeiotic severely underestimates his accomplishments.[1] Born and bred in Cambridge to a family well connected with Brahmin Boston, Peirce's father had the time and money to cultivate and pamper his son's startling intellect.[2] Though these paternal attentions helped produce Peirce's lifelong impatience with those of lesser intelligence (namely, almost everyone), the home tutoring bore early fruit. At age eleven Charles wrote a history of chemistry; at age twelve he began, on his own, a study of Archbishop Whatley's logic; and by the time he was seventeen he was familiar with, if not yet fluent in, the works of Aristotle and Kant. During his adolescent years and throughout his college tenure, Peirce's father drilled him in mathematics; the two often stayed up late into the night working out theorems and debating problems.[3]

After completing his formal education, Peirce yearned for a permanent academic post of the kind awarded his friend William James. His ill temper and a scandal brought on by his insensitivity to the opinions of others, however, made such an appointment impossible. In the 1860s and 1870s his father's connections won Charles employment with the U.S. Coast Survey and the Harvard Observatory. Both positions utilized Peirce's skill in mathematics and physical science, but neither drew upon his greatest love, logic. Finally in 1878, again through his father's influence, Peirce was appointed a part-time lecturer in logic at the new Johns Hopkins University. While still working for the Coast Survey, he maintained this academic position through 1883, the year in which he divorced his first wife, Melusina Fay, and married his second wife, Juliette Froissy. In 1884 the university denied his contract renewal. Though the board of trustees listed academic reasons for releasing him, epistolary evidence suggests that Peirce's "lack of prudence" in regard to his divorce and remarriage shocked the trustees' Victorian sensibilities.[4] Peirce's general reputation for being a difficult colleague did not help matters (he carried on a famous feud with the other logician at Hopkins, J. J. Sylvester), and the fact that his protector, his father, had died in 1880 cut off most options. Hopkins did not renew his contract, and Harvard never again allowed Peirce to lecture at the Cambridge campus. Peirce never attained another academic post.[5] He continued to work for the Coast Survey, but the scandal over his remarriage and his difficult personality undermined him. The survey finally fired him in 1891, and Peirce spent the next twenty years constantly seeking employment, living from one freelance job to the next and relying heavily upon a few sympathetic friends, the most active of whom was William James.[6]

Peirce's forced alienation from the "communities of inquiry" that mattered most to him stands in utter contrast to his philosophical commitment to the communal nature of science and of human life in general.[7] Indeed, the community that was impossible in his life formed so integral a part of Peirce's work that it provides the general frame for this chapter. Notions of and about community inform not only Peirce's reformulations of "science" and ontology, but also the complex theory of continuity (synechism) that structures his pragmatism. Through his theorizing of community and synechism, Peirce's realism will be examined, and I will also assess his attempt to reconcile Kant's idealism with British empiricism, an attempt shared by Hermann von Helmholtz and William Hamilton (discussed in chapters 1 and 3). One consequence of this reconciliation is a theory of truth that posits both the singleness of truth (a characteristic presumed by Helmholtz and Hamilton) and truth's infinite deferral in light of humans' fallible modes of perception and reasoning. Envisioning fallibilism as occurring always within and between communities of inquiry, Peirce develops the famous pragmatic supposition that truth is that which no one has a reason to disbelieve.

The discussion of Peirce's realism includes Peirce's theory of generals and its resonance with Helmholtz's theory of the reality of natural laws. For both thinkers, the reality of a law (or general) differs from individual (and equally real) instances of that law. The difference resides in Peirce's synechism; where Helmholtz attributes the reality of natural laws (such as the conservation of energy) to the overarching action of causality, Peirce argues this reality from a cosmology grounded in virtuality and vagueness. Causality stood as a central theme of Helmholtz's corpus because of its role in defining and redefining the empiricism of natural science. Peirce writes less about causality per se than about how synechism and its concomitant theory of chance (tychism) delineate a field for explaining the relative predictability of the world (efficient causation), the inevitability of irregularities or chance occurrences, and the purposiveness (final causation) constitutive of both regularity and spontaneity. Put differently, Peirce's philosophy presents a cosmology that includes but supersedes a concern for human existence and therefore transforms the presumed orientation of "the empirical" as always directed toward the human.

From this perspective of criticizing a methodological narcissism, Peirce's critical disposition toward psychology is better understood. In my view, Peirce's early comments on psychology place his work in logic and physics within his more general comments about cosmology. By understanding how Peirce's synechism and tychism inform his logic, and how logic and semeiotics invalidate the legitimacy of the individual, we can better grasp the full impact of Peirce's mutation of psychological concepts such as consciousness, mind, feeling, and belief. These mutations form the heart of Peirce's pragmatism and from them we can elicit Peirce's response to the possibilities and limitations of scientifically studying human being. Peirce formulated pragmaticism, his version of pragmatism, primarily as a means of analyzing concepts, but the theory also infers a vision of the self that has important connections to aspects of America's Puritan legacy, specifically the dual obligation to intense self-examination (a form of self-assertion) and to disciplined self-abnegation. Peirce's theories about community and continuity stand as the priorities that lead to his version of pragmatism, a philosophy that stresses both the "inseparable connection between rational cognition and rational purpose"[8] and, coincidentally, the disciplined development of character and conduct through a rigorous process of self-control.

The Necessity of Psychology

Peirce's attitude toward psychology is ambiguous, at best. He read Wilhelm Wundt's 1862 *Beitrage zur Theorie der Sinneswahrnehmung* soon after its publication and closely followed its reception in intellectual circles, but Peirce remained long unconvinced of the need for a separate psychological science. As late as 1893 he records the doubt "that there is any such thing as psychology, apart from logic on the one hand and physiology on the other."[9] Peirce asserts that psychology has the rigor of (natural) "science" only to the extent that it draws from physiology (through the empirical, experimental method) or logic (to the extent that it examines signs and associations) and that rather too few self-designated psychologists are adept in either type of analysis.

Matters of classification, therefore, provide the fuel for Peirce's critique. Three years later (1896) he critiques a new publication in psychology on the grounds of misplaced foundations: "Now, the only sound psychology being a special science, which ought itself to be based upon a well-grounded logic, it is indeed a vicious circle [for the psychologist Peirce is reviewing] to make logic rest upon a theory of cognition so understood."[10] To Peirce, logic grounds cognition, not the other way around. Not only does psychology veil an illegitimate hybrid of methodologies (physiology and logic), it rests on fallacious

assumptions. Logical analyses, Peirce claims, necessarily precede any psychological analysis. Six years later (1902) Peirce seems to concede a modicum of defeat in suggesting that logic and psychology "should be developed separately and side by side."[11] He writes:

> Let me not be understood as having much faith in the current Wundtian monism [of brain physiology and matters of consciousness]. At any rate, however, it is pretty clear that there must be an application of scientific logic in order to separate the precipitate of physiology from the filtrate of logic. In this state of things, or in the real state of things which I am perhaps very mistakenly endeavoring to peer into, it ought, I think, to be admitted that psychological conceptions are not sufficiently matured to afford a safe foundation for any part of logic; and it seems still more evident that it is very much in the interest of psychology itself to restrain it from flowing over into the region of logic.[12]

Since logic does attend to questions of mental process, and since physiology contributes to understanding those same processes, the logician is warranted in pursuing logic's "precipitate of physiology." Admitting some vague connection of neurosensory processes and logical associations, however, does not necessitate a "Wundtian monism." The fact that psychologists currently presume this necessity belies, for Peirce, its immaturity as a science.

These quibbles over discursive boundaries reveal how Peirce's distinction of logic and psychology stems from his views on truth and the status of human knowing:

> Perhaps it may be said that if all our reasonings conform to the laws of logic, this is, at any rate, nothing but a proposition in psychology which my principles ought to forbid my recognizing. But I do not offer it as a principle of psychology only. For a principle of psychology is a contingent truth, while this, as I contend, is a necessary truth.[13]

The truths formed by psychology are contingent; they are particular and hence accidents of the human condition. The truths of logic, on the other hand, are necessary; they form the condition of possibility of human thought and hence of the laws of psychology itself. To Peirce, psychology focuses on the character and content of human knowing, while logic describes the relations that make that character and content possible. Logic studies what would be true under any given set of conditions (regardless of human constraints), while psychology focuses on what is true for human thought and tries to formulate laws about human volition and human character. Logic pursues hypothetical (what Peirce calls "abductive") analyses of what *would be* true in any possible world; psychology hypothesizes ("abduces") what *will be* true in this world.[14] From this perspective, which resonates with Hamilton's, Peirce would view the becoming-sociologist in Wundt as a predictable outcome of psychology's method.

Grasping Peirce's distinction between psychology and logic illuminates his arguments against nominalism, for his suggested antidote to nominalism, "scholastic realism," is a theory of cosmological scope. As described in chapter 1,

Peirce asserts three characteristics of nominalism. First, it claims that laws do not really operate in nature but are merely heuristic categories for organizing human experience. Second, nominalism "blocks the road of inquiry" (and assumes the necessary primacy of an anthropocentric perspective) by assuming that some facets of experience are ultimately inexplicable. Third, nominalism shuns indefiniteness and indeterminateness as a fall from an original definiteness and determinateness, a theoretical stance that results in an absolutist attitude toward truth and fact. Peirce corrects these nominalist "faults" through his synechism (theory of continuity) and semeiotics. Peirce thus reworks Helmholtz's and Hamilton's positions on causality and signification to emphasize purposiveness and vagueness and, as such, he effects a more radical repositioning of Kant by theorizing a complex continuity among all aspects of reality.

Demonstrating how these thinkers' shared terms (logic, causality, signification, consciousness) are grounded in and imply quite different semantic anchorage has been the focus of this book, guided by the question of what makes American pragmatism distinctly American. The distinctiveness of pragmatism does not lie in its vocabulary but rather, I argue, in the rhetoric of Puritanism that forms pragmatism's cultural milieu. Peirce, I contend, was especially drawn to and critical of the Gilded Age's use of the term *Puritan* to evoke an individualistic ethical disposition. In my view, stories about community and ethical accountability that descend from America's Puritan legacy shaped Peirce's responses to Europe's philosophical and scientific concepts and thereby generated his version of American pragmaticism.

The Real Operation of Natural Laws

In his second Cambridge lecture of 1898, Peirce admits that his way of posing the question of nominalism versus realism strays from scholastic formulations:

> Now what was the question of realism and nominalism? I see no objection to defining it as the question of which is the best, the laws or the facts under those laws. It is true that it was not stated in this way. As stated, the question was whether *universals*, such as the Horse, the Ass, the Zebra, and so forth, were *in re* or *in rerum natura*. But that there is no great merit in this formulation of the question is shown by two facts; first, that many different answers were given to it, instead of merely yes and no, and second, that all the disputants divided the question into various parts. It was therefore a broad question and it is proper to look beyond the letter into the spirit of it.[15]

The scholastics debated whether universals are real in themselves (*in re*) or exist only in the things of nature (*in rerum natura*), but Peirce considers this phrasing too broad to enable fruitful discussion. So Peirce rewrites the terms of the debate. Framing the question in terms of axiology ("which is best"), Peirce tosses out the question of how universals relate to individuals and posits a debate about how "laws" relate to "the facts under those laws." He comments further, clarifying why he chooses to examine "laws":

> Most of the scholastics whose works are occasionally read today were matter-of-fact dualists; and when they used the phrase *in re* or *in rerum natura* in formulating the question, they took for granted something in regard to which other disputants, however confusedly, were at odds with them. For some of them regarded the universals as more real than the individuals. Therefore, the reality, or as I would say in order to avoid any begging of the question, the value or worth, not merely of the universals, but also that of the individuals was a part of the broad question. Finally, it was always agreed that there were other sorts of universals besides *genera* and *species*, and in using the word law, or regularity, we bring into prominence the kind of universals to which modern science pays most attention. Roughly speaking, the nominalists conceived the *general* element of cognition to be merely a convenience for understanding this and that fact and to amount to nothing except for cognition, while the realists, still more roughly speaking, looked upon the general, not only as the end and aim of knowledge, but also as the most important element of being.[16]

Peirce is troubled by nominalism because, like psychology, it reduces knowledge about the world to a necessarily human perspective ("the *general* element of cognition . . . amount[s] to nothing except for cognition"). Peirce offers a realism that posits the nonhuman "general" as "the most important element of being." In trying to articulate truths that supersede human cognition, this realism corroborates the aims of natural science to formulate general and true knowledge about the world. Thus Peirce frames the nominalist-realist debate in terms of laws, "the kind of universals to which modern science pays most attention." Importantly, then, Peirce situates his critique of nominalism, the hallmark of his system, squarely within a conversation about the character and purpose of natural science. That character and purpose assume that the lawfulness or regularity of the world logically precedes and conditions the lawfulness of human thought and being. As such Peirce's position seems congruent to that of Helmholtz (the law of causality as the theoretical umbrella that orders the hypotheses of practical science), Hamilton (the basic order of the world guarantees moral order), and Bain (causality operates within a fundamental uniformity of nature). Peirce's difference appears only when one delves further into his specific account of a law or general.

Peirce shares Helmholtz's view that laws are really operative in nature and not simply Kantian constructs of the mind. Peirce also agrees with Helmholtz that laws or generals function regulatively, that is, when humans understand and act according to the regularities of the world, we are able to organize (regulate) human experience and effect a greater control over events and environments. Helmholtz's law of causality, however, includes no *necessary* final causation or teleology.[17] Because of this, he is forced to a position of indeterminacy: since the relation between an instance of a law and the law itself is inexplicable, we must simply "have trust and act." For Peirce a law is not "merely" regulative; regularity fully describes its being.[18] A discussion of Peirce's "universal categories" of "Firstness," "Secondness," and "Thirdness" will clarify this point, for laws, generalities and habits all fall under Thirdness. Firstness, Secondness, and Thirdness are logical categories, but I will explicate them here phenomenologically according to Peirce's 1903 Lowell Lectures on the history of philosophy. "Firstness," he notes, "is the mode of being which consists in its subject's being positively such as it is regardless of aught else. That can only be a possibility."[19] Indeed, virtuality would be a better term since Peirce later admits, "That possibility implies a relation to what exists, while universal Firstness is the mode of being of itself."[20] Firstness is pure quality and pure feeling; it points to the immediacy of perception, before consciousness recognizes or processes that perception.

Secondness is actuality, existence, resistance. "Actuality is something *brute*," Peirce explains. "There is no reason in it. I instance putting your shoulder against a door and trying to force it open against an unseen, silent, and unknown resistance. We have [in this instance] a two-sided consciousness of effort and resistance, which seems to me to come tolerably near to a pure sense of actuality."[21] In terms of cognition, Secondness names the experience of waking in the night, cognizant that one heard something, but as yet unable to classify it. That feeling of otherness, of brute, nameless actuality aptly describes Secondness.

Thirdness is the naming of that noise. Peirce defines it as "the mode of being which *consists*, mind my word if you please, the mode of being which *consists* in the fact that future facts of Secondness will take on a determinate general character."[22] Laws, generals, habits—all are thirds, as are words and other signs. Because Thirdness "consists" in what particular Secondnesses will do in the future, it is a "mode of being" temporally disjunctive from the present; elsewhere Peirce describes it as *esse in futuro*. Firstness, as virtuality, is also temporally disjunctive from the present; it is real without yet being actual. Actuality (Secondness) is the only mode of being in the present; it is the bruteness of *hic et nunc*. Thirdness, however, is both real and actual, both disjunctive from and conjunctive with the present. As regarding its operation in nature, Thirdness is *real*; like Firstness, it is material but not yet actual. But where Firstness is "such as it is regardless of aught else" (a singularity, as its name implies), Thirdness is a relation or series of relations. As such, Thirdness buckles down to actuality. Its mode of being is a relationship that determines how Firstness and Secondness relate to the future. Firstnesses may or may not ever be actualized; their mode of being does not hinge on actualization (though human knowledge of any particular Firstness does require its actualization). But Thirdness *is* conjoined to actuality; it relies on and includes Secondness and Firstness. As Peirce describes it, the reality of a law has the quality of *esse in futuro*; logically, it is a future conditional, a *would-be*.[23]

Humans perceive instances of a law or habit according to the logic of Helmholtz's law of causality. We experience the world as a series of events or effects that have determinable causes, and yet the regularity that we experience is not an accident of human causation and neither—contrary to Helmholtz's musings—is it "inadequate." Laws are not *merely* regulative for Peirce; regularity is their essence and existence. Laws articulate the connected discreteness of life, regardless of the existence of human being; laws thereby illustrate a purposiveness that supersedes human cognition. Whereas Helmholtz suggests that we have trust and act because to do otherwise is to seek fruitlessly for what cannot be understood, Peirce gladly exhorts us to "have trust and act" because to do otherwise is to reject the fundamental purposiveness of the cosmos.[24] Helmholtz, who (unlike Hamilton) avoids nominalism by insisting on the reality of natural law, in the end falls back into nominalism by not recognizing the primacy of the virtual.

The Primacy of the Virtual

As Peirce states early in the second of his 1898 lectures, the question of nominalism is "the question of which is best, the laws or the facts under those laws."[25] The previous section illustrated Peirce's allegiance to the priority of laws and to his claim that they exist as future conditionals. Laws or generals exist both virtually (they are material and real) and as inherently tied to the actual. The individual instances of a law are its actualization, its movement from the indeterminacy of the virtual to the determinacy of the event. By definition, however, a determination is also a limitation since to become determined as x is to close off the opportunity of being not-x. For Peirce, then, indeterminacy is not a fall from an originating determinacy but is rather the state of fullness and completeness that every determination fragments. In this way Peirce counters the nominalist assumption that definiteness logically precedes indefiniteness and argues instead for the primacy of the virtual.[26]

Another way to frame this same counter to nominalism is to ask: which is best, the continuity or discreteness of reality? By asserting the real virtuality of laws, Peirce opts for the real continuity of experience. As noted above, laws really conjoin or assemble the discreteness of life and thereby illustrate a purposiveness that supersedes human cognition. Peirce calls the theory delineating this commitment to continuity, *synechism*. Through it and its accompanying theory of chance (tychism) Peirce theorizes a reconciliation of Kantian idealism and British empiricism. In Baldwin's *Dictionary of Philosophy and Psychology*, Peirce defines synechism as "that tendency of philosophical thought which insists upon the idea of continuity as of prime importance in philosophy and, in particular, upon the necessity of hypotheses involving true continuity."[27] By *continuity*, Peirce at times means simply the commonsense understanding of the term. "We all have some idea of continuity," he notes. "Continuity is fluidity, the merging of part into part."[28] To explain precisely what this familiar experience of continuity implies about reality—much less about the human cognition of reality—is, however, exceedingly difficult.[29]

Peirce draws his musings about continuity from contemporary debates between Georges Cantor and the neo-Kantians. Though he critiques both positions, Peirce avers that each is partially correct. Cantor argues for what Peirce calls the "Aristotelicity" of continuity, which "may be roughly stated thus: a continuum contains the end point belonging to every endless series of points which it contains. An obvious corollary is that every continuum contains its limits."[30] This perspective treats continuity through the use of limits (as, for example, the limit theory employed in basic calculus). Every limit (every "end point") within the continuum simply indicates more "endless series"; limits define discrete points, but points that implicate a range of values. The "Kanticity" of continuity, on the other hand, states that the points of a continuum can be halved or otherwise fractionally divided ad infinitum. These points are individual such that their division delineates the well-known series of rational fractions. As Peirce sees it, Kanticity is "infinite intermediety, or divisibility."[31] Peirce critiques Cantor (and, by default, Aristotle) for "permit[ting] the correlation of [the continuum's] elements with a series of discrete, quantitative units," and he counters that a continuum is composed not of discrete points but of *real*, that is, virtual points.[32] The Kantians' argument pushes the image of discrete points even further; for Peirce, their theory of continuity is too metric. As such, it explains divisibility but not continuity, for it does not demonstrate the relation of continuity between fractions. Peirce asserts that Kanticity introduces gaps or breaks in continuity.

Peirce corrects Cantor (Aristotelicity) by replacing the limit theory of continuity with a theory based on infinitesimals, numbers "greater than zero but less than any number, however, small, you could ever conceive of writing."[33] Peirce modifies Kanticity by suggesting that the perceived gaps or defects in continuity are the points at which virtuality is actualized: the set of infinitesimals (or nonstandard numbers) encircling each real (finite) number creates a vagueness (virtuality) that becomes determined (actualized) in and through a particular function.[34] According to current theories of infinitesimals, "every standard number can be viewed as having its own collection of nearby, nonstandard numbers, each one only an infinitesimal distance from the standard number."[35] Standard numbers include any number one can articulate ("conceive of writing"), including fractions. Each standard number is surrounded by a nonstandard collection of numbers separated by an "infinitesimal distance." Infinitesimals thus form a real, but vague (inarticulable) cloud that overlaps the space *between* real numbers. A point together with its collection of infinitesimals defines a *monad*.[36] It is strictly indeterminable where each monad begins and ends. Hence the monads of a geometrical line shade into each other and constitute it as a continuum.

The fact that the points on the continuum are real might suggest their status as Firstnesses, that is, as pure possibilities, which may or may not be actualized. Peirce, however, intimates in his 1898 lectures that the points of a continuum have a specific order to them, even though they are only real and not yet actual.[37] Orderedness implies a level of determinateness appropriate to Thirdness; the points connote a reality inherently connected to actuality and operating to predict the shape of future events. The points of a continuum are monads. They are partially tied to actuality (finite quantities, standard numbers) and partially embedded in a surrounding vagueness of possibility (infinitesimals, nonstandard numbers). Again, this dual status as both present and temporally disjunctive defines the mode of being of Thirdness. As constituted by thirds, a continuum operates as a law or general; it regulates the behavior of its constituents. To summarize: Peirce's realism argues for the primacy of indefiniteness or vagueness and thus counters the nominalist scorn of indefiniteness as an ontological degeneration. Peirce's synechism employs infinitesimals to construct a cosmological continuity that posits laws (generals, thirds) as (vague) realities that become definite only through a process of actualization. These laws or generals, Peirce asserts, form "the most important element[s] of being."[38]

Peirce's insistence on the ontological priority of laws makes better sense in the context of his struggle to reconcile Kantian idealism and British empiricism, an effort shared by Helmholtz and Hamilton. Because of the primacy of the virtual in his philosophy—that is, because an indeterminate but real continuum is logically prior to the objects and events of actual human experience—Peirce thinks he avoids the Kantian gap between noumenal and phenomenal realms. Our discussion of logic versus psychology helps explain this, for Peirce obviates the noumenal only by establishing a logical continuum that both transcends and enables the human psychology of perception. Laws are real (vague, virtual), and humans experience only particular instances of them. Particularity thus derives from the vagueness of the cosmological continuum. Humans do perceive and experience what is real. There is no ungraspable reality lying behind experience, for "reality" and "experience of reality" lie within the same real (vague, undetermined) continuum.[39]

Continua would be a more appropriate term, for actualization occurs across many dimensions, across many overlapping continua of Thirdnesses. Independent of human cognition, the individual event or object that humans experience (Secondness) actualizes out of states of greater vagueness. Peirce describes this process as a coalescing or "bundling" of habits.[40] In themselves, habits are also thirds; they are real generals out of which particular instances come into being. Thus, an object or event is an instance of one level of Thirdness deriving from another level of Thirdness. The Secondness of human perception, however, describes brute actuality, not a determined thing or event. Thus the process of human perception furthers the process of determination that forms our experience of something.

Peirce's synechism distinguishes him from Helmholtz and Hamilton in clearly demarcating how the reality of natural laws, which guarantees the orderliness of the world, functions through a continuum of ontological and logical continua. Synechism attempts to close the noumenal gap established by Kant while still advocating the empiricist lesson that human knowledge arises out of human experience. Moreover, synechism demonstrates the pragmatic transposition of European "scientific" assumptions in yet another way, namely, in necessitating purpose of final causality in the process of something coming into being. The status of things and events as instances that coalesce through habit best conveys this insertion of purpose, since laws and generals clearly function by an internal logic, but habits, being always habits *of* something or someone, are more obviously purposeful.

Initially, in the formation of the universe, the purpose of habit was simply to persist:

> Out of the womb of indeterminacy we must say that there would have come something, by the principle of Firstness, which we may call a flash. Then by the principle of habit there would have been a second flash. . . . Then there would have come other successions ever more and more closely connected, the habits and the tendency to take them ever strengthen in themselves, until the events would have been bound together into something like a continuous flow.[41]

This passage forms part of Peirce's discussion of how substance originates. Substance arises when habits bundle together and develop "a permanence of some relation."[42] For a stone or a heart, maintaining this permanent relation necessitates only repetition of the habit of taking habits; the purpose of habit is simply to persist. In human subjects, however, this chemical and physiological application of habit combines with the habit of purposive conduct.

Peirce stresses his commitment to synechism in part because his more famous colleague, William James, builds his pragmatism around chance and spontaneous action. Peirce treats chance in a theory he calls *tychism*, but he tends to subsume it within synechism. He writes in 1898:

> I object to having my metaphysical system as a whole called Tychism. For although tychism does enter into it, it only enters as subsidiary to that which is really, as I regard it, the characteristic of my doctrine, namely, that I chiefly insist upon continuity, or Thirdness, and in order to secure to Thirdness its really commanding function, I [find it indispensable] that it is a third, and that Firstness, or chance, and Secondness, or Brute reaction, are other elements without the independence of which Thirdness would not have anything upon which to operate. Accordingly, I like to call my theory Synechism, because it rests on the study of continuity.[43]

Despite the "subsidiary" role of tychism, chance is crucial for Peirce. In his 1892 essay for the *Monist*, "The Doctrine of Necessity," Peirce battles the reigning assumption—common to Helmholtz and others—that efficient causality fully explains the objects and events of the world. Congruent with the accounts concerning the relation of a natural law to its individual instances, Peirce urges his readers to "try to verify any law of nature, and you will find that the more precise your observations, the more certain they will be to show irregular departures from the law. We are accustomed to ascribe these [irregular departures], and I do not say wrongly, to errors of observation; yet we cannot usually account for such errors in any antecedently probable way. Trace their causes back far enough, and you will be forced to admit they are always due to arbitrary determination, or chance."[44] Peirce is aware that in the face of experimental irregularities Helmholtz and other natural scientists will advise us simply to "have trust and act." Peirce, however, traces these "irregular departures" back to chance. The impossibility of exactly duplicating experimental results stems not from instrumental variation or observational error, asserts Peirce, but from a real and independent force operating through the universe, namely, the force of spontaneity or chance.

Through tychism and synechism Peirce refuses to concede complete meaning and effectiveness to the efficient causation assumed by scientists like Helmholtz and philosophers like Hamilton. Generally, the purposeful force of these imbricating theories remains implicit in Peirce's texts. In the same essay just quoted, however, he makes the connection to causality explicit. Countering the *necessitarians*, his term for those who advocate determinism and who assume that only efficient causation is appropriately empirical, Peirce draws out the implications of their theories for studying human nature:

> Necessitarianism cannot logically stop short of making the whole action of the mind a part of the physical universe. Our notion that we decide what we are going to do, if as the necessitarian says, it has been calculable since the earliest times, is reduced to illusion. Indeed, consciousness in general thus becomes a mere illusory aspect of a material system. . . . On the other hand, by supposing the rigid exactitude of causation to yield, I care not how little— be it but by a strictly infinitesimal amount—we gain room to insert mind into our scheme, and to put it into the place where it is needed, into the position which, as the sole self-intelligible thing, it is entitled to occupy, that of the fountain of existence; and in so doing we resolve the problem of the connection of soul and body.[45]

The necessitarians make the defining character of human being (consciousness) an illusion, and they do so by adhering to "the rigid exactitude of causation." Peirce might here be seen as a proponent for psychology, since he obviously does not consider consciousness an illusion. At issue, however, is not consciousness, but mind, a distinction he does not clarify in this passage. *Consciousness,* for Peirce, denotes the inner, personal aspect of mind. *Mind* is a cosmological term, a substitute name for continuity. Peirce argues that chance "flashes" of Firstness spontaneously ("irregular departures from the law") interrupt the continuity of mind and, when those flashes coalesce into states and substances (when they take on even a slight "permanence of relation"), they disrupt the hegemony of efficient causation.

Peirce's expansion of causality to include real, spontaneous events makes a difference for his understanding of science only at the phenomenological level (as opposed to an ontological level), for science depends upon human perception, which itself relies upon the laws of logic. On this phenomenological level, the theory of chance supports Peirce's fallibilism, the assumption that absolute certainty about the objects and events of this world is unattainable. Humans really perceive and experience the world—the Kantian gap is closed—but because chance (tychism) is as real as continuity (synechism), our stance toward and reflections upon our real experiences must remain tentative. Peirce notes that fallibilism affects both the possible quantity and quality of human knowledge: "Not only is our knowledge thus limited in scope, but it is even more important that we should thoroughly realize that the very best of what we, humanly speaking, know [we know] only in an uncertain and inexact way."[46] True scientists, Peirce avers, will concur immediately with these comments on fallibilism and tychism. But, he warns:

There is one class of objectors to [tychism] who are so impressed with what they have read in popular books about the triumphs of science, that they really imagine that science has *proved* that the universe is regulated by law down to every detail. Such men are theologians, perhaps, or perhaps they have been brought up in surroundings where everything was so minutely regulated that they have come to believe that every tendency that exists at all in Nature must be carried to its furthest limit.[47]

Peirce's aversion to institutional religion comes through in this passage. As the conclusions chapter will clarify, Peirce does not oppose religion so much as the attempt by theologians to scientize the religious sentiment. Certainty may be an appropriate desire of the believer, but this desire cannot (should not) be analyzed and codified scientifically, a practice that Peirce attributes to theologians. Indeed, Peirce casts the theological need for certainty in an ironic light, blaming reading habits and upbringing for the apparently absurd notion that science has "proved" anything or that "every tendency . . . in Nature must be carried to its furthest limit."

In an untitled manuscript of uncertain date, Peirce applies these comments about fallibilism and tychism directly to Helmholtz's law of the conservation of energy:

The fourth law of motion was developed about forty years ago by Helmholtz and others. It is called the law of the conservation of energy; but in my opinion that is a very misleading name, implying a peculiar aspect of the law under which the real fact at the bottom of it is not clearly brought out. It is therefore not suitable for an abstract and general statement, although it is a point of view which is very serviceable for many practical applications. But the law generally stated is that the changes in the velocities of particles depend exclusively on their relative positions.

It is not necessary to examine these laws with technical accuracy. It is sufficient to notice that they leave the poor little particle no option at all. Under given circumstances his motion is precisely laid out for him.[48]

Peirce here delivers Helmholtz a deep wound. The German established the law of the conservation of energy as precisely that precept of theoretical science that could encompass the results of the practical sciences. Peirce, however, calls it "misleading" because it is not theoretical enough! The insufficiency arises from Helmholtz resting at the level of the conservation of energy and not pressing the issue to its full explanation in a theory of continuity, such as Peirce's synechism. Moreover, Peirce accuses Helmholtz of being a necessitarian (determinist) because if one follows the law's dictates about particles' relative positions, "the poor little particle [has] no option at all." Helmholtz presents a closed system, one in which chance has no room, precisely because the German upholds the "rigid necessity of causality."

Peirce derives tychism and fallibilism from his theory of continuity, a theory that asserts a primary indefiniteness and thereby counters nominalist claims about primary determinateness. Tychism and fallibilism also critique another nominalist claim. Like the theologians who reject tychism, those who resist fallibilism seek absolute certainty in science and banish spontaneity and freedom from the cosmos. As such they "block the road of inquiry."[49] But is this statement not itself a sort of theological argument, similar to the dogmatic statements of persons who oppose Peirce's tychism? Peirce would say no, that his metaphysics is not based on a dogmatic assumption but on better reasoning, reasoning that is more open to the irregularities of the world and to transcommunal critique. Thus even though he argues forcefully for fallibilism and tychism, he knows that his reasoning remains hypothetical ("abductive") and must be judged according to its logic and to its ability to cover more facts, instances, and experiences than alternate reasonings.

Do Not Block the Road of Inquiry

So important does Peirce hold the maxim that is the title of this section that he terms it the "corollary" to the first "law of reason," which is to desire to learn.[50] He perceives four "bars" to philosophical inquiry, all of them stemming directly from nominalist thinking. The first, the possibility of absolute assertion and perfect formulation, Peirce counters through his fallibilism.[51] The second, "that this, that, and the other never can be known," Peirce critiques with evidence from the history of science. As soon as Auguste Comte declared that the "chemical composition of fixed stars" never could be known, for example, "the spectroscope was discovered and that which he had deemed absolutely unknowable was well on the way of getting ascertained."[52] "The third philosophical stratagem for cutting off inquiry," Peirce continues, "consists in maintaining that this, that, or the other element of science is basic, ultimate, independent of aught else, and utterly inexplicable—not so much from any defect in our knowing as because there is nothing beneath it to know." Peirce critiques this supposition as illogical, pointing out that the position is sustained only by a "retroductive inference": "Now nothing justifies a retroductive inference except its affording an explanation of the facts," but it is hardly an explanation simply to call them inexplicable.[53] Peirce's arguments against nominalist claims of inexplicability further illustrate his deep theoretical commitment to continuity and synechism's corollaries: nothing is inexplicable and no thing or word is ever ultimate or certain. This two-pronged perspective on human knowing forms the kernel of Peirce's "pragmaticism" and the paradox that energizes the bulk of his musings. His epistemology accepts Kant's notion of critique, but refuses Kant's forms of thoughts (which are known immediately and without inference) since Peirce denies validity to a *Ding an sich*; moreover, Peirce's epistemology rejects commonsense notions of certainty and solidity. Peirce labels his stance "critical common-sensism."[54]

The commonsense side of this position counsels a reasoned trust in experience and in the lessons of experience. Common sense bears witness to Secondness, to the sense (physiological and psychological) that the world is real and that humans are an integral part of it, not separated from it by the fact of our self-consciousness. Common sense also bears out the truth of

Thirdness, for a lesson learned is a habit, and to act from habit is to act upon the collective wisdom of history and tradition.[55] Taken in light of Peirce's synechism, such commonsensism obviates any need for a Kantian *Ding an sich* and sounds much more like the Scottish commonsense realists. Like the Scots, Peirce asserts the reality of indubitable beliefs. But akin to Kant's critical disposition, "all the veritably indubitable beliefs are *vague*—often in some directions highly so."[56] By criticism, Peirce notes, our indubitable beliefs or habits are molded, shaped, and made trustworthy. Instead of simply accepting beliefs, as do the Scottish commonsensists, the critical commonsensist "opines that the indubitable beliefs refer to a somewhat primitive mode of life, and that, while they never become dubitable in so far as our mode of life remains that of somewhat primitive man, yet as we develop *degrees of self-control* unknown to that man, occasions of action arise in relation to which the original beliefs, if stretched to cover them, have no sufficient authority. In other words, we outgrow the applicability of instinct."[57] Here, as in Hermann von Helmholtz's writings, Peirce acknowledges that evolution is a process of slowly gaining control over one's environment. But unlike Helmholtz, Peirce attributes this process not to causal efficacy, but rather to the logical and experiential task of responding to a habit's inadequacy by devising a new and better response. Evolution proceeds by criticism, that is, by the causal efficacy of induction and also by the final causation of hypothesis (abduction).[58] Peirce thus uses Kant to counter the nominalist tendency to "block the road of inquiry," though he differs markedly from Helmholtz's return to Kant. According to Peirce, Helmholtz's Kantianism propounds a nominalist appeal to inexplicability and a full dependency on the law of cause and effect. Peirce, on the other hand, employs Kant to move beyond Kant. He rejects the *Ding an sich* (which is the source of Helmholtz's nominalism) by accepting a theory of real, virtual continuity that places human knowledge within a larger semeiotic schema and thus makes purpose real and possible. Moreover, he overlays the cultural success of the law of causality (the basis of the empirical method of the natural sciences) with a logical process that prioritizes the concrete growth of reasonableness. Peirce soundly rejects the notion that Kant's categories rest on some *Ding an sich* that lies completely outside human experience. So Peirce uses Kant's categories and logic to disprove what he considers Kant's primary illogic. And, though Peirce understands the idealism—or conceptualism—of Kant, he moves beyond the latter's synthesis of the sensory manifold by intuition, understanding, and reason to develop a complex cosmology, wherein habits are always real and material, always composite and incessantly assembling, and always, in some sense, mental. In sum, Peirce critiques the nominalists' methods, not simply because they block the road of inquiry, but because erecting such barricades yields an absolutist and mechanical attitude toward truth and fact, as is found in Kant. To Peirce, pragmatism is more fully scientific because it never assumes an a priori, is never content to bow before dogmatism (be it common sense or established powers), and never resists necessary change in the wake of failure, error, or inadequacy.[59]

"Scientific," accordingly, names the process of gaining control over the inferences that constitute our sensations, perceptions, and conceptions, and then solidifying that control in beliefs and habits. Science forms experiments that recognize the real as both constraining and exceeding human cognition. Humans perceive only what is real, but also only part of what is real. Not surprisingly, such an understanding of science has immediate consequences for the notions of truth and fact, most famously the familiar pragmatic claim that truth must be judged as "true for now." Truth congeals around a temporary, warranted consensus. Those beliefs, habits, and propositions considered true are those that are held by so many persons—and that are congruent with so many other beliefs, habits, and propositions—that no one currently has cause or reason to doubt them.[60]

Current scholarship labels this position Peirce's limit theory of truth, a theory that arises directly out of his synechism: truth designates "the real" as completely determined. Truth, that is, covers the fullness of the (real, virtual) continua as they become perfectly actualized. Peirce describes the relation of truth and the real this way: "The opinion which is fated to be ultimately agreed to by all who investigate, is what we mean by the truth, and the object represented in this opinion is the real."[61] At issue is what Peirce means by an opinion "fated to be" universally accepted. Another quotation aids our interpretation: "The real is that which, sooner or later, information and reasoning would finally result in, and which is therefore independent of the vagaries of me and you. Thus, the very origin of the conception of reality shows that this conception essentially involves the notion of a COMMUNITY, without definite limits, and capable of a definite increase of knowledge."[62] These two quotations assert the necessarily communal character of the production of truth and suggest its perpetually future quality. Truth must be a limit, the attainment of which is infinitely deferred, even though communities of inquiry approach the limit asymptotically. Truth "must" be this unattainable limit, for a full end of inquiry would entail a "crystallization of mind," that is, a full and fully determinate state but also a dead and static state. Peirce thus understands truth as real, effective, and yet only articulable in fallibilistic statements.

This theory of truth concludes my explication of the three "faults" of nominalism and contextualizes these faults relative to Helmholtz's and Hamilton's Kantian-influenced empiricism. To summarize: Helmholtz and Peirce agree that laws are not heuristic categories but are really operative in nature. The two scientists differ on this point with respect to their interpretation of reality and their resulting dispositions toward the Kantian *Ding an sich*. For Peirce, reality is virtual—a series of infinitesimally overlapping composites—and, as such, no gap need be assumed between reality and perception of reality. Helmholtz and Hamilton are more literally empiricist in believing that our sensations and instrumental measurements are indeed the most basic elements of perception, though they are not necessarily iconic to (Helmholtz) or fully expressive of (Hamilton) reality itself. This assumed gap between reality and perception leads to the second nominalist fault, which asserts reality to be ultimately inexplicable. This assumption blocks the road of inquiry because it assumes that the human perspective is normative and ultimate. Peirce acknowledges that human knowing is only perspectival, but it is nonetheless real, and it is related—however vaguely, however infinitesimally—to all other perspectives. Peirce argues this position through synechism, according to which indefiniteness and indeterminateness are logically prior to determinateness, just as virtuality logically precedes actuality. Helmholtz and Hamilton, however, follow the mainstream of the history of empiricism and science in assuming that the determinate object exists prior to investigation of it. In their view, science is not about control of inferences through communal efforts, but rather about uncovering the truth that is present but as yet unseen. Science, for Helmholtz and for Hamilton, is the empirical attempt to "get it right," to pinpoint the right methods and the right instruments that will lead the investigator to the one truth that awaits discovery.

Detailing Peirce's three critiques of nominalism might seem a long detour from issues of psychology. Peirce's ambivalence about the need for a separate science of psychology, however, as well as his later criticism of psychology as confusing philosophical and psychological categories and generally lacking in rigor, stem not simply from a dedication to logic over physiology, but from his cosmological theory of continuity that informs both his logic and his physiology and shifts them away from the frame of idealism or empiricism and toward a ground in axiology and purpose. I have already intimated ways in which Peirce's synechism and tychism link up with his pragmatism and his semeiotic. Before turning more directly to Peirce's mutation of psychological concepts, these links need to be clarified.

Semeiotics of the Virtual

In an early and popular essay, Peirce states, "Just as we say that a body is in motion, and not that motion is in a body, we ought to say that we are in thought and not that thoughts are in us."[63] The status of thought as somehow superseding and constitutive of human reality adequately frames a discussion of Peirce's semeiotic, for it immediately draws our attention to the fact that signs are not restricted to an anthropological domain.[64] The whole universe is "perfused with signs," Peirce declares rather poetically.[65] As we know from the previous discussion, however, the universe is not only an unbounded set of objects and events but is also the ever-moving, ever-growing virtuality that underlies and conditions those objects and events. What I call the semeiotics of the virtual, then, describes how human knowledge crystallizes out of the pure Firstness—the vagueness—of the virtual.

Peirce distinguishes semeiotics from Secondness and marks it as a process of Thirdness:

> All dynamical action, or action of brute force, physical or psychical, either takes place between two subjects [whether they react equally upon each other, or one is agent and the other patient, entirely or partially] or at any rate is a resultant of such actions between pairs. But by "semiosis" I mean, on the con-

trary, an action, or influence, which is, or involves, a cooperation of *three* sub-jects, such as a sign, its object, and its interpretant, the tri-relative influence not being in any way resolvable into actions between pairs.[66]

Secondness encompasses physical or psychical actions or effects that are "dynamical"; they follow the pattern of automatic reflex or brute reaction. Semeiosis, as Thirdness, necessarily involves interpretation. The interpreta-tion forms an integral part of the process, for without it the process could be "resolvable into actions between pairs." Peirce terms the three aspects of the semeiotic process the sign, the object, and the interpretant, but it is more complicated than this initial description. Each of those aspects may itself be a third (containing a process of sign, object, and interpretant), and each of those thirds divides into further thirds, and so on, ad infinitum. Thus what persists as a Thirdness in its own right might be felt by humans as a simple quality or Firstness. Peirce's semeiotics always implies multiple selections from infinite layers of virtuality.

Peirce views substance itself as bundles of habits. Cosmologically or ontologically, Firstness arises as a "flash," as a "defect in continuity."[67] Un-less this spontaneity "chance[s] to take habits of persistency,"[68] however, it will be "thunderless and unremembered."[69] By taking habits of persistency, the flash becomes a substance or event, that is, something just permanent enough to be available for human perception. These things or events, which are thirds in themselves (since they have taken habits of persistency), act on our sensory motor systems as firsts and seconds—and so begins another layer of virtuality from which humans perceive (interpret) the world around them. To understand how this process produces human thought requires a discus-sion of Peirce's triadic division of sign, object, and interpretant. Peirce de-picts a sign as something that stands for something else (its object) and deter-mines another sign (the interpretant), which stands in the same relationship to the object as does the first sign.[70] Three examples might suffice; they dem-onstrate, respectively, an iconic sign, an indexical sign, and a symbol. First, a painting of a rabbit is a sign that stands for some rabbit (regardless of whether the author painted from memories of rabbits or from one particular rabbit) and this rabbit is the object of the picture. The picture determines in me the cognition of a rabbit, and this cognition is the interpretant of the picture, which stands in the same relation to the object of the picture as does the picture it-self, namely, both represent or call up the notion of "rabbit." Second, I step outside my door one spring morning and notice that the crocuses have been nibbled down to their greens. The state of the crocuses is a sign, the object of which is some event. My response, "I need to protect my flowers against that rabbit," is the interpretant of the sign (the state of the flowers), which stands in the same relation to the object (the event resulting in the state of the flow-ers) as does the sign itself, namely, both represent or call up the notion of "rabbit" or, more specifically, "rabbit-eating-my-flowers." Third, I tell a friend, "I am going to build a low fence to protect my flowers from those pesky ani-mals," and this sentence is a sign the object of which is my general frustration with rabbits eating from the garden. My friend's reply, "Oh, of course, rabbits! It seemed strange to me that deer would come so close to the front door," is the interpretant of my statement, which stands in the same relation to the object of my statement as does my statement itself, even if she is thinking of the state of *her* crocuses instead of mine.

Though Peirce lists other types of signs, iconic signs, indexical signs, and symbols are most pertinent for explaining human cognition.[71] In each of the examples, the object of the sign and the object of the interpretant are the same but in a general or vague sense, that is, not in the sense of a point-to-point correspondence. Peirce explains this vague relation by stating that a sign relates to its object "not in all respects, but in reference to a sort of idea, which I have sometimes called the *ground* of the representamen." By *idea*, Peirce means "that sense in which we say that one man catches another man's idea."[72] Though Peirce does choose his metaphors carefully, the ground may be considered the *context* of a sign; it allows communication to succeed, despite the occurrence of multiple (and inevitable) semeiotic slippages.

In the conversation with my friend, for example, the common ground or context was the damage done to our gardens. For me, the ground was less vague since, unknown to my friend, I had previously seen a rabbit munching on my crocuses. For my friend, the ground was a vague group of possibilities, a not-quite-satisfactory one of which was "deer." Suppose, however, that my friend had just been visiting a third neighbor, who recently acquired a pair of puppies. Her reply to my proposed low fence might then be, "What will you do when they grow up?" and my returned look of confusion would be a further sign that we had not yet settled on a common ground or context. Thus, the ground functions like any other third or general in that it links a real field of possibilities to the semeiotic matrix that actualizes and interprets those possibilities. In Peirce's words, the ground "is the object as immediate, or as represented for the interpreter";[73] it implicates both the Secondness of the event and the Thirdness of cognizing that event.

In Peirce's later writings he spells out the difference between the immediate and the dynamical objects of a sign. We can regard the dynamical object as the object in its pure Firstness relative to the human mind, and the immediate object as a third, that is, as the relation that links the sign and the (dynamical) object through the interpretant. As a third, the immediate object is both real and actual; it participates in the interpretive process but also, simultaneously, remains independent of it. As a third, the immediate object contains within it—and simultaneously is an interpretation of—a second and a first, namely, the dynamical object as the brute fact of the event (Secondness) and the pure quality and possibility of the event (Firstness).

An object or event that in its own right is a third (because it is a repetition of events, a habit) exists as part of the field of possibility for human perception. Actual in itself, it remains as a Firstness or real possibility prior to a person's encountering it. At the moment of encounter, the object or event opposes, resists, stimulates effort, or affects the person with force. Put cosmologically, some of the infinite possibilities (pure Firstness) of the dynamical object are selected and actualized. This Secondness belongs to both the dynamical and immediate objects. As the sensory motor system and memory interpret the resistance (or effort, and so on), the immediate object operates as a sign (a third) to constrain a particular interpretant. I call the interpretants of the sensory motor system *material interpretants* to distinguish them from the more strictly cognitive interpretants of conscious thought.[74] One material interpretant determines another through a series of inferences the result of which Peirce labels the *perceptual judgment*. He defines this as "a judgment asserting in propositional form what a character of a percept directly present to the mind is."[75] Perceptual judgments derive from percepts, which are their pre-conscious grounds,[76] and on them "all our knowledge rests."[77] Perceptual judgments name the first layer of conscious interpretation, which itself rests upon many prior layers of actualization.

As this discussion indicates, Peirce's semeiotic differs considerably from Helmholtz's physical sign theory. Both thinkers stress semiotic relationality, and in doing so they reposition Kant's transcendental project in response to the nineteenth-century cultural valuing of *Naturwissenschaft*, joining the semiotic synthesis of the manifold to physicalist explications of nerve operation, memory, and reflection. Helmholtz, however, employs relationality as a means of countering the notion that signs are necessarily iconic. As a result he inserts a gap between reality and perception that remains thoroughly Kantian. Signs, for Helmholtz, indicate but do not represent objects, for objects in themselves are always fully inaccessible to human cognition. Peirce, on the other hand, offers a semeiotic of unceasing actualizations from real, overlapping continua. Each actualization per se—assuming it is not an instantaneous and unknown flash of pure spontaneity—is a third; relative to human consciousness, Thirdness is the basic state. But human consciousness is itself formed through series of inferences of signs, where each sign and each inference is a third. Relationality, therefore, not only pins the transcendental project to a culture increasingly dominated by the empiricist assumptions of the natural sciences—by which Peirce's schema, like Helmholtz's, guarantees the reality and materiality of all signs—but relationality also nullifies the theoretical need for a *Ding an sich* since each actualization occurs out of the preceding ones. Peirce's semeiotic thus requires iconicity, even if only in an infinitesimal sense, that is, even if only at the ontological level of habits, the iconic repetition of which forms substance itself. While this iconicity may be negligible or insignificant relative to processes of human cognitive representation, still it is the crux of Peirce's pragmaticism. It is the means by which his Kantianism—his insistence on the omnipresence of thought and on the subjectivism of the construction of human thoughts—is balanced by his empiricism, his claim that there are actual objects and events, which exist separately from human thought and which constrain human interpretation, however vaguely.

If the kernel of Peirce's pragmaticism is the dual truth that nothing is inexplicable and that no thing or word is ever ultimate or certain, then iconicity is the ground of this truth. By obviating the Kantian noumenal, iconicity guarantees that nothing is inexplicable, and by keeping iconicity at an infinitesimal level, Peirce focuses on the interpretive character of human cognition and thereby guarantees the fallibility of every conclusion. Like Helmholtz and Hamilton, Peirce's philosophy follows Kant's *pragmatisch* aim both in attempting to bridge the apparent gap between mind and world and in judging signs according to their ability effectively to navigate the interpreter through life. But unlike his European colleagues, Peirce insists that the scientist must yield the results of thought and action to a community for assessment and emendation. Science is necessarily a communal pursuit, because "truth" does not lie waiting to be discovered, but subsists within vague and constraining fields of possibilities that pull the community toward it. Truth is not neutral and objective, but active and purposeful.[78] Peirce's repositioning of science thus balances empiricism with purposiveness and embeds both in a complex theory of continuity that promulgates and ontologizes the necessity of community. Having explicated Peirce's philosophy in light of science, this chapter now turns to his pragmatism in order to demonstrate the connection between logic and human conduct and character. This brief discussion sets the stage for a closer examination of Peirce's treatment of certain psychological concepts, which will lead us directly into his paradoxical theory of subjectivity and to my argument that an effective Puritan imaginary informs each of these facets of his system.

By Their Fruits Ye Shall Know Them

So far I have established the centrality of logic for Peirce and its grounding of psychology and all "human sciences." Because the humanities (as we call the human sciences today) centrally involve the question of how to live a good life, it is not surprising that Peirce's version of pragmatism asserts a dependency between logic and ethics. One essay narrates the development of pragmaticism in terms of an extended reflection on self-control. "Now the theory of Pragmaticism," he writes, "was originally based . . . upon a study of that experience of the phenomena [*sic*] of self-control which is common to all grown men and women; and it seems evident that to some extent, at least, it must always be so based."[79] The second half of this chapter starts from this assertion and expounds the connection between right thinking and right acting, which not only portrays pragmaticism as a theory of selfless, community-produced subjectivity, but also links that theory to the Puritan imaginary operative in the late nineteenth century. As Joseph Conforti notes, the Gilded Age displayed an "interest in and appreciation for the virile character, rock-ribbed sense of duty, and spiritual aspirations embodied in the lives of Puritan leaders."[80] Character, duty, and spirituality are the key words of Conforti's chapter on the late nineteenth century, and they operate as key words in Peirce's corpus, too.[81] For the pragmatist, the important questions are how to distinguish and maintain the contradictory obligations of being ethical and being scientific, how these conflicting duties require distinct modes of self-control, and how the horizon of thought and being superseding human being can contravene what he calls America's "gospel of greed."[82]

Pragmatism, Peirce notes, is primarily a theory about the meaning of concepts.[83] This logical pursuit, however, soon bumps into the question of what difference it makes—practically—to think one way instead of another: "For it is to conceptions of deliberate conduct that Pragmaticism would trace the intellectual purport of symbols; and deliberate conduct is self-controlled conduct."[84] Peirce claims that logic teaches us to reason well by discerning "the intellectual purport of symbols," and inevitably this discernment leads to the logical connection between the meaning of concepts and "conceptions of deliberate conduct." Peirce here implies his so-called pragmatic maxim, which states that the meaning of a concept is fully encompassed by our conceptions of the concept's conceivable practical effects.[85] The repetition of "concept" in that maxim conveys the embedding of both meaning and action in the rules of logic, an important nuance since the rules of logic express themselves in persons as dispositions and habits of thought. "Intellectual purport" leads to "deliberate conduct" instead of singular, intentioned acts because conduct denotes a habit of action. Unlike single acts, habits can be examined and "controlled." By linking logic and ethics, Peirce offers his pragmaticism as a theory about the development of human moral character.

Peirce's contemporaries, most notably William James, miss the import of embedding meaning and action in the rules of logic. In Peirce's view, they put forward single acts as the "be-all and end-all of life." This misreading of the pragmatic maxim infuriates Peirce and leads him to rename his philosophy "pragmaticism."[86] The anger stems from Peirce's conviction that focusing on acts over conduct dissociates moral character from logic. Such a tenet would be the "death" of pragmatism: "For to say that we live for the mere sake of action, as action, regardless of the thought it carries out, would be to say that there is no such thing as rational purport."[87] Rational purport names the end (telos) of logic, and logic, as the early part of this chapter demonstrated, articulates the rules of thought and being that supersede individual human existence. Denying or minimizing the force of rational purport, Peirce suggests, allows humans to deny the continuity of which they all are a part.

Self-control, on the other hand, develops skills whereby thoughts and actions are aesthetically judged and logically critiqued. This judgment and critique proceed by the scientific method of abduction, deduction, and induction (a further use of science not limited to the causal efficacy of physical events), that is, by the rules and method of logic. Logic thus mediates between the physical narrative of our actions' conditions and the psychical narrative of our actions' motives in a manner that, under Peirce's rubric, subsumes individual desires to communally held standards of beauty, truth, and goodness. Peirce employs the gospel maxim "by their fruits ye shall know them" to indicate how an individual's acts are generally indicative of the person's character.[88] As such the brute reality of an action—its singularity relative to the virtual fullness of habits—is turned on its head, for in this light an action is a sign of some habit of which it is an actualization to either oneself or another. Actions form the data of self-reflection as well as of community judgment.[89]

Peirce's pragmaticism thus differs from James's pragmatism in de-emphasizing effects, acts, and utility and arguing for the development of moral character and conduct through a logical process of self-control. Put in this frame, Peirce's pragmaticism constructs an ethos of what one scholar calls the seventeenth-century Puritan "culture of discipline."[90] In Peirce's day what I term the Puritan imaginary is seen in poignant and contested images of the American self and nation. Multiply received and multiply transmuted, the stories about America's Puritan origins intermingle with the technological, political, and social changes of the nineteenth century and are changed by them as much as they critique them. I will examine these interactions later in this chapter. First, though, I wish to clarify how Peirce's construal of self-control (as the link between logic and conduct) has specific consequences for the psychological concepts of mind, consciousness, and feeling.

Psychology Revisited

Peirce asserts that one of the confusions of contemporary psychologists is their claim to be studying consciousness. Actually, he says, they study mind: "consciousness is really in itself nothing but feeling," and feeling "is nothing but the inward aspect of things, while mind on the contrary is essentially an external phenomenon." The methods of psychology cannot address the internal, "inward" aspect of consciousness, but only the "external phenomenon" of mind. Peirce exemplifies this relationship through the analogous one of an electrical current to a wire. For many years, he notes, it was thought that electricity "moved *through* the metallic wire; while it is now known that is just the only place from which it is cut off, being wholly external to the wire." Strictly speaking, electricity is not a current through a static material, but rather exists as a field around the wire. Mind is to consciousness as electricity is to the wire, that is, mind is like an effective field that is not consciousness and not created by consciousness, but is created by interactions or relations between consciousness and the rules and method of logic.[91]

"The psychologists," however, "have not yet made it clear what Mind is,"[92] and in confusing mind and consciousness they imply that one can investigate consciousness without depending on the rules of logic. Peirce counters this view by restricting consciousness most generally to feeling and labeling mind as the continuity of consciousness or feeling. In examining mind, psychologists observe the external effects of consciousness over time; they stand external to consciousness, treat its effects as the objects and data of an exact science, and then organize that data around hypotheses of the structure and process of human cognition. This method of studying mind thus borrows the method by which a physicist studies objects and events in the world, only in psychology, the objects are less tangible and the events do not lend themselves to repetition. Psychological events, that is, are not constrained by efficient causation. These inherent limitations of structuring psychology as the empirical study of human thought loom behind Peirce's definition of *general psychology* as "the study of the law of final causation."[93] Peirce admits that no contemporary psychologist would agree to such a definition, for "psychologists say that consciousness is the essential attribute of mind; and that purpose is only a special modification." Peirce, on the other hand, asserts that "purpose, or rather, final causation, of which purpose is the conscious modification, is the essential subject of psychologists' own studies; and that consciousness is a special, and not a universal, accompaniment of mind."[94] Peirce thus redefines *psychology* as the study of mind that transmutes the concept of causality inherent to science to include the purposiveness of final causation. He preserves consciousness within the domain of logic, but he further mutates the received understanding of this concept.

Peirce delimits three types of consciousness, in parallel with his three ontological categories. As a first, consciousness is simply feeling. It is the backdrop of being alive, which can be sensed in a moment but cannot be cognized or articulated. Peirce also terms first consciousness *immediate feeling*, *primisense*, and *qualisense*. As a second, consciousness is the sense of opposition, otherness, or duality. It is altersense, "the mere consciousness of *exertion* of any kind," which Peirce also calls *molition*, that is, "volition minus all desire and purpose."[95] Purpose and desire introject Thirdness into consciousness. As a third, consciousness is thought. Peirce describes it as the "sense of learning," *medisense*, and "the recognition of Habit of any kind in consciousness."[96]

Consciousness as a third best conveys Peirce's repositioning of psychological terms. He equates third consciousness with thought, but thoughts are not in us; rather, we are in thought.[97] This inversion underscores the semeiotic character of thought and indicates the material and public character of signs. Peirce beautifully portrays how this interaction of shared signs constructs human consciousness. "Consciousness," he writes:

> is like a bottomless lake in which ideas are suspended at different depths. Indeed, these ideas themselves constitute the very medium of consciousness itself. Percepts alone are uncovered by the medium. We must imagine that there is a continual fall of rain upon the lake; which images the constant inflow of percepts in experience. All ideas other than percepts are more or less deep, and we may conceive that there is a force of gravitation, so that the deeper ideas are, the more work will be required to bring them to the surface.[98]

Consciousness is of the same "substance" as percepts (water), and ideas are percepts unified in the body of the lake. Percepts stem from a continual "rain" of external experience (our sensory motor systems and the rules of logic guiding perceptual judgments). Although consciousness is of a single substance (water), real differences (ideas) exist at each level, and these affect the activity of and on the lake's surface (the present moment of consciousness). As Peirce continues this metaphor, he stresses that ideas react to one another and associate habitually; like waves and currents in a lake, ideas function in rule-like but not necessarily predictable ways. He also notes that the work of raising ideas toward the surface of the lake proceeds according to purposes and that "mind has but a finite area at each level; so that the bringing of a mass of ideas up inevitably involves the carrying of other ideas down." He concludes, "The control which we exercise over our thoughts in reasoning consists in our purpose holding certain thoughts up where they may be scrutinized. The levels of easily controlled ideas are those that are so near the surface as to be strongly affected by present purposes. The aptness of this metaphor is very great."[99] Peirce's typology of consciousness and his metaphor of the bottomless lake together reposition the "proper" study of psychology. If psychologists were to study consciousness and not mind, he suggests, they would investigate consciousness as the construction of human thought from the communal nexus of signs that derives out of a cosmological continuity. Detouring from standard inquiries within scientific psychology, such as attention response times and memory capacities, Peirce's mandate for psychology entreats scientists to go beyond formulating laws about human thought and being, by showing the inherent purposiveness within those laws and the grounding of human being in community. In short, an inquiry into the semeiotic elements of consciousness and their logic of relations defines a *pragmatic* psychology, pregnant with purposeful consequence.

What Is It to "Know" a Self?

> *If individualism, tolerance, equality, and liberty are great American virtues of our day, we must go elsewhere other than Puritan New England for their origins. What our Puritan forebears valued was far different: a communal ideal consisting of unity by means of exclusiveness, intolerance for ungodliness and dissent, self-denial, subordination, and a public spirit for the common good, and all motivated, at least theoretically, by Christian love one for another.*
> —Allen Carden, Puritan Christianity in America

The metaphor of the bottomless lake suggests that the uniqueness of a person lies not in anything substantial, but in the particular relations or assemblages made among substances. The combinatory engine, so to speak, is the collaborative effort of purpose and self-control. Alongside this vision of consciousness, Peirce's writings weave an intriguing vision of human selfhood, one that resonates strikingly with the epigraph's description of Puritan community. At the heart of Peirce's vision stands a paradox between self-assertion and self-abnegation, and he translates the paradox into one between the character of the good scientist and the character of the good person, respectively. Any differences between persons, Peirce claims, are negligible and attributable to the vaguenesses of semeiosis, but those differences make *the* difference between someone who is a good scientist and a good person, and someone who is not. The working of this antinomy—between asserting that there are no separate selves and asserting that the distinctions that do exist between persons are crucially ethical—reveals a dual focus on ascesis or disciplined self-production. Disciplined persons mold themselves through intricate attention to their habits of thought and action, *and* disciplined persons deny themselves by submitting to the larger truths of community, cosmos, and God.

This antinomy and its resulting focus on discipline resonate strongly with America's Puritan imaginary.[100] Institutional, Calvinist Puritanism was rejected in Peirce's day as a relic of America's unenlightened past, but the moral and cultural force exemplified by Puritan individuals became increasingly idealized and mythologized by preachers, politicians, and social critics. The Puritan past was rewritten and presented as the model for (perhaps especially New Englanders') narratives about the mission and purpose of self and nation. The contradictory exhortations about the self, which one Puritan scholar phrases as "the yearning for rebirth [that] involves a felt loss of identity,"[101] work themselves out, in Peirce's pragmatism as well as other cultural locations, through an ideal "community of discipline."[102]

This ascetic ideal gathers a string of virtues we now stereotype as the Protestant work ethic under a depiction of community that is voluntary, Godserving, and held together by scrupulous conduct and Christian love. According to Stephen Innes, the disciplined culture focuses primarily on avoiding "immiserating vices" and developing an ascetic disposition toward time. Taken together, these foci cut across all aspects of Puritan society, including family, church, government, agriculture, trade, attitudes about free time and holidays, and customs regarding cooking, traveling, and gift giving. The paradox arises through the fact that cultivating the habits of correct conduct (virtuous character and godly asceticism) inevitably requires a constant and exacting assertion of (attention to) the self for the sake of (or to the end of) denying that same self.[103] Recognizing the profound entrenchment of the ideal of a community of discipline, however, does not argue for its actual existence. In the seventeenth and eighteenth centuries as truly as in the nineteenth century, "Puritan" was a code word for certain attitudes, a mythic entity that continually fissured from within as its objects (the citizens of Puritan New England, the citizens of America's Gilded Age) continually failed to be as orthodox and homogeneous as the myth required. Prior to the nineteenth century, more persons accepted themselves as institutionally Puritan, and this graced the myth with a certain social presence and power. But the imaginative power of the myth persisted even when its political power faded away. Peirce's theory of subjectivity demonstrates this poignantly.

Peirce's "Puritan" antinomy of self-assertion and self-denial within the context of community discipline refracts across many levels of his theories of self and society. Just as differences between persons distinguish ethical from non-ethical individuals, so, from another perspective, they distinguish ethical from non-ethical facets of a single person (for example, the degree of self-control one possesses), and, from a third perspective, they distinguish the ethical person from the scientific person generally. The boundaries between these distinctions define the specific dispositions toward life. For example, an ethical person possesses self-control and purpose, which a non-ethical person does not. Even within an ethical person, however, strains of chaos and irrationality persist, so that it becomes a matter of the degree of self-control possessed. To be a good scientist also requires self-control and purpose but molded in different ways and toward different ends. Since Peirce believes that everyone should be both scientific and highly ethical, his stance results in a call to cultivate paradoxical dispositions. In short, Peirce both calls for persons to abdicate selfhood, to examine themselves strictly and incessantly for the sake of greater self-control, *and* he calls on them to mold themselves into highly ethical persons, who conservatively cling to the habits that constitute their characters, and highly scientific persons, who anarchically fling aside any habit that seems to conflict with current inductive evidence.[104]

This section will proceed by first offering some quotations that indicate Peirce's aversion to any notion of substantial selfhood or individualism, and then by displaying Peirce's stance toward self-control and responsibility in order to question whether any kind of reconciliation can be brought to this antinomy of self-dissolution and self-construction. To the extent that Peirce's writings share a moral tenor with Puritan ethical injunctions and perspectives on subjectivity, my goal is to indicate this moral tenor and to demonstrate the resulting "American" sense of consciousness and purpose.[105]

In his 1893 "Grand Logic," amid a discussion of the faults of traditional propositional logic, Peirce scoffs yet again at the nominalist tendency to shrug off lines of inquiry on account of their being "inconceivable." Then he makes the following exhortation:

> Nothing is "inconceivable" to a man who sets seriously about the conceiving of it. There are those who believe in their own existence, because its opposite is inconceivable; yet the most balsamic of all the sweets of sweet philosophy is the lesson that personal existence is an illusion and a practical joke. Those that have loved themselves and not their neighbors will find themselves April fools when the great April opens the truth that neither selves nor neighborselves were anything more than vicinities; while the love they would not entertain was the essence of every scent.[106]

This is a striking sentence in a paragraph that otherwise berates nominalists and asserts the reality of possibility in a familiar Peircean manner. On the face of it, it is an outrageous claim. What can it mean to say that selves are nothing but "vicinities"? What is the connection of "love" to such an assertion? And why does Peirce, in a treatise on logic, insert this odd allusion to the Christian eschaton?

According to Peirce's theory of infinitesimals, every finite number is actually a monad composed of that finite number plus its surrounding set(s) of infinitesimal numbers. Extending this logicomathematical theory to cosmology, it aptly describes continuity itself. A substance or event, then, is analogous to a finite number, it is a third that demonstrates both determinateness and vagueness, for it is always surrounded by overlapping series of continua, which are themselves analogous to the sets of infinitesimal numbers surrounding finite numbers. By this view, a self or person is at once a substance and an ever-changing event; a person is only partially determined, is a great deal vague, and exists in continuity with all that surrounds the self. This use of infinitesimals asserts a logical and ontological continuity between mind and matter and thus explains how selves, for Peirce, are only vicinities.

But why does Peirce argue this view of the self in the context of "love"? One scholar of pragmatism comments that love is an "issue that troubled the modern mind at the end of the nineteenth century," but he offers no argument for why this might be so.[107] Studies have been done of the late millennial turn to the East, especially to the thought and faith of Buddhism, and to the romanticizing (and appropriation) of the "Orient."[108] Certainly Peirce is part of this cultural yearning: he raises love to a cosmic power of evolution, and he sometimes expresses the sentiment that the heart of the Gospels is equal to the Buddha's teachings on selflessness and compassion.[109] To him, thought and love and God are synonymous:

> If a pragmaticist is asked what he means by the word "God," he can only say that just as long acquaintance with a man of great character may deeply influence one's whole manner of conduct, so that a glance at his portrait may make a difference, . . . so if contemplation and study of the physico-psychical universe can imbue a man with principles of conduct analogous to the influence of a great man's works or conversation, then that analogue of a mind . . . is what he means by "God."[110]

God remains a thought literally too big and too vague to think. A good "analogue" for this concept, however, is the "mind" of a "great man," which we tap into through long acquaintance with his "works or conversation" and which "influence our whole manner of conduct."[111] God is this thought, this analogous thought, which comes to us through our musings and disciplined studies of the "physico-psychical universe." To the theologians' question of "whether there really *is* such a being," Peirce responds:

> The only guide to the answer to this question lies in the power of the passion of love which more or less overmasters every agnostic scientist and everybody who seriously and deeply considers the universe. But whatever there may be of *argument* in all this is as nothing, the merest nothing, in comparison to its force as an appeal to one's own instinct, which is to argument what substance is to shadow, what bed-rock is to the built foundations of a cathedral.[112]

God, who is too big and too vague for humans to think, can be felt as "the power of the passion of love," a power that is nonrational but overwhelming, a power that affects not the logic of consciousness but the sentiment of instinct. Since Peirce here infers that instinct is more ontologically important than reason, we can understand why Peirce frames our opening quotation on the self in terms of love. As thought, God can barely be conceived, but as love, God can be felt. Persons who sequester this love and turn it on themselves, however, will be found "a fool" when they realize that not the self but love in its virtual fullness illuminates the true reality and designates the community (the continuum) as the creating force of human being.

Peirce directly connects subjectivity and synechism in his essay "What Pragmatism Is" by extracting two claims of synechism and using them as the basis for the beliefs on which the logic of pragmatism rests. The first claim is that "a person is not absolutely an individual. His thoughts are what he is 'saying to himself,' that is, is saying to that other self that is just coming into life in the flow of time." The second claim is that "the man's circle of society (however widely or narrowly this phrase may be understood) is a sort of loosely compact person, in some respects of higher rank than the person of an individual organism."[113] Peirce thus derives pragmatism from two assertions about the self. The first statement rejects the temporal stability of the self since the self is always growing and changing; the second denies the spatial stability of the self, in that its society has a greater claim to stability (as an organism that depends upon but also always supersedes single selves) than does the person as an individual.[114] Peirce warns that holding on to the self and examining it for its unique constitution results only in watching the self dissolve in its becoming-other.

For the Puritans of the Gilded Age, personal identity also was temporally ruptured by the catastrophes of conscience and trial. As I suggested in the prologue, the term *Puritan* at this time became increasingly inflected with the terms of psychology (consciousness and will) and phrenology (character). The Puritan character was tough-minded, strenuous, and highly self-disciplined. Nonetheless, a person's conversion to the Puritan temper was not expected to occur without setback. Even during the first generation of Puritans, a definite experience of grace was expected as the sign that God drew them to conversion. Unlike the clarity and distinctness of a Cartesian (or scientific?) experience, however, Puritan conversion was followed by trials and periods of doubt. The prescribed remedies for doubt and despair for both periods included reflection on one's deeds and thoughts and allegiance to the dictates of conscience. This commitment to reflection and conscience is parallel to that which Peirce recommends. He notes that in a period of real, existential doubt (not the methodological doubt of the Cartesians), habits fragment or fracture, and a struggle ensues to sift through the resulting confusion until new habits are formed.[115] The sifting process is, for Peirce, the three-pronged one of abduction, deduction, and induction, and the new habits are evidence of a new level of self-control (higher or lower, depending on whether the process was more or less successful).

This three-tiered and incessant process of human cognition also functioned for Peirce on a nonconscious, cosmological level. On this level he abandons the terminology of abduction, deduction, and induction and replaces it with a description of the relentless process of forming, breaking up, and acting upon habits. The process holds both for the constitution of substance (rocks are habits) and for the meaning of the concepts used by humans. Peirce explains this span from cosmological to phenomenological in "Man's Glassy Essence," a late essay in which he quips that he has always known that "a person is nothing but a symbol involving a general idea," but can only recently confess that his "too nominalistic" past disallowed the insight "that every general idea has the unified living feeling of a person."[116] Each of these assertions needs to be examined in turn.

First, a person is a symbol, a Thirdness of Thirdness. Since a symbol is conventional and unmotivated—meaning it is formed largely through arbitrary processes and tends to spread to increasingly arbitrary applications—it "involves" a general idea of an even greater level of vagueness than the symbol itself. This general idea is the symbol's ground, or the context whereby the arbitrariness can still signify in predictable ways. An individual person is thus but a symbol or representation of a larger idea, the idea of "person," or the social aspect of being human. Second, every general idea is real; as such, it is a third that contains a second and a first within it. The second is the brute experience of the general idea before its meaning is extracted. The first is the feeling of first consciousness, of pure virtuality, that is a part of the second and hence of the third. Peirce makes an ontological claim that feeling is the most fundamental aspect of being; this feeling, as Firstness, is the pulse and vibration of all life and all possibility. Since that feeling is included in and presupposed by the Thirdness of the real general, the general has the "living feeling of a person," which is "unified" by the fact of being a third, a general or law.

It does not take an extended digression to suggest a resonance between these two statements from Peirce and the Christian tenets that persons are created *imago dei* and that the Holy Trinity is the unity of three divine persons. As is well known, Calvin's *Institutes* opens with an allusion to the *imago dei* by insisting that knowledge of self can only come through knowledge of God. "No man," Calvin writes, "can survey himself without forthwith turning his thoughts towards the God in whom he lives and moves; because it is perfectly obvious . . . that our very being is nothing else than subsistence in God alone."[117] To translate this into Peircean terms, God is the general that functions as the ground of human being, and each human is the image or symbol involving this general.

Peirce claims that selves are only vicinities and that persons are nothing but symbols. Both descriptions require Peirce's theory of synechism as he makes clear in another oft-quoted passage:

> Nor must any synechist say, "I am altogether myself, and not at all you." If you embrace synechism, you must abjure this metaphysics of wickedness. In the first place, your neighbors are, in a measure, yourself, and in far greater measure than, without deep studies in psychology, you would believe. Really, the selfhood you like to attribute to yourself is, for the most part the vulgarest delusion of vanity. In the second place, all men who resemble you and are in analogous circumstances are, in a measure, yourself, though not quite in the same way in which your neighbors are you.[118]

Peirce's seemingly complete dissolution of subjectivity in this passage stands in stark contrast to the stereotypically autonomous individual sanctioned by Puritan culture. According to at least some scholars of Puritanism, however, the "individual" of that culture is but an epiphenomenon of the community:

In seventeenth-century New England, Protestant salvation theology helped create the ethically autonomous (male) individual even as it rooted all labor and enterprise in communal and other-worldly obligation. This, of course, was emphatically not the case of "individualism" rising at the expense of a declining "communalism." *The New England individual was imbedded in community.* Inner-worldly individualism emerged as a consequence of, not at the expense of, a revived collective identity and social solidarity within the community of the elect.[119]

What Innes claims about the seventeenth century, I see Peirce nostalgically asserting for the nineteenth century. For Peirce, the Puritan call to examine one's conscience—the prototypically individual experience of a believer before her God—is enabled and conditioned by public practices of mutual inquiry and accountability. Puritan "conscience" is not a free and private relation to God, and the "individual" does not condone the glorification and assertion of selfhood. Rather, "self-examination serves not to liberate but to constrict; selfhood appears as a state to be overcome, obliterated; and identity is asserted through an act of submission to a transcendent absolute."[120] Peirce's claim that to call one's mind one's own is a grammatical mistake ("an egotistical anacoluthon") can be heard as a faithful echo of the Puritan submission to God and community, rather than as a radical negation of identity.[121] Like the Puritan, Peirce carves out a legitimate arena for the self, but he emphasizes its limitations over its scope.

To this point I have been emphasizing Peirce's dissolving, perforated, and relativized notion of the self. Peirce beautifully summarizes this perspective on subjectivity, in his 1898 lectures on "vitally important topics":

> I would not advise a man to devote much time to observations of oneself. The great [thing] is to become emancipated from oneself. [Γνωθι] σεαυτον [To know thyself], to make your own acquaintance, does not mean Introspect your soul. It means see yourself as others would see you if they were intimate enough with you. Introspection[,] I mean a certain kind of fascinated introspection[,] on the contrary, is looking at yourself as nobody else will ever look at you, from a nar row, detached, and illusory point of view. Of course, a man must search his heart somewhat. It is highly needful. Only don't make a pursuit of it.[122]

Let us turn now to the other half of the antinomy. Where the previous passages break down the barriers between bodied selves and revel in the inefficacy of self-examination, this and the following passages enjoin the self to gather and fasten the loose ends of thought and being, and thereby gain control over one's determinate and determining habits. As we shall see, Peirce insists that the better mark of personality is not what a person expresses, but what control a person has over her expressions. This aspect of subjectivity reveals itself clearly in a passage touched on earlier in this chapter:

> Now the theory of pragmaticism was originally based . . . upon a study of that experience of the phenomena of self-control which is common to all grown men and women. . . . Now control may itself be controlled, criticism itself subjected to criticism; and ideally there is no obvious definite limit to the sequence. But if one seriously inquires whether it is possible that a completed

series of actual efforts should have been endless or beginningless (I will spare the reader the discussion), I think he can only conclude that (with some vagueness as to what constitutes an effort) this must be regarded as impossible.[123]

I am most interested in how Peirce here points to the recursive character of control and criticism: "Now control may itself be controlled, criticism itself subjected to criticism; and ideally there is no obvious definite limit to the sequence." Peirce seems to be anticipating a challenge to his call for self-control. Since control can itself be controlled, when can one claim ever to possess true control? Since criticism itself can be criticized, when can one claim ever to possess true knowledge? In response, Peirce denies that control or criticism can be final or absolute and thereby derails the entire debate before it has begun; he simply rejects the notion that any sort of "first" or ultimate control can be attained.[124]

Peirce decides that self-control is vague, both in its injunction and in its operation. He speaks to this conclusion in a 1908 *Monist* essay by again implying the distinction between specific acts and the generality (vagueness) of conduct: "our power of self-control certainly does not reside in the smallest bits of our conduct, but is an effect of building up a character."[125] Peirce specifies the procedure of "building up a character" in an undated letter to F. C. S. Schiller:

> The power of self-control is certainly not a power over what one is doing at the very instant the operation of self-control is commenced. It consists (to mention only the leading constituents) first, in comparing one's past deeds with standards, second, in rational deliberation concerning how one will act in the future, in itself a highly complicated operation, third, in the formation of a resolve, fourth, in the creation, on the basis of the resolve, of a strong determination, or modification of habit.[126]

Self-control is a constituent of conduct, not an attribute of individual actions. Indeed, Peirce at one point defines conduct as "action under an intention of self-control."[127] For this reason Peirce does not emphasize action in the sense of a series of acts, but suggests rather that generals are embodied through the development of conduct, that is, through self-control, which itself is a general.[128]

The vague notion of conduct that attaches to a person results from multiple, vague layers of self-control, which themselves can always be further controlled. Far from being a detriment, however, the endlessness of the series of control is hailed as the mark that separates human from beast: "There are certainly more grades [of self-control] than I have enumerated. Perhaps their number is indefinite. The brutes are certainly capable of more than one grade of control; but it seems to me that our superiority to them is more due to our greater number of grades of self-control than it is to our versatility."[129] Peirce openly declares the seeming endlessness of recursive self-control to be the very mark of selfhood. In "Consequences of Pragmaticism" (1906), referring to the works of Josiah Royce, F. C. S. Schiller, F. Schiller, and Henry James, Sr., he states, "It is by the indefinite replication of self-control upon self-control that the *vir* is begotten, and by action, through thought, he grows an esthetic [*sic*] ideal, not for the behoof of his own poor noddle merely, but as the share which God permits him to have in the work of creation."[130] Formed by self-control, the very concept of the self thus enjoins a moral judgment: a self is a creature with some modicum of self-control, and the greater the self-control, the more human is the creature. On the other hand, self-control is a multilayered and vague event or state, and the self formed through self-control is equally vague and multilayered. In the end, it can be questioned how a self can exercise control over itself if the self is only constituted through self-control. The more determined we are to focus on the source of control, the further out we are flung to family, neighbors, society, and natural selection. Likewise, the more closely we examine the product of control (the self), the more fully do we realize that one does not strive for selfhood "for the behoof of his own poor noddle merely," but that the becoming of self is the abdication of uniqueness and an acknowledgment of the blurred boundaries between self and community, between self and the nonself of the continuum.[131]

I am arguing that the self-control rhetorically demanded of and by the Gilded Age's Puritan resonates beautifully with Peirce's vision of the self and with his critique of what he called his culture's "gospel of greed" (what we might call an intensification of capitalism). Puritan obligations of self-control were not the means of sculpting a unique individuality, but publicly accountable methods of overcoming the self for the sake of the community. In the seventeenth century the seesaw between the desire for the visible fruits of self-control (that is, wealth) and the suspicion and repudiation of materiality disposed the Puritans at once to tolerate, sustain, and critique the burgeoning market economy of capitalism.[132] Ambivalence toward capitalism only grew in strength in the eighteenth and nineteenth centuries, even as institutional Christianity in America veered increasingly away from its Puritan origins. For instance, Benjamin Franklin's developed morality has been called "a secular version of Mather's Puritan ethics," that is, an "ethics of benevolence" greatly influenced by Quakers such as John Woolman. Woolman's tract *Remarks on Sundry Subjects* eloquently argues against economic exploitation in a manner that is "particularly interesting because of the way in which the doctrine of stewardship of wealth and love for one's fellowmen are tied together with approbation for a moderate capitalism, kept moderate by a religious self-control rather than by any form of social intervention."[133] Of course religious self-control was, for the Puritans, a "form of social intervention," but more to the point, certain habits and dispositions of the Puritan way of life persisted into the eighteenth and nineteenth centuries and functioned as a Puritan imaginary, even as the institutions of American Puritanism were being increasingly muted, dismantled, and dismissed.

To recapitulate the argument of this section: Peirce's view of the self exhibits a tension between self-abdication and self-control. Though the tension is never overtly resolved in his writings, it is typologized in the contrasting dispositions of the good scientist and the ethical person. On the one hand, Peirce sneers at those who would turn to science for a proper guide to conduct. Ethical guides to conduct permit "no room for doubt, which can only paralyze action. But the scientific spirit requires a man to be at all times ready to dump his whole cartload of beliefs, the moment experience is against them."[134] Since beliefs are the habits upon which a self is prepared to act, and since habits constitute the self that is acting, Peirce's scientist exemplifies a throwing off of the self through a readiness to throw out one's "whole cartload of beliefs." On the other hand Peirce directly contrasts the abandonment required by the scientific method with the ethical need for self-control: "In short, as morality supposes self-control, men learn that they must not surrender themselves unreservedly to any method, without considering to what conclusions it will lead them. But this is utterly contrary to the single-mindedness that is requisite in science. In order that science may be successful, its votaries must hasten to surrender themselves at discretion to experimental inquiry, in advance of knowing what its decisions may be. There must be no reservations."[135] To be ethical, persons should cling conservatively to the beliefs and habits that have successfully molded them and cull or reshape those that hinder the formation of an ethical character.[136]

Whether or not reconciliation is necessary or warranted, the incommensurable positions do highlight the role of purposiveness in Peirce's pragmaticism and its tight connection to self-control. This role can be highlighted with respect to habit, causality and signification. In terms of habit, of the three types of a sign's interpretants, the final one is conduct, that is, the disposition toward action or the purposeful habits that surround individual acts. In terms of causality Peirce stresses the role of final causality in human constitution, development, and existence. In terms of signification, Peirce concurs that signs, as thirds, are employed conventionally or without motivation, but he also insists that the formation of the sign is necessarily motivated—that is, has purpose and connection to the real—no matter how vaguely or infinitesimally that motivation is retained. Peirce's views on nature, habit, and language contrast sharply with those of Hermann von Helmholtz and William Hamilton, whose conceptual reliance on the Kantian *Ding an sich* voids any necessary motivation of a sign and whose narrowing of causality to the efficient causation of empiricism eradicates from discussion any necessary purpose or final causality. This contrast of Helmholtz and Hamilton to Peirce marks the contours of how the reception of scientific development by American intellectuals differs from that of their continental counterparts. Consequently, even though Helmholtz and Hamilton—like Peirce—stress the fundamental importance of theoretical inquiry loosed from the economic reigns of technical application, their understandings of science constrain the scientist with the requirements of sufficient "objectivity" and strict reproducibility of data. Both Europeans capitulated to the philosophic and economic forces that were reshaping European science, while trying to encase those forces in their cultures' more traditional values (Kantian idealism, Scottish Calvinism).

Peirce longed for philosophy to become "scientific." But as that term came to denote less the general acquisition of precise knowledge (*Wissenschaft*) and more the narrower and highly professional role granted empirical technicians, he quickly intuited the constraints of a continental notion of "science" and rejected them. He rejected them not by refusing the concept but by insisting that science is a way of life, an attitude, and a disposition. If science is the mark of precision, then philosophy should be scientific, but not at the cost of creativity or generality. Peirce thus exemplifies the possibility of being both a good person (ethical) and a good scientist (radical), for he radically accepts—always with criticism, always with modifications—each new discovery coughed up by the Continent, from Darwin's evolution to the Curies' discovery of radium. Yet he conservatively and stubbornly holds on to the idea that science is not simply the pursuit of truth, but also and concurrently the pursuit of goodness and beauty and the acknowledgment of realms of purpose superseding the human. As the next chapter narrates, James is not oblivious to these issues and problems, but he solves them in drastically different ways.

6 ♫

William James

The axis of reality runs solely through the egotistic places—they are strung upon it like so many beads.
      —William James, *Varieties of Religious Experience*

Pragmatic Psychology: A Man of Purpose

William James (1842–1910) shared with Peirce a Boston Brahmin upbringing. The first son of a large and vivacious family, William (like Charles) was spoiled by his father and his education was given scrupulous attention both in Cambridge and abroad.[1] Instead of being a father brimming with mathematics and physical science, however, Henry James, Sr., bestowed on William an insistence on the legitimacy of "spirituality" and a mandate to prove that matters of the heart were congruent with matters of science. William rejected his father's mystical religious sentimentality, but his father's religious passion colored his pursuits, from his early desires to be a painter, to his study of medicine, to his move into psychology, and finally to his turn from experimental science to philosophy and ethics.

Throughout this restless career, James doggedly insisted on the importance of the individual. The last chapter noted Peirce's ambiguous disposition toward subjectivity, but no such ambiguity marks the writings of James: the centrality of the individual self remains constant throughout his broad and varying corpus. James's delight in and struggle with the possibilities and limitations of individual selves motivates his move from medicine to psychology and sustains his jump into philosophy and ethics. Indeed, psychology and ethics lie on a continuum for him, for though James spent more than a decade composing his scientific treatise, *The Principles of Psychology*, he soon distanced himself from the actual practice of the new science. He either applied the theories of the *Principles* to nonlaboratory settings (for example, culture, politics, and psychic mediums), or he applied the moral consequences of the *Principles* to his defense of radical empiricism and pragmatism.[2] During each of these phases, the centrality of the individual self remained constant, and each new turn spurred the formation of new theories regarding the familiar psychological concepts of consciousness, empiricism, and causality. This chapter will demonstrate how James inserts these psychological concepts into a personal cosmos sustaining purposeful consciousness and enjoining a tough-minded attempt to live a strenuous life.

The centrality James accords to the individual under the aegis of a scientific psychology is a gauge of the social triumph of the self-reflexivity of epistemology. James acquired his intellectual credentials during the period in which scientific psychology was evolving. As discussed in chapters 1 and 3, undertakings in human physics (Helmholtz) and philosophy (Hamilton) first encouraged and then competed with psychological inquiries, such as those made respectable and popular by Wilhelm Wundt and Alexander Bain (chapters 2 and 4). In James's day psychology's status as a separate and legitimate natural science was still being debated, but its development was grudgingly tolerated because of its ability to discover new "facts" about the human self.[3] James follows Wundt and Bain in developing a psychological science, but he diverges from both in yielding to the transmuting presence of distinctly American and residually Puritan habits. A brief characterization should be given of the theoretical relationships between James and his European counterparts.

Wundt and James both rework the concept of empiricism that the British empiricists take for granted. Wundt's repositioning of this concept results in a nonmaterialist schema that attempts to extend the understanding of what can be included under "empirical science." James critiques the British empiricists through a "radical" empiricism that asserts the reality of both relations and relata. Counter to this resonance with Wundt, James struggles with the German's theory of parallel causality, especially as it concerns consciousness. As was argued in chapter 2, Wundt asserts a single causality that can be interpreted either physically or psychically; this so-called parallel causality reworks the terms *consciousness* and *causality* to fit the specific requirements of a scientific psychology. In *The Principles of Psychology* James concedes a similar parallelism, but he claims that it functions as a heuristic device. Later, through his radical empiricism, James still upholds a parallel causality that denies any real distinction between knower and known, but he attempts to theorize this parallel physical/psychical causality empirically instead of resorting to Wundt's nonmaterialism. Most important, Wundt uses *purpose* as a social concept to analyze feeling and volition, and he incorporates it into his concept of the social self. James regards purpose through the lens of the individual, as the means of negotiating moral interactions and personal interests. He never disregards the subjective basis of existence. Wundt's construction of a social self leads his research toward the new field of sociology, but James leaves the laboratory for ethics by insisting that the frame of human purpose is at once individual and divine.[4] As far as the relation between James and Bain is concerned, both men exhibit a tension between what might be called intuition and empiricism. Both reject innate beliefs for the sake of a more "scientific" approach to studying human nature, and yet both appeal to an innate or instinctual human tendency to believe and to have trust in one's beliefs. To mitigate this tension, both men resort to sets of dualisms and hybrid methodologies that unsettle the definition of *science* as results acquired through empirically repeatable efficient causation.

As the last chapter suggested, the differences between Peirce and James are marked. First, James lacks Peirce's sense of pure possibility (what Peirce terms *Firstness*). The Jamesian subject starts his engagement with the world at something like brute fact, or the feeling of resistance and otherness (what Peirce terms *Secondness*). Second, James views *vagueness* as relating only to interactions between selves or linguistic signs, while Peirce theorizes vagueness as a cosmological category. Third, James desubstantializes consciousness, denying its status as an "entity" and calling it "an external relation." Peirce considers consciousness an internal semeiotic relation; to him, psychology studies mind, a concept entailing the external relations between signs and actions.[5] Fourth, James's focus on individual purpose raises the question of the extent to which he is a voluntarist. His use of *willing* appears to restructure the subject, despite the critique of certain Cartesian and Kantian depictions of subjectivity in his account of consciousness. By contrast, the concept of *will* is almost completely absent in Peirce. As shall be seen, "the difference made by the difference that is James" to the evolution of pragmatism is an unwillingness to venture into ontology.[6] This refusal expresses both his resolve to be scientific and his conviction that science cannot speak to the purposes of life. Peirce may discover purposiveness unfolding within the processes of life, but for James, purpose is imposed, either by individual will or by a consciousness connected to and superseding the individual.

Few commentators doubt James's voluntarism. Yet none of whom I am aware have traced the workings of this voluntarism to his psychological writings on consciousness, or demonstrated how the will anchors the swing between monism and dualism, between a consciousness that is open to the universe and a consciousness that is disjunctive and private. Voluntarism, which gains scientific support from the professionalization of psychologies such as Wilhelm Wundt's, thus acts as a web, the strands of which conjoin James's psychology, philosophy, and what might be called his moral theory and views on religion. It protects the individual from the growing impersonality of the natural sciences and expresses his conviction in the reality of individual and universal purpose. James's typical pragmatic emphasis on purpose, then, becomes a concept that ties together the many facets of his writing. In the individual, purpose signifies will and freedom of will. In the universe, purpose signifies mystery and the reality of promise and moral order. From one perspective, James's promotion of individual volition and cosmic mystery resonates with the Romantic transformation of Puritanism discussed in the prologue. From another perspective, it harks back to an epistemologically informed, inward-directed piety common to both Puritan and pragmatist: humans can use the newly formulated empirical method to seek and feel God in nature (where "nature" includes our embodied selves), though humans can never know the transcendent mysteries of God.

This chapter will clarify how James's commitments to both scientific respectability and the psychological need for a personal universe trap him in an epistemological pendulum swing between monism and dualism. Drawn to dualism (or functional dualism) both because of its tough-minded empiricism and because it protects the real disjunction (and therefore sanctity) of individual will and action, James nevertheless covers it with a monistic canopy. The monism asserts the reality of spheres of consciousness with which our consciousness continually conjoins, and it functions to guarantee the personal character of the universe. I will show the swing between dualism and monism through James's psychological writings on will and consciousness, through his epistemological struggles within radical empiricism, and through his philosophical presentation of pragmatism. Through each facet of his writings, James exhibits the conviction that the mystery of the world transcends individual experience and, simultaneously, that individual experience is the best manner in which to both probe and assist the mystery.

Willing Individuality: Empirical Consciousness

James's position on consciousness during his years of writing *The Principles of Psychology* is aptly demonstrated in the following passage:

> The conception of consciousness as a purely cognitive form of being, which is the pet way of regarding it in many idealistic schools, modern as well as ancient, is thoroughly anti-psychological, as the remainder of this book will show. Every actually existing consciousness seems to itself at any rate to be a *fighter for ends*, of which many, but for its presence, would not be ends at all. Its powers of cognition are mainly subservient to these ends, discerning which facts further them and which do not.[7]

Here, consciousness is presented as the active agent of a self, if not the self entirely. Consciousness is not "a purely cognitive form of being," that is, not a Kantian place in which, or a function whereby, sensations are assembled or synthesized into percepts and concepts. Consciousness does not wait upon sensation. Rather, it is "a fighter for ends"; it reaches out and anticipates experience. Indeed, James even suggests that consciousness creates the very goals for which it fights ("but for its presence . . . [they] would not be ends at all"), an indication that consciousness is, or acts on behalf of, a purpose-oriented agency.

Besides conveying James's early position on subjectivity, this passage also distinguishes him from his philosophical and psychological opponents. In disdaining the "idealistic schools," James secures one of his primary objectives: to differentiate psychology from philosophy and to present psychology as an 'empirical' science. Like Wundt, James struggles with natural science's criterion of "empiricism." On the one hand *Principles* overtly accepts the dominant scientific understanding of the empirical as emphasizing the material and as demonstrated through efficient causality. Since a scientific psychology can only ask which conditions of the brain yield which ranges of thought or feeling, it must presume an efficient causality—which is putatively physiological—operating between brain and thought.[8] On the other hand, presenting consciousness as a stream and fighter for ends suggests a causality that supersedes efficient causation. Teleology, or purposeful causality, appears in James's assertions that consciousness is "at all times primarily *a selecting agency*" and that consciousness "loads its dice" in order to exert "a more or less constant pressure . . . in favor of *those* of its performances which make for the most permanent interests of the brain's owner."[9] Such assertions beg the question of who or what is guiding the selecting activity, and who or what is loading the dice of consciousness with personal or subjective purposes. James recognizes that if the claim for an active consciousness is to pass muster, then some*thing* or some*one* must control its stream, much as the level and flow of a dam are controlled by active agents according to tangible needs.

James thus faces the difficulty of reconciling the image of a purposeful consciousness with his own methodological decision to exclude metaphysical considerations from his purview. After stating that psychology cannot extend beyond the limits set by natural science, James writes, "The theories both of a spiritual agent and of associated 'ideas' are, as they figure in the psychology books, just such metaphysics as this. Even if their results be true, it would be as well to keep them, *as thus presented*, out of psychology as it is to keep the results of idealism out of physics."[10] The specter of his idealist opponents rises again, this time to threaten the sanctity of physics. The intrusion of idealism into physics, James maintains, is as unacceptable as the incursion of metaphysics into psychology. Both errors compromise the scientific priority of empirical investigation. James's one possible escape from this dilemma resides in the italicized phrase "as thus presented." Perhaps the problem is not with metaphysics per se, but only with the way in which his philosophical and scientific colleagues present it. If so, either James has concluded that, while metaphysical truths may be attainable, the discussion of this possibility must be curtailed in scientific texts since such discussion would not be empirically based, or James has, to some degree, adopted Wundt's extension of the very concept of empiricism, so that the problem with the presentations of metaphysics by others is their failure to take into account this amplification of "empirical." Both of these options are apparent throughout *Principles*. James does define empiricism by the scientific method (as Francis Bacon codified it in his *Novum Organum*) and considers it the proper means and mode of scientific expression. James also controverts this point by acknowledging realms of reality that cannot be encapsulated by this understanding of science and empiricism, like his references to the agency and teleologic force of or behind consciousness. These allusions are treated as more than signposts to other, more metaphysical investigations. Indeed, his claim that consciousness is a fighter for ends is followed by an empirical proof based on an appeal to the actions of nerve currents and nerve fibers, and he concludes that "consciousness . . . is only intense when nerve-processes are hesitant." Consciousness, the active agency choosing on behalf of the interests of its "owner," is most alert when a choice or problem confronts it, proving its ability to aim for ends instead of passively enabling them.[11] For James, this proof empirically accounts for teleology and extends the notion of empiricism to include purpose.

As discussed in chapter 2, Wundt repositions empiricism by defining *empirical* as that which involves the examination of the entire contents of experience; since psychology encompasses the "entirety" of experience, it is more broadly empirical than the physical sciences.[12] James's proof in terms of nerve currents belies his interest in maintaining a material basis for empiricism. Since purpose ultimately cannot be accounted for materially, however, *Principles* cannot resolve the tension between James's reference to the metaphysics of teleology and his use of teleology to explain psychological data. Five years after the publication of his psychological treatise, in an essay entitled "The Knowing of Things Together," James concedes the theoretical trouble of the book:

> I have become convinced since publishing that book that no conventional restrictions *can* keep metaphysical and so-called epistemological inquiries out of the psychology books. I see, moreover, better now than then that my proposal to designate mental states merely by their cognitive function leads to a somewhat strained way of talking of dreams and reveries, and to quite an unnatural way of talking of some emotional states.[13]

Of those who would agree with him—his metaphysically inclined colleagues— James mandates "a long inquiry into conditions as the one I have just failed in," that is, a methodological refusal to employ metaphysical language without interrogating the implications and assumptions of that language. James acknowledges that he has failed to account satisfactorily for the most commonly employed metaphysical terms within psychology (attention, reminiscence, synergy, relating to self and others, the individual soul, and the world soul), but says he has at least indicated the direction future research should take. At any rate, James's concession to metaphysics enables him to elaborate on the metaphysical transformations he devises for European scientific concepts. The most important of these is his mutation of consciousness into an epistemology that might be called a "functional dualism" premised on the need to uphold both empiricism and purposefulness.

James sets out this dualism in two articles on radical empiricism, "Does 'Consciousness' Exist?" (1904) and "The Notion of Consciousness" (1905). In the former and more detailed article, James unexpectedly presents his theory as a type of monism:

> My thesis is that if we start with the supposition that there is only one primal stuff or material in the world, a stuff of which everything is composed, and if we call that stuff "pure experience," then knowing can easily be explained as

a particular sort of relation towards one another into which portions of pure experience may enter. The relation itself is a part of pure experience; one of its "terms" becomes the subject or bearer of the knowledge, the knower, the other becomes the object known.[14]

According to this description, the subject and object of experience are simply two aspects or "terms" of the same moment, the same drop of "pure experience." The latter is equated with the "primal stuff or material in the world" and thus seems to be the basic building block of a monistic universe. As with other monisms, this putatively basic ontological unit still has parts or "portions," which "relate" to other portions in ways that yield either a knowing subject or a known object. Though James does not indicate what enacts the relatings, or from what stance the perspectives of knower and known are effected, he pointedly claims that the relating of one segment of pure experience to another segment is not external to pure experience but is itself another portion of it. Here James expresses the mature version of radical empiricism: relations are as real as anything else in the system of knowledge and being, that is, they are not mental constructs transcending material reality, but are themselves real and material.[15]

James then suggests how his monism is a dualism of function and how pluralism is generated out of "pure experience":

> As "subjective" we say that the experience represents; as "objective" it is represented. What represents and what is represented is here numerically the same; but we must remember that no dualism of being represented and representing resides in the experience *per se*. In its pure state, or when isolated, there is no self-splitting of it into consciousness and what consciousness is "of. " Its subjectivity and objectivity are functional attributes solely, realized only when the experience is "taken, " *i.e.*, talked of, twice, considered along with its two differing contexts respectively, by a new retrospective experience, of which that whole past complication now forms the fresh content.
>
> The instant field of the present is at all times what I call the "pure" experience. It is only virtually or potentially either object or subject as yet. For the time being, it is plain, unqualified actuality, or existence, a simple *that*.[16]

James does not address the question of what is resolving the pure flow of experience into discrete moments. Writing in an article to dereify and reposition the concept of consciousness, James is perhaps reluctant to acknowledge that his functional split between the subject and object of knowledge is useful only to conscious beings. He can elide the concept of consciousness only by presuming a personal consciousness preceding the moment of pure experience. Here James opposes Peirce, who accounts for experience by arguing that the mentality or purposiveness of the cosmos becomes personalized and conscious only through a complicated process of habit formation. Against Peirce, James might well contend that the only element preceding pure experience is the previous thought (no thinker need be posited behind the flow of thought), but this contention underscores the priority of the thinker and consciousness for James's schema. For Peirce, by contrast, the prior element to conscious thought is not another conscious thought but pure possibility (Firstness), or what he calls *mind*. James's hypothesized rebuttal is problematic in another sense, since he claims (in *Principles* and elsewhere) that the direction of the flow of consciousness is controlled by interest or purpose.[17] But what or who controls interest and purpose? Peirce's answer would come in the form of his cosmology of vagueness and purposiveness (positing a pure virtuality in which God is thought and love). James never tackles the question; however, he presumes he has overcome the classical mind-object dualism of "being" or essence by admitting a dualism that is "solely functional." This functionalism secures his desired monistic pluralism by having each relation create a new context for pure experience, so that the universe will be plural since there are plural sentient beings constructing these contexts. Though the world consists of a single substance or state—pure experience— the very experience of pure experience is necessarily plural.[18]

How empirical is this epistemological schema? In "Does 'Consciousness' Exist?" James explicitly resolves to "expel neo-Kantianism" and its attendant dualisms.[19] Moreover, he baldly asserts that the functional dualism achieves his goal, since "instead of being mysterious and elusive, it becomes verifiable and concrete."[20] *Verifiable* and *concrete* are coded expressions for empiricism, but in what sense do they apply to James's functionalism? James does not say. Instead, he gestures at the commonsense empiricisms of Locke and Berkeley and to the obviousness of personal experience: "If the reader will take his own experiences, he will see what I mean."[21] James's presuppositions surface in this appeal. Not only does a mentality stand behind the moment of pure experience, but the mentality is possessed by a personal self. In this sense, James's empiricism capitulates to a Kantian idealism much more than does Wundt's. Both psychologists work to redefine the concept of empiricism, to widen its scope and application. Wundt's repositioning produces an idealistic parallelism that is then dispersed over the social plane, so that subjectivity is socially derived. James desires a materialist dualism that is "verifiable and concrete"— that fits the hard sciences' understandings of the empirical—but he places the criterion for empiricity within the personal, conscious experience of an individual subject. In James, as in Kant, the world emerges out of the subject, but for James the world is not pure, cold reason, but the intoxication of personal purpose.

An article from 1904 clearly demonstrates the tight connections among radical empiricism, individuality, and James's prioritizing of purpose. James's "The Experience of Activity" is his presidential address to the American Psychological Association. In it he applies radical empiricism—his version of pragmatism—to the psychological and philosophical problem of activity. The topic brings him inevitably to the question of who or what is instigating activity. He asks, "How is this feat performed? How does the pulling *pull*? How do I get my hold on words not yet existent, and when they come by what means have I *made* them come?" As is typical, James sidesteps these questions: "Arrived at this point, I can do little more than indicate the principles on which . . . a radically empirical philosophy is obliged to rely in handling such a dispute."[22] The principles he invokes are those of the vitality of immediate experience and its ostensible and real materiality. He revisits examples suggested in other articles of 1904, stating that mental entities and physical entities designate the same reality, even if the paths of thought and action stemming from them differ radically.[23] He then provides a summarizing description of causality:

> Sustaining, persevering, striving, paying with effort as we go, hanging on, and finally achieving our intention—this *is* action, this *is* effectuation in the only shape in which by a pure experience-philosophy [radical empiricism], the whereabouts of it anywhere can be discussed. Here is creation in its first intention, here is causality at work.[24]

Where is this causality working? And how can this description encompass bodily as well as psychological causation? James, too, must have been dissatisfied with this description since the text immediately proceeds to a footnote in which he hurriedly denies that the above statement is at variance with any of the arguments presented in "Does 'Consciousness' Exist?" an article in which James claims that although both "thoughts" and 'things' are composed of pure experience, things can act upon each other while thoughts can only "associate." James details the various senses of association, of which the following is one: "One thought in every developed activity-series is a desire or thought of purpose, and all the other thoughts acquire a feeling tone from their relation of harmony or oppugnancy to this."[25] Purpose (final causality) thus stands as the foundation for thought and activity, and again, James avoids any explanation of the origin, construction, or maintenance of this implied agency.

James ends this footnote with a whimper: "The subject needs careful working out; but I can see no inconsistency [between "The Experience of Activity" and "Does 'Consciousness' Exist?"]." Perhaps he could not see it, but he sensed it. Indeed, the same inconsistency persists throughout *Principles* and in his mature writings on pragmatism. What subtends the Jamesian continuum that is functional dualism is an encapsulated voluntarism, a claim I shall argue in the next section. So far, I have shown how James's work from the *Principles* to his essays on radical empiricism change the meanings of the European psychological concepts of empiricism and consciousness in order to make room and voice for individual purpose.

Owned Thoughts and Branded Cows

In "The Consciousness of Self," the tenth chapter of his *Principles*, James sets up a theory of subjectivity that seems to recognize the fluidity and social contingency of the self. For instance, he writes, "In its widest possible sense . . . a man's Self is the sum total of all that he CAN call his, not only his body and his psychic powers, but his clothes and his house, his wife and children, his ancestors and friends, his reputation and works, his lands and horses, and yacht and bank-account."[26] James calls this a description of the "empirical self," the self for which, as he puts it, the line between me and mine is blurred.[27] James emphasizes that the self spreads through its social sphere according to ability ("all that he CAN call his"). This phrasing indicates that James is not advocating a social constitution of the self, but a willed social extension of the self, a conception of things and persons based on their infusion with the self's labor, love, and will. The extended self is thus less an actuality than a representation, a "calling" of the self's boundaries.

James clarifies this position when he specifically describes the social self. "A man's Social Self," he writes, "is the recognition which he gets from his mates." Here James exploits an ambiguity in "recognition," which can be taken as either "basic acknowledgment" or "esteem." In either sense of the word, recognition is a person's ability to create in another's mind an image of herself. "Properly speaking," James concludes, *"a man has as many social selves as there are individuals who recognize him* and carry an image of him in their mind."[28] Quite unlike Peirce's layered account of subjectivity, according to which subjectivity grows out of habits acting upon habits, James's subject is a comparatively isolated will that motivates the attention (recognition) of other wills. James defines the self's sociality in terms of the persons whose responses to the self generate "an image" of him: the social self is that which is recognized, re-cognized, and represented in the minds of others. To cement the idealistic tone of this discussion, James explicitly relates it to Wundt's account of self-consciousness, though he does so in a way that displays his continuing struggle with the concept of "empiricism."

Positing that each self has a core or "nuclear" self that is the "sanctuary within the citadel" of consciousness,[29] James suggests that this core self is the sum of physiological "adjustments collectively considered" or "a feeling of bodily activities whose exact nature is by most men overlooked."[30] This account suggests that physiological changes generate an epiphenomenon—the nuclear self—and that some aspect of the "me" can, in some unexplained way, act to "feel" this nuclear self as the "sanctuary within the citadel of personal identity." The description concedes a type of parallelism similar to Wundt's (see chapter 2), though James does not admit to borrowing from his German colleague. His note merely states, "Wundt's account of Self-consciousness deserves to be compared with this [account]. What I have called 'adjustments' he calls processes of 'Apperception.'"[31] Apperceptions in Wundt are mental: they are equivalent to attention, or the process by which consciousness selects a part of the world with which to connect the sensory-motor system and memory in order to generate a percept.[32] James continues in this note with a long quotation from Wundt's *Physiologische Psychologie*, a passage that mirrors James's own discussion of consciousness. In the quoted passage Wundt first states that a select set of percepts acquires priority over others, specifically, as James translates it, "those of which the spring lies in ourselves."[33] Wundt then describes these percepts as "images" and "representations" that "distinguish themselves from all others by forming a *perma-*

nent group." He defines this stable group of percepts as those responsive to the will. Thus, Wundt understands self-consciousness as a set of percepts that are both stable and able to be willfully manipulated. Finally, Wundt admits that his presentation shares much with classical faculty psychology, except that the latter begins by positing an abstract ego, whereas his account ends with positing only the possibility of an abstract ego. The possibility is never realized, he notes, because "the process of apperception itself comes to our knowledge chiefly through those feelings of tension [what I have above called inward adjustments] which accompany it." The notion of an abstract concept can only be projected from the concrete feelings that constitute the process of apperception, or consciousness; since continuity of feeling is experienced but can never be proven, an "abstract ego" (the wholeness and continuity of the self) can only remain a possibility. Like James, Wundt subordinates the mental process of apperception to physical feelings, or affect, though in James the attempt comes off feebly because he never resolves the problem of agency, that is, the problem of how identity remains continuous throughout thought and action.

To articulate the "more subtle aspects of the Unity of Consciousness,"[34] James employs a metaphor that relies on the claim that each thought is "owned" and claims that thought can be compared with a herd of cattle.[35] Cows are "brought together into one herd because their owner found on each of them his brand. The 'owner' symbolizes here that 'section' of consciousness, or pulse of thought, which we have all along represented as the vehicle of the judgment of identity; and the 'brand' symbolizes the characters of warmth and continuity, by reason of which the judgment is made."[36] If consciousness is a series of pulses, a stream of thoughts, what does it mean to cordon off one part of a pulse as "the vehicle of the judgment of identity"? The extended metaphor attempts to answer this question by turning first to an imagined rebuttal of common sense, which "is sure that [the unity of all the selves] involves a real belonging to a real Owner, to a pure spiritual entity of some kind." Further, "the herd's unity is only potential, its centre ideal, like the 'centre of gravity' in physics, until the herdsman or owner comes. He furnishes a real centre of accretion to which the beasts are driven and by which they are held."[37] James likes the cogency of such a commonsense account, clarifying as it does the gaps in the empiricist and associationist conceptions by providing a "medium" through which thoughts "gum" together. Nonetheless, James rejects common sense since it requires an ostensible nonempirical agent behind consciousness. In James's words, "in our own account the medium is fully assigned, the herdsman is there, in the shape of something not among the things collected, but superior to them all, namely, the real, present, onlooking, remembering, 'judging thought' or identifying 'section' of the stream."[38] But this description simply begs the same question posed above: what does it mean to call a part of a "pulse" of thought "superior" to any other part of the same pulse? James admits that his claim does not satisfy the basic demands of common sense, demands he wants to appease:

> The unity into which the Thought . . . binds the individual past facts with each other and with itself, does not exist until the Thought is there. It is as if wild cattle were lassoed by a newly-created settler and then owned for the first time. But the essence of the matter to common-sense is that the past thoughts never were wild cattle, they were always owned. The Thought does not capture them, but as soon as it comes into existence it finds them already its own.[39]

A strange shift occurs in this quotation. The unity of consciousness is no longer a superior section of the pulse of consciousness, but is the present thought in and of itself. As it comes into existence, it seems to have the power to function not as another cow marked by the same brand as the rest of the herd, but rather as the herdsman, the one who holds the legal title of ownership. James adheres to this new perspective and expands it: "We can imagine a long succession of herdsmen coming rapidly into possession of the same cattle by transmission of an original title by bequest. May not the 'title' of a collective self be passed from one Thought to another in some analogous way?" Not satisfied to leave the matter rhetorically framed, James concludes, "It is a patent fact of consciousness that a transmission like this actually occurs."[40] He seems not to notice the contradiction. What began with an assertion that each thought is an owned part of consciousness, interestedly interpreting a world external to thought and in need of unification with other thoughts, here becomes an insistence that each passing thought is somehow the owner of all past thoughts, less an interpreter of the world than an interpreter of the rest of consciousness. As James concludes his metaphor, "Who owns the last self owns the self before the last, for what possesses the possessor possesses the possessed."[41] To resolve this contradiction James needs to say that something is connected to thought without being thought, that there is some thing or process that can unify thought by providing it with purpose. Though he leaves the matter standing in "The Consciousness of Self," his chapter on the will indicates that volition serves this purpose: "To sum it all up in a word, the terminus of the psychological process in volition, the point to which the will is directly applied, is always an idea. . . . The only resistance which our will can possibly experience is the resistance which such an idea offers to being attended to at all. To attend to it is the volitional act, and the only inward volitional act which we ever perform."[42] Apparently, some ideas are hard to grasp and thus "resist" the will's attempt to select them. Still, whatever selection or attention occurs constitutes the direct action of volition. As such, volition—and not a "superior section of consciousness"—functions as the selecting agent of consciousness. James thus arrives at the same position as Wundt in that extended footnote: the glue between independent thoughts and actions is the will.

Since James avers that volition forms not a separate faculty but simply another operation of consciousness, this picture of the will can be reconciled with his earlier assertions about a managing component of consciousness. At least, it seems plausible until one tries to fit volition into James's metaphor of thought as the herdsman who owns the cattle (the previous thoughts). If James had a theory of habits akin to but perhaps more individualistic than Peirce's, he could have argued that volition is a set of established habits that maintains personal identity through conjunction with memory, so that the current flow of thought occurs through a process of continual actualization. Without such a theory, James's account pulls in two opposing directions. It edges toward an idealistic faculty psychology, in which volition functions as the banks of the stream of thought (banks that both contain and control the flow). At the same time, it teeters toward an atomistic empiricism in which each thought is both owner and owned, both willer and that which is willed. Of these options, the former better suits James since it rectifies British empiricism's failure to account for the unity of consciousness. The result, however, is an unacknowledged voluntarism that guarantees both the unity of consciousness and the inviolateness of the individual self.

The ramifications of James's implicit voluntarism appear most directly in his phenomenology of experience. To explain this, the next section further compares Peirce and James, with specific reference to the lack of pure possibility (Peirce's Firstness) in James and the consequent difference in the concept of vagueness. I shall show how James theorizes vagueness so as to ensure the clarity of purpose within consciousness.

External Relations and the Fringe: Vagueness

Of all his writings, James's essays on radical empiricism most clearly demonstrate a lack of Peircean pure possibility (Firstness). His earlier writings on psychology do discuss relations "firstlike" relations between instances of consciousness, and these relations frame his later, radical empiricist accounts of general, human experience. In *Principles* James terms these relations of consciousness *the fringe*. In a passage just preceding his account of the fringe, James notes explicitly, "It is . . . the reinstatement of the vague to its proper place in our mental life which I am so anxious to press on the attention."[43] James's notion of the vague (as the fringe) differs from Peirce's (chapter 5) and thereby leads to different accounts of consciousness, habit, and the self. I shall specify links between James's writings on psychology and the phenomenology of experience in his radical empiricism in order to show how James's consistent preference for individual psychology and Peirce's reliance on a more cosmically oriented metaphysics generate different horizons for subjectivity and ethics, even while the two pragmatists have affinities in countering the increasingly secular enterprises of their European colleagues.

James describes the fringe as a "psychic overtone" or "suffusion" that indicates "a faint brain-process upon our thought, as it makes it aware of relations and objects but dimly perceived."[44] Less cryptically, he characterizes the fringe as constituting the "dynamic meaning" of a word, by which he means all the associations and shades of meaning that make language rich and complex.[45] Such shades and associations fire from parts of the brain other than the one engaged in the moment's word or image, that is, they are not in the stream of consciousness, though they form part of the energy that pushes it along. Restricting the fringe to words and images, then, James uses the concept to indicate how a sign's virtual meanings and associations (other words and images) continually push on its boundaries. Peirce, too, recognizes a dynamic characteristic of signs, though he registers it as the ontological connection of a sign (Thirdness) to both the habitual paths of the sensory-motor system (Secondness) and the nonconceptualized, material world apart from the self (Firstness). He also expresses semiotic dynamism as the sign's ability to become unmoored from brute reality (Secondness) and run, in a sense, from sign to sign (Thirdness to Thirdness) producing what today's semioticians call *unlimited semiosis*.[46] Opposing this, James acknowledges a sign's connection to sensory input only in what he terms the "static meaning" of a "concrete" word, such as "table" or "Boston"; for James, it is the meaning that directly links experience to thought. The fringe or "dynamic meaning," however, is always mental; it is another word or image lying just out of the range of present consciousness.

The fringe operates for James as a transitional consciousness, a set of relations between thoughts (but which are *not* thought) that are as real as those thoughts themselves. Stating the matter in this way recalls James's mature position of radical empiricism, in which relations between experiences are asserted to be as real as the relata, and moves us from psychology per se to James's more general, philosophical statement about human experience. "In radical empiricism," James writes in the conclusion to "A World of Pure Experience," "there is no bedding; it is as if the pieces [of the mosaic of experience] clung together by their edges, the transitions experienced between them forming their cement."[47] Unlike an actual mosaic, which is glued together by some kind of substratum, the philosophy of radical empiricism asserts no foundation for human experience. The only glue, the only assurance of continuity, rests in the transitions that are experienced between experiences. In essence, then, James has taken his psychological position on the fringe and here extended it beyond words and images to a theory of general experience.

"A World of Pure Experience" offers another poignant image of how the fringe guarantees the continuity and discontinuity of consciousness: "We live, as it were, upon the front edge of an advancing wave-crest, and our sense of a determinate direction in falling forward is all we cover of the future of our path."[48] According to this description our experiences are punctual, individual, and discrete; they occur on "the front edge." Yet the movement of experience is made coherent and purposive by being part of a larger wave crest, a more general continuity that provides a vague feeling of "a determinate direction," a purpose or plan. From this description we sense how the fringe, or the set of transitional experiences carried by the "advancing wave-crest," depends upon volition. These transitional experiences ensure that the "front edge" of our experience is not a random zigzag but is rather a series of actions that can be narrated in terms of reason or purpose. With his usual double-edged sword, then, James uses the fringe to signify a mental vagueness that ensures the purposive clarity of experience.

We can now examine the consequences of invoking the concept of the fringe, paying particular attention to what can be termed a lack of pure possibility (Firstness) in James. In asserting Firstness or pure possibility as one of his universal or cosmological categories, Peirce opts for the position that possibility is real and material, but not actual. The position defines what Peirce means by realism, and he opposes it to nominalism, which does not acknowledge the reality of possibility.[49] Though James has no place for real possibility and is, in this sense, a nominalist by Peirce's criteria, he does at times believe in the reality of tendency or potential. The difference between his position and Peirce's argument for real possibility lies in the fact that vagueness in James remains a mental concept, a way of accounting for actual mental events that willfully affect the present moment of consciousness without being in that moment.

At times James seems to imply that the world of experience is the only world there is, but his investment in the ability of science to narrate the facts of the world (as opposed to truths about the world) contravenes this assumption. Facts belong to the world as it really is, and truths to the ways humans appropriate and use those facts. Thus consciousness actively "carves" or "sculpts" the world we experience out of the initial chaos of pure experience:

> The world *we* feel and live in will be that which our ancestors and we, by slowly cumulative strokes of choice, have extricated out of this, like sculptors, by simply rejecting certain portions of the given stuff. Other sculptors, other statues from the same stone! Other minds, other worlds from the same monotonous and inexpressive chaos! My world is but one in a million alike embedded, alike real to those who may abstract them. How different must be the worlds *in the consciousness* of ant, cuttle-fish, or crab![50]

In one sense this passage sounds much like Peirce, for whom the indeterminateness of the cosmos becomes actualized in different ways according to the capacities of the entity accomplishing the actualization.[51] For Peirce, however, these capacities have been evolved over millennia through the slow pressures of natural selection, while James specifically inserts "strokes of choice" as the mechanism of selection. Where does this choice originate? The short answer is from the fringe. Since consciousness both is experience and appropriates the world as "pure experience" or an undifferentiated *that*, it is the task of consciousness—with the push of the fringe—to sort out what is interesting and determinate in that pure experience and what is uninteresting or indeterminate. In other words, the vagueness of the fringe provides a tentative plan or purpose to the conscious movement through an undifferentiated world, turning the world into objects of interest or necessity.

The combination of James's monism of pure experience with his functional dualism of consciousness and world highlights the human self and its sanctity as the generator and consumer of experience. The fringe generates the conscious, selecting choice that acts to determine pure experience. As such it is not only the concept through which James's somewhat veiled voluntarism operates in his psychology and radical empiricism; it also is the defining quality of the ethical character. "An act has no ethical quality whatever unless it be *chosen* out of several all equally possible," writes James.[52] But for the human subject to be claimed as ethical, choice about action and character must exist at every instance: "[a person's] choice really lies between one of several equally possible future Characters. What he shall *become* is fixed by the conduct of this moment."[53] Though habits form our characters, James here suggests that the choice of an instant can overturn habit, wipe clean the slate, and remake a person's character. The philosopher who once credited so much power to habit that he called it "the great fly-wheel of society"[54] here relativizes the omnipresence of habit with the omnipotence of choice. We will return to this perspective when we consider the legacy and imaginary of Puritan conversion. James's assertions about will and choice—as well as the pragmatic temper of fallible belief for the sake of effective action—promulgate the notion of a paradigmatic American subject who is able to choose her future without constraint and who upholds the ethical right to execute that free choice for the sake of personal character development.[55]

This section has underscored differences between Peirce and James, yet they do share common goals relative to the German psychologists. Though the pragmatists' differ in their writings about consciousness, causality, and subjectivity, both are anxious to uphold human purpose or purposiveness as a real element in the world, an element not reducible to an epiphenomenon of efficient causality. In tandem with this stress on purpose lies a serious attention to ethics. Though James is much more individualistic than Peirce, both pragmatists draw the ramifications of human purpose into discussions of the self's moral character. In comparison, Helmholtz and Wundt both extend what interest they have in ethics in a social direction. Even before James turns to philosophical and ethical concerns over psychological investigations, his interest in the ethical consequences of his psychological views is evident, whether it be the ethical implications of "the law of habit" or the psychological reasons why cramming does not lead to the desired end of education. Though Peirce did not systematically examine ethics and aesthetics until late in his life, his writings are scattered with ethical insights, such as the moral ramifications of viewing science in one way versus another or how the ability to imagine scenarios builds human character and even saves lives.

In the following section I turn more specifically to James's statements on ethics and religion as they inform his commitments to will and choice. Like the chapter on Peirce, this chapter will end with the third goal of this book, namely, to suggest the connection between James's focus on purpose and America's nineteenth-century Puritan imaginary by examining a possible analogy between the icon of James in American philosophy and the icon of Jonathan Edwards in American religious history.

Puritan Matters of the Heart: A Tough-Minded Philosophy

*I now see, as I have seen in his other books that I have read, that the aim
and end of the whole business is religious.*
— *Oliver Wendell Holmes, Jr., in* Writings of William James

The relation between Edwards and James can only be a possible analogy. True,
certain intellectual impulses are shared by the two. But the benefit of a tentative comparison resides in attempting to articulate what can be designated as
American in James's pragmatism. Like others of his generation, James found
Edwards useful in ways Edwards might never have embraced as his own. The
comparison I want to make between Edwardsian Puritanism and Jamesian
pragmatism constructs the third or pragmatic part of this book's three-part
investigation. Having generated the German, Scottish, and pragmatic intellectual territories and having indicated the ways in which the pragmatists transformed their European counterparts, I will now account for that transformation and demonstrate its effects. The question is whether it is possible to point
out the cultural values and assumptions according to which the pragmatisms
of Peirce and James initiated new intellectual formations in America.

In the chapter on Peirce, I extracted his notions of community and self
formation and compared these intellectual emphases to narratives and scholarship about Puritan theories of community, subjectivity, and accountability.
I argued that Peirce draws upon a Puritan imaginary more familiar to his
father's times and uses it to critique what he calls the Gilded Age's "gospel
of greed." In this chapter, I deal with James's notions of personal experience
and his assertions of the ultimate mystery and singularity of human existence
and compare them with Jonathan Edwards's theories of experience and the
personal. Both the prevalence of these notions in the texts of the pragmatists
(and Puritans) and the argument that this prevalence is sustained by a persistent Puritan imaginary motivates and justifies these comparisons. Despite the
many differences between the intellectual and social cultures of James and
Edwards, the pragmatist reads Edwards's philosophical theology for its realism and its affect. Better put, James breathes in and leans upon a Puritanism
that his own Gilded Age swept up into images of America and held tightly
and sacredly.

Let it be admitted that in the most obvious respects "James was less a
Puritan than any other American pragmatist."[56] His voluntarism and individualism make him a true candidate for Arminianism (those who assert a radical
free will), and he is not a religionist in any traditional, institutional sense.
Though later in his life he would begin many of his days at Appleton Chapel
in Cambridge,[57] that attendance does not reflect adherence to any doctrine or
creed. Rather, James downplays the entire question of God's existence in favor
of the evidence of God's usefulness, or at least the usefulness of the idea of
God. In other words, James cares less about what a person believes than about
the consequences of that belief. What are the practical effects of a person's

religion? How does one's faith affect the choices one makes, the goals one sets, the acts one attempts? Stated in terms of consequences, questions such as these are often attributed to the Puritans. As the prologue showed, the late nineteenth-century place and meaning of "Puritan" carried on the Romantic exhortation to moral purity. Puritan implied "tough-minded" persons who act with propriety and integrity,[58] persons of strenuous character who could hold themselves to a heartfelt, inward discipline and thereby effect private reform for the sake of the public good. Both tough-mindedness and matters of the heart apply to James's pragmatism.

In his lectures on pragmatism James praises the tough-mindedness of the Puritans, those who were willing to be damned for God's greater glory.[59] James distinguishes between two philosophical temperaments, the "tender-minded" and the "tough-minded,"[60] and since being "irreligious" lies on James's list with tough-mindedness, it may seem a strange epithet to apply to Puritanism. To James, tough-mindedness highlights Puritanism's realism over against the abstract idealism of contemporaries (like Fechner and Fiske) whose religious treatises analyze concepts such as the "absolute," for which James can find no religious feeling or understanding. To James, Edwards and other Puritans exemplify how strong faith can yield a realistic, material, tough-minded disposition toward life. In fact, practice is the only evidence of a person's faith. As James comments on Edwards's *Treatise on Religious Affections*, "The *roots* of a man's virtue are inaccessible to us. No appearances whatever are infallible proofs of grace. Our practice is the only sure evidence, even to ourselves, that we are genuinely Christians."[61]

The second characteristic—valuing matters of the heart—stems from the Romantic mutation of the Puritan imaginary that foregrounds emotion and affect; certainly what James recognizes as "genuine" religion centers in affect or matters of the heart much more than in doctrine or theological reflection. Edwards's famous distinction between understanding (the head) and apprehension (the heart) effectively claims that a purported experience of God will affect behavior; a new "spiritual" sense will create a change of heart. In more Jamesian terms, the changed disposition affects subsequent actions and habits.[62] In *The Varieties of Religious Experience*, James describes Edwards as a Puritan who values emotion and theorizes (theologizes) personal experiences of God by analyzing affect and aesthetics.[63] Edwards's injunctions to probe one's conscience and to seek a conversion of the heart through prayer and meditation strongly resemble James's conviction that the intense (and private) experiences of prayer and mystical revelation preserve the crucible of religion.

A third resonance between James and Edwards lies in their shared conviction that an experience (especially an experience of religious conversion) can be immediately life changing, bypassing the accretions of habits and producing an "entirely different kind of natural man."[64] I showed this aspect of James's psychology earlier in this chapter; it is also present in the chapter on "Conversion" in *The Varieties of Religious Experience*, where James uses Edwardsian Puritanism to expound on the possibility of sudden and radical change. Invoking Edwards, James calls conversion an "original and unborrowed experience,"[65] and life after conversion as one marked by "delightful conviction" and "clean and beautiful newness."[66] This text also treats the sick soul and darker aspects of religious experience. But in the end both Edwards and James accept that moral rectitude requires dispositions of love, goodness, and benevolence, since these are the aspects of "true virtue."[67] While Edwards opposes these dispositions to free will, James suggests a causal link between them: free will, a person's choices, and the will to believe can cause the growth of love, goodness, and benevolence.

The most clear-cut inheritance from Puritan to pragmatist is a certain epistemologically informed piety. John Winthrop and Jonathan Edwards, as much as Peirce and James, claim both that humans cannot know the transcendent God and that humans can nonetheless find and feel God revealed in creation.[68] This piety together with an emphasis on good works and practical effects enables a heightened prioritizing of personal experience, which attracts James. James and Edwards (and other Puritans) differ profoundly in their accounts of personal experience, but they agree on its fundamental importance, especially as it upholds the mystery of the cosmos and the fallibility and uncertainty of human existence.

James's Experience of God

James's later, pragmatic views of God find their seeds in *The Principles of Psychology*. As discussed, James models various "constituents" of the self, and part of that schema includes the "rivalry and conflict of the different selves."[69] To James, what motivates each choice or decision about hierarchization between these different selves is a person's future or "potential" self.[70] He goes on to link this potential self "with our moral and religious life" and states that, as our "ideal social self," the potential self "is at least *worthy* of approving recognition by the highest *possible* judging companion, if such companion there be." Evidently, for James, God stands as a "*possible* judging companion." One could interpret this phrase as indicating that already James subordinates the question of God's actual existence to God's possible existence. The effect and necessity of prayer follow from the mere possibility of a "judging companion" since that possibility embraces our ideal image of our self, namely, our potential self. James continues:

> This self is the true, the intimate, the ultimate, the permanent Me which I seek. This judge is God, the Absolute Mind, the "Great Companion." We hear, in these days of scientific enlightenment, a great deal of discussion about the efficacy of prayer. . . . But in all this very little is said of the reason why we *do* pray, which is simply that we cannot *help* praying. It seems probable that, in spite of all that "science" may do to the contrary, men will continue to pray to the end of time. . . . The impulse to pray is a necessary consequence of the fact that whilst the innermost of the empirical selves of a man is a Self of the *social* sort, it yet can find its only adequate *Socius* in an ideal world.[71]

James places God firmly in an ideal world, here acting as the concept that secures the "adequate *Socius*" of the potential self. Resonant with Feuerbach, James implies that humans project the best and most virtuous aspects of ourselves into an ideal character (God) that then acts as both companion and judge. Prayer functions as an acknowledgment of our ideal, potential self and of our continual inability to live up to it. The inability is necessary to James since the gap between the actual and potential self—and the obvious superiority of the latter—motivates our moral and religious lives.

Little more is said about God in *Principles*, and "God" and "religion" are completely absent from James's index, which further indicates his ambivalence toward reconciling issues of science and religion throughout his psychological writings.[72] As he moves into his writings on radical empiricism (which overtly combine his psychological and philosophical interests), James devotes more space to discussing religion, morality, and issues handily grouped under the term *spirituality*. As mentioned in the previous section, a primary goal in these essays is to demystify or de-intellectualize religious speculation of the kind best represented by Fechner's "absolute." Instead of proposing a complex theological schema—which, James scoffs, is impossible to employ in one's life—he suggests we should first ponder whether "any superhuman consciousness" is at all "probable." Before diving into a sea of theological generalities, one should question why such a task is at all useful or interesting. Offering an answer to this preliminary question, James asserts without argument and quite contrary to his usual nominalism that "there *are* religious experiences of a specific nature, not deducible by analogy or psychological reasoning from our other sorts of experience." The reality of such experiences "point with reasonable probability to the continuity of our consciousness with a wider spiritual environment."[73] James thus unequivocally responds to the reality and abstractness of theological enterprises with the primacy and irrefutability of personal experience. Since people claim to have religious experiences, these must be upheld as valid evidence of a superior consciousness with which our consciousness is linked. The response exhibits the same dualism present in other aspects of his psychology and radical empiricism: all is one (all is consciousness) and yet the one is appropriated in pluralistic ways (we become conscious of the one consciousness through varied, private experiences).

From this asserted primacy of private religious experience—and hence of personal consciousness—it is not a far jump to James's statement in "The Essence of Humanism" that God, if existent at all, "is no absolute all-experiencer, but simply the experiencer of widest actual conscious span."[74] To understand this claim requires a closer look at James's pragmatism, such as his famous 1898 essay "Philosophical Conceptions and Practical Results." In this essay James presents his version of Peirce's pragmatic maxim, which he feels "should be expressed more broadly" than his colleague did. He restates Peirce's maxim as asserting that the meaning of a "truth" is "the conduct it dictates or inspires." But a "truth" can affect conduct, James insists, only because it first "foretells some particular turn to our experience which shall call for just that conduct from us." In this version of the Jamesian pragmatic maxim, meaning boils down to "some particular consequence" rather than to Peirce's assertion of a general (vague or virtual) tendency toward some conduct.[75] The more important difference between the two maxims lies in the implied range of operation of each. The Jamesian maxim seeks the meaning of truths while the Peircean one simply seeks the meaning of ideas or concepts. James does not explicitly note this divergence from (or misreading of) Peirce, but it makes all the difference in terms of how the maxims are applied. For example, instead of using examples of meaning or logic, James chooses to demonstrate his pragmatic maxim through the concept of God: What difference does believing in God make? What is the particular consequence of that belief?[76] For James, the status of God as a truth is what is at issue, not simply the meaning of the term. Moreover, James never specifies a particular consequence of belief in God, as he stipulates by his maxim, but offers only a general consequence and a set of possible individual responses that might be grouped under the rubric of personal religious experience. For instance he suggests that the idea of God satisfies some of our deepest hopes and needs, such as the "need of an eternal moral order."[77] And he offers a list of "concrete religious experiences" that derive from belief or instigate belief, including "conversations with the unseen, voices and visions, responses to prayer, changes of heart, deliverances from fear, inflowings of help, [and] assurances of support."[78] "God," then, sustains our most ideal realms and deepest hopes, and James implies that God *is* true so long as these consequences of belief in God are forthcoming.[79]

Quite distinct from Peirce's concerns about logical meaning and its relation to actual existence, James's pragmatic maxim suspends questions of whether such religious experiences have any basis outside of the experiencer's own psychological reality. Peirce's schema attempts to plot a line (however jagged and incomplete) between a virtual Firstness (possibility), an irresistible, felt Secondness (reality), and Thirdness (concept, thought). James does not acknowledge Firstness, and due to his monism (or functional dualism), which reduces reality to that which is experienced, he somewhat collapses Secondness and Thirdness.[80] Thus while Peirce directly or indirectly comments on the mind/not-mind problem through his insistence on the connection of thought (Thirdness) to reality (Secondness), James in essence declares all of reality the province of human experience and sets up personal experience as reality's standard, not its derivative.

Since human experience is temporal and always reaching beyond itself, James indicates the need for concepts that express our experiences of hope, promise, and the ideals for which we strive and that can ground them in ideas like an "eternal moral order." Religion and God serve just this need. Later essays in pragmatism further this vision of religion and expound on its usefulness for human existence. For instance, in his first lecture in *Pragmatism*, James acknowledges the popular appeal of his two lists (the tender- and the tough-minded) by stating that though "we" (presumably, educated men like himself) are attracted to "facts" and the successes of the empirical method, still he claims "we" cannot relinquish religion. Its values and ideals cling too tightly. Pragmatism, he suggests, offers a way of synthesizing the two mental dispositions in a way that preserves the best of both.[81] Following James's pragmatic path, one can better understand how truth cannot exist as an absolute or universal correspondence between belief and reality—for if reality names a wider sphere of experience, then reality and hence belief changes as life proceeds. Rather, truth signifies a sense of the expedient or the good. Therefore, humans believe in God not because we can prove God exists, but because belief in God "proves itself to be good in the way of belief," that is, belief in God results in practical consequences that enable and support a better life, such as confidence in a moral order or the ability to hope for the future.[82]

Despite its reliance on personal experience, this picture of religion would have dismayed Jonathan Edwards, and probably will not be very convincing to anyone who actually believes in God. Indeed James's *Pragmatism* received sharp critique from his friends and colleagues. *Pragmatism* anticipates their criticism, and James responds not according to Puritan doctrine or historical truth, but according to the Puritan imaginary, which aligns Puritanism with James's own critique of idealism, rationalism, and an inability to choose "the strenuous mood."[83] The critics are but tender-minded thinkers, James implies, persons who need to assert the actual existence of God so as to believe that "the cares of the world are in better hands" than humans can provide. James scorns such a reaction to pragmatism, calling that type of religion a license to take "a moral holiday." Religionists inappropriately extend their confidence in an eternal moral order to a belief that God alone sustains and controls this moral order.[84] James's utter rejection of the orthodox Christian position explains his claim that pragmatism shifts philosophical authority as surely as did the Protestant reformation.[85] Distinct from the Kant's 'second Copernican revolution,' which was epistemological, James's shift in authority centers in willing, in the individual's freedom to command action:

> Does our act then *create* the world's salvation so far as it makes room for itself, so far as it leaps into the gap? Does it create, not the whole world's salvation of course, but just so much of this as itself covers of the world's extent?
>
> Here I take the bull by the horns, and in spite of the whole crew of rationalists and monists, of whatever brand they be, I ask *why not*?[86]

Instead of resting on the superior power and compassion of a transcendent God, James suggests that humans take matters into our own hands. Think not that the world will be saved but only that it might be saved; it is a possibility left to us, to our choices, struggles, and abilities. James calls this position *meliorism* and on it depend his views not only of God and religion but also of ethics. Meliorism is neither optimistic nor pessimistic, he cautions, but straddles both attitudes with the conviction of possibility. When the question arises of achieving a particular goal or ideal, meliorism assumes that the possibility of success depends on the extent to which each human being acts toward its realization. "The religion of humanity," James quips, "affords a basis for ethics as well as theism does."[87]

One might think that this position would open up James to a theory of community or society, in which various goals or ideas are articulated and possible strategies for attaining them are advanced. Despite his pluralism, however, James remains doggedly individualistic, seeming to believe that life experiences themselves will steer a person toward the best ideals and goals, if only that person is seeking them sincerely.[88] Thus instead of turning to a social ethic, as does Wundt, or to a philosophical account of community, as does Peirce, James insists that "the only way to be true to our Maker is to be loyal to ourselves."[89] This position, relying as it does upon the voluntarism of his psychology, is only made more evident in James's most directly religious work, *The Varieties of Religious Experience*.[90] In this text James presumes the philosophical priorities of experience (radical empiricism) and the individual (pragmatism) by methodologically setting out to examine personal religious experience over against any sort of institutional embodiment of that experience. James goes so far as to define religion, for the purposes of the lectures, as "the feelings, acts, and experiences of individual men in their solitude, so far as they apprehend themselves to stand in relation to whatever they may consider the divine."[91] The definition not only stresses the private and experiential fulcrum of religion, but also the primacy of individual judgment: one decides for oneself both what is divine and when one is in relation to it. Thus nothing in this definition exceeds the will—and therefore the action and judgment—of the individual.

Not until the "conclusions" to the *Varieties* does James indicate how his prioritizing of individual religious experience relates to his former vocation as a scientist. In response to scientific striving toward that which is ever more general and universal, James writes:

> In spite of the appeal which this impersonality of the scientific attitude makes to a certain magnanimity of temper, I believe it to be shallow, and I can now state my reason in comparatively few words. That reason is that, so long as we deal with the cosmic and the general, we deal only with the symbols of reality, but *as soon as we deal with private and personal phenomena as such, we deal with realities in the completest sense of the term*.[92]

As "appealing" as science may be, it does not pragmatically satisfy the deeper yearnings for a universe that caters to the personal. Not only does it not satisfy such yearnings, it also seeks to bar them at the gate of scientific inquiry.

Conclusions

Many commentators on James and his family tell a biographical story to explain his commitment to religious values. The secondary literature on both James and Peirce overflows with biographical exposés, often employed as causal explanations for various aspects of their philosophical thought. For instance, Henry James, Sr.'s unorthodox but fervent religiosity (inspired by the writings of Charles Fourier and Emanuel Swedenborg) is usually discussed as a kind of permanent scar on William's development. Just as a scar never integrates with the surrounding skin but for just this reason can act as a reliable identity marker, James is said to have been unable to accept his father's piety and yet continually to be haunted by it. Along these same lines, one often reads that Henry, Sr., pushed his eldest son into a career in science in the hopes that William would come to reconcile science with religion, a task the unscientific father could not perform himself.[93]

I am making an argument not about the James family, but about the construction of America as an idea and practice. I have steered away from the particular and well-rehearsed details of James's and Peirce's biographies and kept my focus on their philosophical texts. The lesson of deconstruction is that every text offers clues to the assumptions that construct it. With this in mind I have analyzed a series of texts by the pragmatists in order to illuminate the proclivities and investments that anchor their status as a philosophical movement. In the last chapter I argued that in Peirce's texts, his reception of European natural science reveals an unwavering commitment to purposiveness against deterministic readings of those sciences. Unlike James's struggle with the place of purpose, and his consequent division of the world into public (scientific) and private (individual) spheres, Peirce presents a sweeping ontological vision that finds purposiveness unfolding in the center of scientific inquiries, and strips the personal struggle to live a good, true, and beautiful life of any individual basis. I related Peirce's central concept of community—a crucial religious, ethical, scientific, and aesthetic category for him—to Puritan visions of self and community that were formed during the Second Great Awakening and that gave Peirce a means to imagine a society not built around greed and individuality. In this chapter I have compared James's analyses of purpose and the consequences of his resolutions about purpose for subjectivity to the theological legacy of Jonathan Edwards, a theology that grows in prominence and authority during the nineteenth century. Edwards and James have the dubious privilege of historical commendation. Their works are now considered both as representing their times and as pushing beyond them. Without pausing to debate this inherited perspective, we can use it to aid our search for stories about "America." The volume of commentary on James and Edwards solidifies their status as mythic figures, and their works can be approached as important statements about the formation and constitution of the myths of our national history and heritage.[94] But more important, Edwards stands to James as a type of Puritan that his culture valued more generally, a man whose Puritanism displays itself through integrity, inner strength, heartfelt sensitivity, moral discipline, and a strenuous life. James sees in Edwards an appeal for the reality of mystery, human fallibility, and epistemological uncertainty. Edwards attributes all of these to the omnipotence of God; James, to the individual self's controlled and active relation to its world. For the Puritan, God's providence relativizes human existence and human ability, while for the pragmatist the individual relativizes scientific certainties.[95] But for both the theologian and the psychologist-turned-philosopher, the fulcrum of this relativizing is personal experience. As we have seen, James regards as most real those experiences that are the most private and individual. Science, with its striving for generality and universality, is derivative at best. Whereas science seeks to demystify reality and unveil its workings, James sees in the individual person's experiences the basic mystery of life. For James, marking the individual as the locus of the most real links his arguments for free will with his confidence that nothing can capture the singularity and mystery of an individual human being standing before the hugeness and personal exhortation of the cosmos. Faith is real and crucial but its very seclusion (in the heart) renders it fundamentally mysterious, the mystery of faith thus perfectly paralleling the mystery of God.

Since religious experience is shrouded in mystery, both Edwards and James recognize the imperative for interpreting experience. Personal experience is continuously on trial. Thus the crucible of personal experience leads both thinkers rapidly to discussions of freedom and morality. Where James's emphasis pushes the individual into a solitary relationship with the world, Edwards's emphasis pulls the experiencer back into a community. Edwards urges that all personal experience must be interpreted and all spiritual emotions tempered, actions best accomplished in a church that holds its members mutually accountable. One might say that the need to interpret private experience encourages both thinkers to opt for "the strenuous life" and to concede that to strive for this life is to fail over and again, not because of a *flawed* human nature but because of a *fallible* human nature, that is, a nature that can only proffer limited interpretations and thus must rely on future experiences to challenge and amend them. Obviously, this position encompasses James's pragmatism and his conviction that the "will to believe" will mold an effective philosophy and ethic. In Edwards, it steers us toward his doctrines of sin and salvation and to the importance he places on communal structures of interpretation and guidance.[96] In short, while Edwards meets personal experience with humility and the need for moral accountability, James embraces it as the backbone of self-confidence and self-control.

The option for the strenuous life means a stress on the fruits of experience, on action or behavior. Assurance of the fallibility of human knowledge and being yields an existential uncertainty in both thinkers. In James the uncertainty leads him to insist on free will and to argue for a meliorism that exhorts everyone to claim freedom of will and actively to reform the world. Edwards's long and complex treatise on free will has an equally long and complex history of interpretation. Suffice it to say that he upholds a more orthodox Calvinism that balances absolute human dependence on God with a moral culpability that begins with self-reflection and ends with community judgment. For Edwards, uncertainty over interpretations of religious experience lead him to focus on overt practices as visible signs of the believer's mysterious new heart. What might be called the shared religiosity of Edwards and James—a purpose transcendent to efficient causation, the mystery of the universe, the priority of personal, religious experience, the acknowledgment of fallibility and uncertainty—signifies differently in their respective eras. Yet, the continuity of this religiosity speaks to continuities within the stories

America tells about itself through this Puritan imaginary. Edwards and James alike perceive America as a land forged from the wilderness by individuals of conscience, persons who were not afraid to assert their differences from the status quo and yet who also did not hesitate to face their own limitations and failures. Both believe in the ability of individuals to accomplish tremendous things in the world and to overcome their shortcomings—James through a will that chooses to assist the personal cosmos, Edwards through God's gracious bestowal of the right dispositions. Edwards's Puritan Calvinism devolves into James's "varieties of religious experience," and yet both thinkers assume an unknowable transcendence that is sought and found through irrefutable personal experience. Finally, though Edwards never stoops to a "proof" of God and James considers such efforts quite beside the point, both men focus on the effects of faith, on the movements of the heart that lead to changes of habits, and hence on the human struggle to live the best life possible. As we saw with Peirce, whose paradoxical views of the self and whose theories of community also echo America's Puritan imaginary, James's reception of European thought flows through the funnel of inherited Puritan sentiments. He transmutes one according to the other in a manner that spells out a new and popular myth of America. It is to this myth that we now turn.

Conclusions

The Mythology of Self and Nation

The United States of America,—bounded on the north by the North Pole; on the South by the Antarctic Region; on the east by the first Chapter of the Book of Genesis and on the west by the Day of Judgment. . . . The Supreme Ruler of the Universe . . . has marked out the line this nation must follow and our duty must be done. America is destined to become the Light of the world.

—*Arthur Bird,* Looking Forward

This book has explored the development of American pragmatism out of the pragmatists' engagements with certain European currents of thought. Specifically, I have argued that the pragmatists resisted positivistic and simplistically empirical accounts of natural science and that this resistance shaped their epistemologies, logics, phenomenologies, and psychologies. I chose to focus especially on the American reception of psychology, since the evolution in Europe of a discourse of psychology separate from physiology and philosophy, and the subsequent anxieties about whether or not psychology is "scientific," efficiently encapsulate much broader cultural and scientific debates on the nature and method of science and the nature and method of studying the human. Articulating the intellectual spaces of German and Scottish psychology prepared the way for examining the American repositioning of psychology and science within theories of human knowing and being that emphasize the disciplined production of the self (ascesis) either through habits (Peirce) or the will (James). Such repositioning is the constitutive mark of American pragmatism.

If the detailed readings I have offered of the concepts of consciousness, causality, will, and belief in the texts of Helmholtz, Wundt, Hamilton, Bain, and the pragmatists do nothing more than situate the genealogy of American pragmatism firmly within European psychology, I will have contributed a new argument for students and scholars of pragmatism. I hope to have accomplished more than that, however, for I have argued that the conditions of possibility of the pragmatists' mutations of the psychological concepts of consciousness, causality, will, and belief reside in the cultural legacy of American Puritanism. The enduring Puritan imaginary affects numerous aspects of American mythology, including that of the American self.[1] The preceding chapters have made clear that American pragmatism, like Puritanism, articulates ethical and religious narratives about the self. These narratives inform pragmatism's accounts of science and human knowing and, I have argued, they disclose the urgency behind the Americans' insistent repositioning of the European concepts. Viewed in this light, one can regard American pragmatism—particularly the version made popular by William James—as a general term for certain versions of the myth of the American self, a myth that purports to trace its lineage back to seventeenth-century American Puritanism.

The strangeness of asserting links among American pragmatism, American mythology, and American Puritanism resides in the common assumption that Puritanism no longer existed in the nineteenth century. I have addressed this assumption and countered it with arguments that the Puritan imaginary worked both *mythologically*, as that which shaped understandings of the ideal self and of America's purpose and mission, and *practically* (at least in the pragmatists' New England), as the cultural context in which questions of science and God were debated.

The chapters in part III began with psychological concepts and ended with discussions of self, God, and nation. This chapter inverts the direction of analysis. I offer a close reading of lectures written almost contemporaneously by James and Peirce. First I clarify James's Puritan image of self, God, and nation, and then I argue how these visions arise out of and/or parallel to James's understandings of consciousness, causality, will, and belief. Having established that Jamesian pragmatism delineates a strong version of the myth of the American self, I conclude with a reading of Peirce that demonstrates how his pragmaticism offers an alternate version of this myth. Peirce stands as the operative unthought of James; his views on self and nation engage the Puritan imaginary as surely as those of James, but with less triumphalism and more humility. Perhaps the recent renewed interest in Peirce's complicated vision of the world can be attributed, at least in part, to precisely this sobriety and to the alternative genealogy he offers of the self and its relations to community and cosmos.

The Scales Seemed to Fall from My Eyes

In 1899, the same year that produced this chapter's epigraph, James's collection of *Talks for Teachers* was published. One of these talks, "What Makes a Life Significant," so thoroughly displays James's disgust with bourgeois malaise and his fascination with the swelling masses of immigrant labor that the historian James Livingston finds it an irresistible template for his arguments about the interactions of late nineteenth-century corporate capitalism and theories of subjectivity.[2] I am indebteded to Livingston's insightful analysis, and I turn to the same talk for depicting my own, quite different, analysis of Jamesian subjectivity.

James opens his talk with a depiction of the bourgeois retreat center at Chautauqua Lake in upstate New York. He acknowledges the beauty and peacefulness of the place but admits a growing restlessness and irritation during the course of his stay. After some reflection on the possible causes of his discomfort, he attributes it to an "absence of human nature *in extremis* anywhere."[3] He then recounts an experience on the journey back home:

> I was speeding with the train toward Buffalo, when, near that city, the sight of a workman doing something on the dizzy edge of a sky-scaling iron construction brought me to my senses very suddenly. . . . Wishing for heroism and the spectacle of human nature on the rack, I had never noticed the great fields of heroism lying round about me, I had failed to see it present and alive. I could only think of it as dead and embalmed, labeled and costumed, as it is in the pages of romance. And yet there it was before me in the daily lives of the laboring classes. Not in clanging fights and desperate marches only is heroism to be looked for, but on every railway bridge and fire-proof building that is going up to-day. . . . There, every day of the year somewhere, is human nature *in extremis* for you. And wherever a scythe, an axe, a pick, or a shovel is wielded, you have it sweating and aching and with its powers of patient endurance racked to the utmost under the length of hours of strain.[4]

James betrays nothing that could immediately be identified as "religious" in this paragraph, but his view of the self comes through clearly. The virtue, even the worth, of a person, James implies, resides not in the degree to which she takes up and mirrors the causes prescribed by the nation or other large social bodies, but rather in the mundane personal experiences that articulate and achieve the person's individual goals.[5] James calls the diligent attention to this individual agenda "human nature *in extremis*": a person's willed effort extends directly to specific actions that yield visible, pragmatic results, and this connection of action and effort forms the person's consciousness through "sweating and aching and with its powers of patient endurance." As we saw in chapter 6, will subtends consciousness in James's psychology and functions teleologically in his pragmatism to shape a person through separate, individual acts. James continues:

> As I awoke to all this unidealized heroic life around me, the scales seemed to fall from my eyes; and a wave of sympathy greater than anything I had ever before felt with the common life of common men began to fill my soul. It began to seem as if virtue with horny hands and dirty skin were the only virtue genuine and vital enough to take account of. Every other virtue poses; none is absolutely unconscious and simple, and unexpectant of decoration or recognition, like this. These are our soldiers, thought I, these our sustainers, these the very parents of our life.[6]

James here suggests the religious subtext of his thought by structuring his turn to the salvific power of the laboring classes ("common men") in terms resonant with Paul's conversion after his encounter with Jesus on the road to Damascus (Acts 9:1–19). Indeed, we now can perceive that the analogy to Paul began in the previous paragraph, in that James, like Paul, was on a journey at the time of his encounter with the divine; he was, as he puts it, "speeding with the train toward Buffalo." For both men, conversion occurs away from home and in the middle of things; for both, conversion interrupts a journey to a city (Damascus, Buffalo) outside the holy city (Jerusalem, Cambridge).

In the pragmatist's version of the story, Paul's collision with the world's sole transcendent savior becomes an "encounter" with America's seemingly infinite mass of immanent saviors, and the infusing Holy Spirit that propelled the apostle to baptism is replaced with an overwhelming "wave of sympathy" that motivates James's propitious change of heart. The strategy of framing his prophetic word about human nature in terms of this famous Christian conversion shows how Christian (if not yet evidently Puritan) discourses make possible the development of American pragmatism. What more do the narrative twists on Paul's conversion illuminate about James?

First, James's experience is not an encounter but an "encounter." Instead of falling to his feet, jolted and stunned by the presence of the divine, James calmly absorbs the revelation from his window seat. The separation is not only physical. The speed of the train—a technological and temporal separation—protects him from any actual contact with "our sustainers." The windowpane and the train's movement exemplify, respectively, the individuality and plurality of the Jamesian self. Quintessentially, that self stands in isolation from its peers and world. As he writes in *The Varieties of Religious Experience*, "as soon as we deal with private and personal phenomena as such, we deal with realities in the completest sense of the term."[7] Appropriately, then, James's conversion remains a private affair. The external world, the world of the nonself, stands as the object of his attention, and the windowpane—the barrier between self and other—is transparent. James recognizes no complexity in the hermeneutics or epistemology of the world. The passing scenes are assimilated into his stream of consciousness and are given importance based on the attention and will accorded to them.[8] This Jamesian self stands as the stable point in consciousness's flow of experience, and I argued in chapter 6 that this stability is effected by the will. The will functions as the banks of the stream of consciousness, guiding the direction of the stream through the purposive operations of selection, attention, and habit. From the point of view of the external world, however, the self is the one in movement (imaged by the speeding train) and is thus a plurality. James labels this plural being the *social self* and asserts, "a man has as many social selves as there are individuals who recognize him and carry an image of him in their mind."[9] As such, the plurality of the self is real only in the sense that different perspectives are real, but the plurality is not actually existent. Rather, the actual existence of the self occurs in the will underlying consciousness; the will enables the consciousness purposively to assimilate the external world.

The second lesson from James's renarration of Paul's conversion centers on his perception of the divine. For the pragmatist, the world's saviors are immanent, multiple, and ordinary. Such saviors exemplify James's meliorism, the so-called tough-minded philosophy, which insists on the necessity and effectiveness of human action to make the world a better place. Only weak-willed rationalists and spiritualists, he notes, leave the salvation of the world to transcendent powers. As in his view of the self, in James's perception of divinity, we see how the cooperating forces of will, consciousness, and action impinge on and constitute both the self and the beliefs of the self. Willing to believe in the human capacity for effective action motivates a person to that action. Performing those acts further shapes consciousness and will and thereby patterns that person's belief system and character. Because James upholds every person's ability and duty to effect such world-saving action, he responds to his "encounter" not with a submission to divine authority (as is signaled in Paul's baptism), but with an "overwhelming sympathy." He confesses he has fallen short of the "the common life of common men." Such a life represents for him the fullest humanity and, therefore, the fullest divinity, and in his confession he identifies with persons whose lives are untrammeled by the satiety and mediocrity ("flatness and lack of zest"[10]) of bourgeois existence. Again, the self that James advocates is a self of volition and action, a self whose individual willed efforts form consciousness and belief, and, consequently, a self fully responsible for the failures of its life and world.

In using Paul's conversion as a frame for his own, James seems to be setting himself up as a new prophet or a new apostle. Of what or to whom is he an apostle, though? James's talk anticipates these questions by comparing his sympathy for the common person to the attitude displayed in Tolstoy's writings, an attitude constitutive of the Russian character. James especially embraces Tolstoy's "deification of the bravery, patience, kindliness, and dumbness of the unconscious natural man."[11] Directly after this statement, James discloses to the reader an internal dialogue: "Where now is *our* Tolstoi, I said, to bring the truth of all this home to our American bosoms, fill us with a better insight, and wean us away from that spurious literary romanticism on which our wretched culture—as it calls itself—is fed? Divinity lies all about us, and culture is too hide-bound to even suspect the fact. . . . Must we wait for some one born and bred and living as a laborer himself, but who, by grace of Heaven, shall also find a literary voice?"[12] No, we need not wait. James will gladly be the American Tolstoy, illuminating the national character in his stirring portraits of the laboring masses. James will be the prophet of America, revealing to its citizens the particular qualities of the American self. James will be an apostle for the simple ("natural") person, who wills hard work and honest living and exemplifies "the only virtue genuine," a person whose will and effort are so unclouded by the superficialities of the world that his virtue seems "unconscious" and "unexpectant of decoration." The American self, James proclaims, does the right thing for the sake of its being right, that is, for the sake of its producing worthy and useful effects. As we saw in chapter 6, the Jamesian mutations of psychological concepts (consciousness, causality, will, and belief) produce an account of subjectivity that emphasizes purposive action. The ability to choose such action forms the cornerstone of an ethical individual, a person whose willed acts produce world-saving (useful and worthy) ends.

The next paragraph of James's lecture further manifests the American character and places it solidly within a religious frame:

> And there I rested on that day, with a sense of widening of vision, and with what it is surely fair to call an increase of religious insight into life. In God's eyes the differences of social position, of intellect, of culture, of cleanliness, of dress, which different men exhibit, and all their pride, must be so small as practically quite to vanish; and all that should remain is the common fact that here we are, a countless multitude of vessels of life, each of us pent in to peculiar difficulties, with which we must severally struggle by using whatever of fortitude and goodness we can summon up. . . . At this rate, the deepest human life is everywhere, is eternal. And, if any human attributes exist only in particular individuals, they must belong to the mere trapping and decoration of the surface-show.[13]

Like God on the seventh day of creation, James pauses and surveys his new understanding of self and virtue. His comments at this point, however, appear contradictory to the Jamesian pragmatism that insists on the uniqueness and moral accountability of the individual. The American self, he suggests, is at once individual ("each of us pent in to peculiar difficulties") and prototypical ("the deepest human life is everywhere"), at once particular and universal. This apparent contradiction actually resonates with the larger facets of James's philosophy that I ground in his culture's Puritan imaginary. At the end of chapter 6 I discussed James's commitments to a purpose transcendent to efficient causation, to the mystery of the universe, to the priority of personal, religious experience, and to the acknowledgment of fallibility and uncertainty. I summarized these priorities as tough-mindedness and a concern for matters of the heart, and I linked them to the Gilded Age's use of *Puritan* to evoke just such a strong but sensitive character. James did center his philosophy on the individual self, and yet the link in the quotation between "self and social assertion" is reminiscent of Peirce's deployment of the Puritan imaginary, that is, of what Sacvan Berkovitch has called typical of the Puritan myth. "The colonial Puritan myth," he writes, "linked self and social assertion in a way that lent special support to the American Way."[14] In chapter 5, I discussed a number of ways in which Puritanism exerted opposing demands on its adherents, including by forcing self-abdication through intense introspection, by obligating a frugality that inevitably produced a problematic wealth, by dogmatically asserting human fallibility, and by preaching both epistemological uncertainty and theological certainty. Each of these demands simultaneously centers on the self and denies or empties the self for the sake of God and community. Berkovitch extends his claim:

> The same Puritan myth, differently adapted, encouraged Edwards to equate conversion, national commerce, and the treasures of a renovated earth, Franklin

to record his rise to wealth as a moral vindication of the new nation, . . . Thoreau to declare self-reliance an economic model of "the only true America," Horatio Alger to extol conformity as an act of supreme individualism, and Melville, in *Moby-Dick*, to create an epic hero who represents in extremis both the claims of Romantic isolation and the thrust of industrial capitalism.[15]

I would also argue that what I term the *Puritan imaginary* "encouraged" William James to respond to European disputes about the concepts of science and the human by repositioning familiar psychological terms within an account of human knowing and being that becomes the constitutive mark of America's only indigenous philosophical movement. Unlike Peirce's pragmaticism, which retains the tension between the mandate to self-assertion and the mandate to self-immolation, James's pragmatism portrays a well-known and widely accepted version of the American self, a self that holds personal, private experience as the most real, that universalizes individual experience as prototypical, and that protects this claim by wrapping it in the legitimizing mantle of America's Puritan imaginary.

America and Europe: Lines of Flight and Considered Mutations

The Puritan imaginary is in no way monolithic or stable; indeed, its constitutive flux is what validates my claim that it continued to exert a strong hold on Americans throughout the nineteenth century. Recent social histories indicate that Puritanism never denoted a homogeneous or fully hegemonic entity; from the first Puritan's step on New England soil, the concepts of Puritanism and Puritan community fissured from within. Certainly the semantic anchoring became increasingly tangential as the contingencies of the nineteenth century deployed Puritanism for causes that would likely seem foreign and non-Puritan to the likes of Winthrop, Mather, and Edwards.[16] Despite its perpetual semantic flux, the Puritan imaginary did consistently engage debates over the relation of the spiritual and the material, sometimes described as religion versus science, sometimes as belief versus practice. One scholar of American culture speculates, "The practical and the spiritual remain primary antithetical categories in American experience."[17] But I contend that the antithesis is sublated—cancelled out and preserved—in American pragmatism by its double repositioning, first of Puritanism and then of European notions of both science and methods of studying the human.

The double horizon for the pragmatists' intellectual agenda—how to reconcile the changes within European natural science with the religious values current in their culture—can thus be attributed both to a Puritan imaginary that had long been a factor in defining America to itself (despite its internal fracturing) and to the new scientific theories about subjectivity and truth that were being formulated and debated in Europe. Additionally, Peirce's and James's critical receptions of European science were framed by another continuity within the nexus of American mythology, namely, America's historically fetishistic relationship to all things European. In setting out to determine what is American about American pragmatism, this book necessarily drew from both horizons of fracturing continuity: the Puritan past and the attraction to/repulsion from Europe. The pragmatists looked to Europe for intellectual conversation, edification, and inspiration, but they appropriated the coveted European currents of thought only through the cultural context and valuation of the Puritan imaginary and through a pride and faith in the uniqueness and success of the American experiment.

The concepts of consciousness, causality, will, action, and belief form integral parts of mid–nineteenth century scientific discourse in Germany and Scotland. Through these concepts, natural scientists and philosophers tried to embrace faithfully the increasingly accepted explanatory capacity of a strict efficient causation, while recognizing the impossibility of applying that explanatory framework directly to the study of human beings. In chapter 1, I offered the most basic example of this struggle in Hermann von Helmholtz's application of the law of causality (efficient causation) to human consciousness. Though Helmholtz does stress the mechanistic functions of the brain's sensory-motor system, he also acknowledges processes of "unconscious inference" and semiosis that somehow stand outside of or parallel to that motor system. Helmholtz's institutional and disciplinary position in physics enable him to avoid the contradictions implicit in his accounts of consciousness, semiosis and causality. Wilhelm Wundt, however, dedicates his life to carving out an institutional space for a scientific psychology and thus his questions and investigations of the human inevitably engage debates about the nature and method of science. Responding to natural scientists whose inquiries assumed the necessity of the empirical (efficient causation) for all scientific enterprises, Wundt extends the definition of *empirical* to include elements of final causation. As I demonstrated in chapter 2, Wundt's solution entails a parallel causality, the effects of which are the assertion of consciousness as an independent entity deserving of investigation and a stress on process instead of natural science's more typical stress on isolated events and/or entities. Being a psychologist and not simply a philosopher of science, Wundt directs his new understandings of consciousness and causality to delineating the parameters of being human. Chapter 2 examined how his redefining the terms empiricism, objectivity, and causality affected his understanding of the self as a volitional, purposeful, active, and social creature.

William Hamilton professes neither physics nor scientific psychology, but his philosophical psychology still assumes the dominance of efficient causation and Hamilton struggles to reconcile that assumption with his concomitant commitment to the "testimony of consciousness." Hamilton asserts that this testimony both affirms and supersedes efficient causation on the evidence of common sense. In chapter 3, I demonstrated how Hamilton's resolution of this conundrum through the philosophy of the conditioned asserts understandings of science and causality typical of natural scientists, but he argues their truthfulness through their nonmechanistic, purposeful consequences for the moral nature of humans and the omnipotence of God. Less trained than

Hamilton in medicine or the natural sciences and yet interested in psychology
as a scientific enterprise, Alexander Bain completely rejects his compatriot's
Calvinist frame and reintroduces confusion about and ambiguity in applying
causality to human objects of study. Chapter 4 showed how Bain avoids typical
formulations of efficient causation in recognition of their implicit demand for
certainty; instead Bain portrays causation in terms of successive relations and
grounds its logic in the wider logic of the uniformity of nature. This uniformity also functions as the logical horizon for Bain's depictions of consciousness, will, belief, and action by forming a canvas of predictability for unpredictable and fallible human nature.

In the 1870s Peirce and James encounter these debates through their relatively informal Cambridge Metaphysical Club. Over the next two decades their
works display a constant theme that was barely discussed by the Germans
and Scots, namely, the concept of purpose or purposiveness as a defining
characteristic of human thought and being. Holding to that ontological claim
as an uncritical foundation, the pragmatists continue their training in and
reflection upon the natural sciences. That training, work, and reflection inspire them to try to reconcile Europe's dominant image of a good scientist
with their American image of human nature. For James the tension between
the two images determines the questions of his magnum opus, *The Principles
of Psychology*, and eventually compels him to attend more fully to questions
of philosophy and ethics. In *Principles* James does not follow Wundt's lead
in extending the definitions of empiricism and objectivity. Consequently the
text oscillates between what James felt to be the dry, unfeeling strictures of
natural science and the passionate demands of philosophy and ethics. I have
argued that the inability to resolve this oscillation steers James out of psychology and into the philosophical speculation that eventually yields his
pragmatism, which reconciles science and ethics within the crucible of individual experience. Peirce's writings, I have argued, never relinquish the
tension between the obligations of a good scientist and the obligations of
an ethical person. I suggested in chapter 5 that this sustained tension acts as
a tempering dialectic in Peirce's work, functionally advocating that communities of scientific inquiry need to be checked by communities of ethical lay-
people, and vice versa.

Before focusing more directly on their differences, let me underscore what
the pragmatists' shared. First and most generally, James and Peirce share a
commitment to embedding the processes of human knowing in bodily action
and social interaction. This physical and social context does not reduce consciousness to the sensory-motor system, but asserts a complex and purposeful set of phenomenological and epistemological relations that insists on the
concomitant importance of mind and body. By this view psychology is as
much about the physical as about the mental components of being human, as
is shown by the pragmatic stress on habit and/or willed action as the direct
consequence and constituent of consciousness. Second, both pragmatists display ethical sentiments or subtexts in their writings, especially in their attention to the ethical ramifications of our habits of knowing and being. Thus the

body and mind studied by psychology together determine a subject formed by ascesis, that is, by a disciplined and disciplining attention to one's habits and willed actions. Third, the pragmatists insist on the value of scientific inquiry for treating matters of the heart, and indeed this insistence propels their simultaneous deference to and repositioning of the scientific enterprise.[18]

The pragmatic assertion of final causation as both inherent to human nature and inherently scientific conjoins these shared aspects. Peirce and James argue that final causation is a scientific character of human nature, and this has direct consequences for their mutations of consciousness, will, action, and belief. Moreover, for both men, action, belief, and will shape consciousness, and consciousness shapes action and belief. The two thinkers differ in the methods by which each concept affects the others. James prioritizes the will; volition and choice subtend and constitute the other concepts. Peirce, however, hardly treats will at all, and for him the other concepts describe aspects of subjectivity that are sculpted from a slow and continuous process of semeiosis. The cosmology he erects asserts different boundaries of the self than we saw in James and, hence, promulgates a different image of self and nation. I turn now to this alternative imaginary as the conclusion of my book.

Asserting the Unclaimed Self

Peirce was a sinner and desperately needed the assurance of salvation. Few Puritans, and no other pragmatist, so well understood what this meant—the sacrifice of pride, of ego, of self.
—*Paul Conkin*, Puritans and Pragmatists

The self-transcendent self is an autonomous power: Such a self depends upon the most complete surrender of egoism. Its self-transcendence alone leads to self-possession.
—*Vincent M. Colapietro*, Peirce's Approach to the Self

James's portrayal of the American Self follows the mythic pattern of sustaining individual and societal interpretations and, as such, fits Berkovitch's depiction of the Puritan origins of the American self as a self that "interweaves personal and corporate self-fulfillment."[19] Peirce's account of the self engages more directly the paradoxical Puritan obligation to deny the self through intensive self-examination. Thus Peirce might be favorably compared with Jonathan Edwards, whose life and work also center on this Puritan paradox.[20] Where Edwards and James stand as "winners" in the American pantheon, however, Peirce is an acknowledged loser. His formulations of science, logic, and the nature of human thought and being did not become popular, did not become mythic. Nonetheless, they are just as assuredly "American" in the senses outlined above, that is, in revaluing both the two horizons of continuity (the Puritan imaginary and the ambiguous relationship to Europe) and the new theories generated by European natural scientists.

Next I offer an extended reading of a lecture written (but never delivered) for Peirce's famous 1898 Cambridge lectures, the lectures that encouraged James to reintroduce (really, fully to introduce) the notion of 'pragmatism' in his 1898 Berkeley lectures. My exegesis purports to evidence how Peirce's pragmaticism encircles James's pragmatism as the latter's operative unthought. According to Gilles Deleuze, the "unthought," a concept theorized by Michel Foucault, is "not external to thought but lies at its very heart, as that impossibility of thinking which doubles or hollows out the outside [of thought]."[21] As Deleuze would have it, the unthought is a "fold" of thought. This vivid metaphor posits that all thought comes from the "outside"—compare Peirce's assertion that "we ought to say that we are in thought and not that thoughts are in us"[22]—and yet the very process of thought (which Peirce calls semeiosis) bends and twists thought, thereby forming pockets of "interiority."[23] In claiming Peirce as the operative unthought of James, I am suggesting that Peirce's pragmaticism is the fold of thought that lies at the very heart of James's pragmatism. It is at once the condition of possibility of James's philosophy and its fundamental Other, or opposite. To exemplify this relation of Peirce to James, and the ramifications of their differences in terms of America's Puritan imaginary, I offer a reading that will clarify how even the most abstract elements of Peirce's philosophy are influenced by his culture's valuing a Puritan character. His portrait of this Puritan self, however, does not support the popular imaginary of the American self. Rather, his theory of the self asserts itself only through self-abnegation.

The circumstances of the lecture series and the particular section I have chosen are significant. Together they indicate in three ways Peirce's tenuous situation in relation to both intellectual and popular society. First, James himself arranged for the presentation of these lectures. A popular and successful Harvard professor, James took on this task not only in hopes of introducing Peirce's thought to his students, but more urgently in an effort to provide needed income for his friend. By 1898, Peirce was unaffiliated with any institution, in debt, caring for an ill wife, and weak from the stresses of poverty. Second, James had petitioned Harvard's president, Charles Eliot, and the Harvard Corporation (the university's board of directors) to allow Peirce to lecture on Harvard's campus. The corporation denied this request.[24] The resounding denial testifies to the extent of Peirce's isolation. He had been turned down for a Johns Hopkins professorship for reasons that were murky, even insupportable. But between the walls of the academy ran the uncompromising gaze of social propriety. The scandal of Peirce's love affair with the woman who would be his second wife, an affair that began long before his first marriage was legally dissolved, ousted him from Hopkins and from any other academic post and, indeed, made him virtually unemployable. Third, these 1898 lectures were not the lectures Peirce wanted to give. He had planned a series of talks detailing his logic of relatives, but James insisted on a "more popular plan."[25] Specifically, James encouraged Peirce to abandon the theme of logic altogether and construct a series around "vitally important topics." Peirce was insulted but, desperate for both money and attention, he started over and soon sent James an outline for a series entitled "Detached Ideas on Vitally Important Topics." The sarcastic repetition of James's casual phrase bubbles up throughout Peirce's eight lectures. Finally, the selection I present is from an alternate version of his first lecture and hence was never delivered. Peirce wrote and rewrote these lectures, sending versions to James for approval and trying to meet his friend's dual demand for clarity and popularity. Of course the two thinkers registered clarity and popular interest according to widely different criteria, and one can sense in Peirce's letters to James the former's frustration that his colleagues in philosophy could not stomach what Peirce considered a necessary level of abstraction and neologism. One imagines that even if Peirce had had an academic career, his isolation would have been just as great.

That the passage to which I turn is an alternative version does not negate its importance, but rather underscores two critical marks of Peirce's writings. First, Peirce always tries to display both logical and personal relationality. Thus the version of the lecture he actually delivered necessarily was the one approved by James and engages his logic of relatives, the logic that bridges his universal categories to his semeiotic. Second, Peirce both asserts fallibilism and lives it. Assertion, emendation—assertion, emendation: such is the pattern of all of Peirce's formulations. Rarely are the changes dramatic shifts. Instead they usually consist of nuances of perspective, a slow process of fine-tuning semantics and broadening applications. Thus the following, undelivered selection aptly mediates Peirce's account of the American self, despite and because of its status as an alternate.

The last section of the lecture illuminates Peirce's familiar opposition between science and ethics or between matters of reason and matters of "vital importance":

> True conservatism, I say, means not trusting to reasonings about questions of vital importance but rather to hereditary instincts and traditional sentiments. Place before the conservative arguments to which he can find no adequate reply and which go, let us say, to demonstrate that wisdom and virtue call upon him to offer to marry his own sister, and though he be unable to answer the arguments, he will not act upon their conclusion, because he believes that tradition and the feelings that tradition and custom have developed in him are safer guides than his own feeble ratiocination. Thus true conservatism is sentimentalism. . . . On the whole, he [the conservative] thinks his wisest plan is to reverence his deepest sentiments as his highest and ultimate authority, which is regarding them as *for him practically infallible*—that is, to say infallible in the only sense of the word in which *infallible* has any consistent meaning.[26]

Peirce, who today is often accused of being scientistic, here clearly grounds subjectivity in sentiment. No matter how convincing and indisputable a particular course of action may be, he asserts, its logic must and will be subjected to the "highest and ultimate authority" of the sentiments inculcated by "tradition and custom." Though his pragmaticism often presents logic as the cornerstone of human knowing and being, Peirce here disdains "feeble ratiocination" in light of the "practical infallibility" of learned sentiment. The assurance of practical infallibility is noteworthy on two counts. First, it contrasts starkly with Peirce's more usual assertion that all human endeavors are fallible. To salvage a "practical" infallibility as the only "consistent meaning" of infallible, then, marks for Peirce the intractability of sentiment. Tradition and custom do change, of course; but they change slowly, so that within the course, of a person's life their recommended habits of thought and action seem immutable. As such, the sentiments formed out of those habits lodge deeply and firmly within the larger network of habits that constitutes the self. For a course of action to be adopted, it must agree with those habits. In this way the sentiments form a sort of intractable barrier that resists any quick or easy change of social mores. As was argued in chapter 5, the ethical person conservatively clings to her beliefs and in so doing ensures that the self-control that steers her conduct arises not from a purposeful will but from a deep and permeating structure of purposive habit.

Second, proclaiming a practical infallibility puts the acquisition and maintenance of the foundational sentiments within a patently religious frame. Indeed Peirce depicts the human attitude toward sentiment in terms theologians would use to describe a believer's attitude toward God. A person "reverences" her deepest sentiments; they are her "highest and ultimate authority." In such phrases we can discern a repositioning of the Puritan obligation to examine closely one's feelings for the sake of disciplining the self into a more perfect relationship with God. Similarly, Edwards's sermons and musings present detailed reflections on the duties and trials of the heart and attempt to reconcile this Puritan focus with Locke's discourse on the understanding. Contemporary commentators argue that this reconciliation of heart and head forms a general characterization of American Puritanism and its discussions of self and community.[27]

As Peirce continues, he acknowledges his own penchant for scientific thought and situates himself with respect to his assertions about sentiment:

> Uncompromising radical though I be upon some questions, inhabiting all my life an atmosphere of science, and not reckoned as particularly credulous, I must confess that the conservative sentimentalism I have defined recommends itself to my mind as eminently sane and wholesome. Commendable as it undoubtedly is to reason out matters of detail, yet to allow mere reasoning and reason's self-conceit to overslaw [over-slaugh? over-awe?] the normal and manly sentimentalism which ought to lie at the cornerstone of all our conduct seems to me to be foolish and despicable.[28]

In naming himself a "radical" Peirce separates himself from the "true conservative" of the previous paragraph.[29] As was presented in chapter 5, *radical* characterizes the proper disposition of scientists who must be prepared to overthrow their "whole cartload of beliefs" at the moment any empirical datum or respected scientific peer throws a shred of doubt upon them. Peirce intends *radical* in the etymological sense of "root"; radical persons must be prepared to cut off their beliefs at the root if a scientific community or their own scientific investigation so advises. This disposition opposes sentimentalism, the conservative quality of which positions it as the optimum "cornerstone of all our conduct." Both the anticipated pointillism of the radical and the ingrained consistency of the conservative rely for their proper functioning on the establishment of habits that form two admittedly contradictory dispositions. Emphasizing conduct over James's acts, Peirce repeatedly sets forth a view of the self that is dependent on the character-building effects of habit.

This quotation suggests America's Puritan imaginary in three ways. First, Peirce "confesses" that the person he seems to be is not the truth of his being. He presents this contradiction between the self's appearance (logical or scientific) and reality (sentimental) as a public confession. Indeed, his life apparently requires this brutal honesty (Peirce is a long-time scientist and "not reckoned as particularly credulous"). Confessing this contradiction of appearance and reality prefaces Peirce's seeming desire to resolve it through a further confession of reason's "self-conceit." He repents of reason's arrogance by naming sentimentalism a "sane and wholesome" disposition, resistance to which would be "foolish and despicable." Second, the problem with the scientific disposition is not its radicality but precisely that tendency to "self-conceit." That is, the stakes involved circulate around the vanities of self-assertion and the necessity of ruthlessly gutting such vanities from one's soul. Third, and most obviously in contrast to James, Peirce labels the priority of sentimentalism "manly." James considers sentimentality to be tender-minded and is the more typical nineteenth-century bourgeois in ascribing tenderness and sentimentality a feminine voice. Peirce resists feminizing sentiment and in calling it "manly" encases it with overtones of strength and duty, tones befitting the Puritan call to self-examination and self-critique.[30] Indeed, all three of these points resonate with the Puritan character that exemplifies exacting self-examination, public confession or accountability, and repentance.

The lecture's following paragraphs slowly extract Peirce's understanding of "vital importance." He begins by denying that epithet to philosophy:

> Philosophy after all is, at its highest valuation, nothing more than a branch of science, and as such is not a matter of vital importance; and those who represent it as being so are simply offering us a stone when we ask for bread. Mind, I do not deny that a philosophical or other scientific error may be fraught with disastrous consequences for the whole people. It might conceivably bring about the extirpation of the human race. Importance in that sense it might have in any degree. Nevertheless, in no case is it of *vital* importance.[31]

The end of the following paragraph clarifies this position: "Certainly, any task which lies before us to be done has its importance. But there our responsibility ends. Nor is it the philosophy itself, *qua* cognition, that is vital, so much as it is our playing the part that is allotted to us."[32] Matters of vital importance are intimately personal; they bracket the self from other selves. Indeed, the nonvital nature of philosophy and other sciences lies precisely in their focus across and beyond individuals. Where science aims for the universal expression of generalities, vitally important matters remain particular and individual. As Peirce indicates, they determine "the part that is allotted to us." This phrase evokes the Calvinist doctrine of election or predestination and is one of two tokens of the continuing Christian subtext in these paragraphs. The paraphrase of Matthew 7:9 ("Or what man of you, if his son asks him for bread, will give him a stone?") forms the other Christian token. The impact of this biblical line carries more punch if one knows that it prefaces the so-called Golden Rule: "So whatever you wish that men would do to you, do so to them; for this is the law and the prophets" (Matt. 7:12). This rule and its earlier, altruistic (parental) instantiation pointedly focus on the self and its actions. Peirce's grounding of "vital matters" in the uniquely personal resonates unexpectedly with the individualism of William James. One crucial difference displayed by the paragraph under consideration is the end or telos toward which the personal or individual self acts. For James, "world-saving" actions chosen by the individual form the highest end. For Peirce, duty dictates our action, "playing the part that is allotted to us." James's self centers on the will and its ability to choose and directly guide the self's purposeful framework for action. Peirce's self receives its purposeful framework from outside itself and incorporates it into a vague network of habits that mold not actions but conduct.

The quoted paragraph highlights yet another difference between the pragmatists. Peirce designates philosophy as a science, whereas James views philosophy as an alternative to science, as the proper place for "metaphysical" inquiries that presume a reality beyond that assessed by the efficient causality of natural science. James places matters of the heart, of "vital importance," squarely within philosophy; Peirce critiques that view by outlining philosophy's function as a science, as a field of inquiry entailing particular methods, rules, and goals. As such, philosophy can only concern what is general, but matters of vital importance, both pragmatists agree, are the least general of matters. What is vital is that which is most private. On that point, Peirce and James concur. The abyss that divides them appears when Peirce asserts that what is most private is that which is the least real of all human matters. Peirce, however, has not yet illuminated this abyss. First he extends his comments about science and philosophy to the philosophy of religion:

> You will observe that I have not said a single word in disparagement of the philosophy of religion, in general, which seems to me a most interesting study, at any rate, and possibly likely to lead to some useful result. . . . It is not the philosophy which I hold to be baleful, but the representing it to be of vital importance, as if any genuine religion could come from the head instead of from the heart.[33]

To the extent that one approaches religion as a science, Peirce offers no complaints about it. His critiques resound only when a philosopher—like James—seeks to promote the scientific study of religion as a matter of vital importance. Invoking the Puritan separation of head and heart, he again asserts sentiment to be the province of religion and logic the method of philosophy (and every science). Peirce extends these comments to ethics:

> Somewhat allied to the philosophy of religion is the science of ethics. It is equally useless. Now books of casuistry, indeed, using the word "casuistry" not in any technical sense, but merely to signify discussions of what ought to be done in various difficult situations, might be made at once extremely entertaining and positively useful. But casuistry is just what the ordinary treatises upon ethics do not touch, at least not seriously. . . . To be a moral man is to obey the traditional maxims of your community without hesitation or discussion. Hence, ethics, which is reasoning out an explanation of morality is—I will not say immoral, [for] that would be going too far—composed of the very substance of immorality.[34]

Peirce condemns ethics for purporting to rationalize the very antithesis of rationality. Because beliefs about right and wrong are sculpted not out of the choices of a rational will but from the slow titration and distillation of habit, the study of human conduct—the stuff of ethics—cannot be gathered into a scientific enterprise. Casuistry, the nearest ethics gets to a science, presents case studies not for the purpose of deriving universal rules of action, but in an effort to image concretely the habits recommended by tradition and custom. Only through casuistry does the alliance of ethics to the philosophy of religion appear clearly. Each generalizes from matters of vital importance to matters of communal importance. Viewed as an inquiry that always falls short of science, casuistry also demonstrates the inherent kinship of religion and morality as matters of the heart.

The next paragraphs of the lecture further contrast the practicality of vital inquiries and the uselessness of science. Then he inserts a paragraph that only partially flows from the previous discussion:

> It would be useless to enumerate the other sciences since it would only be to reiterate the same declaration. As long as they are not looked at as practical, and so degraded to pot-boiling arts—as our modern writers degrade the philosophy of religion, in claiming that it is practical—for what difference does it make whether the pot to be boiled is today's or the hereafter's? They are all such that it would be far too little to say that they are valuable to us. Rather let our hearts murmur "blessed are we" if the immolation of our being can weld together the smallest part of the great cosmos of ideas to which the sciences belong.[35]

The first part of this paragraph continues Peirce's previous argument. Science is not unconditionally useless, rather its practicality simply should not be of immediate focus. Science investigates a problem and then debates the cogency of its results. Usefulness may fall from these investigations, but that does not define their goal. Peirce admires the classical scientists (for example, Newton and Galileo) whose experiments only found practical application centuries later. If this explains the first part of this paragraph, confusion still resides in the last sentences. What does Peirce mean when he says, "it would be far too little to say that [the sciences] are valuable to us"? Perhaps this statement asserts that looking only to the value of science, that is, to its practicality, narrows its focus to the particularities of the here and now and demeans its greater task, which is to examine the world ceaselessly and to articulate hypothesized laws or generalities. Scientific examination generates ideas about the world, and Peirce claims that "weld[ing] together" these ideas on the "the smallest part of the great cosmos of ideas" defines the duty incumbent on every scientist. Performing this noble duty, however, seems to require "the immolation of our being"; indeed Peirce counsels us to consider ourselves "blessed" if we sacrifice ourselves in contributing to this "welding" project.

I contend that these sentences directly apply Peirce's anti-nominalism to his theories about science and to his views of the self.[36] Nominalists, who perceive reality only in the particularities of life, assert such particularity as the value of science, its clear usefulness in and for the here and now. Nominalists extend the individualism inherent to issues of "vital importance" to what Peirce claims are the general inquiries of science. Analogously, Peirce's realism (antinominalism) embraces the real generality of concepts like science, human or person. Both general concepts negate or immolate the individual self; one (science) negates the self's particular needs for the sake of producing truths that may not be "of value" for generations; the other (person) negates the self's particular sense of self ("vital interests") for the sake of that examination (science) that forms part of the "great cosmos of ideas." The reality or truth of the self is not its individuality but its self-transcending generality. Only through immolation, however, can one attain self-transcendence, and only through self-transcendence can one reach self-possession.

Peirce's portrait of the self is refined a bit later in his lecture. In the following paragraph, he collapses the dichotomy he has carefully set up between science and matters of vital importance:

> Were I willing to make a single exception to the principle I thus enunciate, and to admit that there was one study which was at once scientific and yet vitally important, I should make that exception in favor of logic; for the reason that if we fall into the error of believing that vitally important questions are to be decided by reasoning, the only hope of salvation lies in formal logic, which demonstrates in the clearest manner that reasoning itself testifies to its own ultimate subordination to sentiment. It is like a Pope who should declare *ex cathedra* and call upon all the faithful to implicitly believe on pain of damnation by the power of the keys that he was *not* the supreme authority.[37]

Logic acts as the translator—or interpretant—for sentiment and science. Logic can function in this manner because of its essential connection to psychology or, as Peirce would prefer, phenomenology. Chapter 5 reviewed Peirce's early resistance to a separate science of psychology and his eventual capitulation to its success in proving itself a science. Never, though, does he grant that psychology supersedes logic. His precise demarcation of consciousness and mind delegates only the latter to psychology. Logic concerns itself with consciousness because logic depends for its operations upon the perceptual judgments of consciousness. These judgments constitute the Secondness of consciousness and themselves depend upon the Firstness of consciousness, that is, pure feeling. Peirce images feeling or virtual consciousness as the bottomless lake that forms the base of his metaphor for how signs—always public and always material—become literally incorporated in and by this first consciousness. He articulates how signs, through mediation with and by other signs, constitute second consciousness (the level of perceptual judgments) and third consciousness (the level of self-consciousness or reasoning). Distinct from continental psychologists and from James, Peirce's quest is not to reconcile the study of consciousness to the empirical demands of natural science, but to focus on the construction from external signs of consciousness itself. He calls consciousness "that inward aspect of mind, which we egotistically call *ours*; though in truth it is we who float upon its surface and belong to it more than it belongs to us."[38] Peirce mutates a defining question of psychology into one of ontology and solves it in two ways. First he diagrams the evolution of logic (Thirdness) from feeling (Firstness) and then he insists that since the components of consciousness are signs, and since signs are generals, the self as an individual is itself just a component of that semeiotic generality. Logic is the most general, non-individual aspect of the self. Yet according to Peirce it is only through logic that one can perceive the dependence of logic on feeling (sentiment) and the ultimate nonreality of all that is particular in the self (matters of vital importance). Just as the Roman Catholic faithful accept the pope as the highest authority who is yet not the ultimate authority, so Peirce counsels persons to accept logic as the authority in the self that deconstructs its authority about the self. Logic, like the Pope, is the medium of salvation.

Through the above extended reading I have been arguing that Peirce's so-called scientism, his anti-nominalism and his prioritizing of logical analysis all structure a view of the self whose only reality is grounded in public signs and communally shared traditions and customs. By this view of the self, the only legitimate self-assertion is self-immolation. If there be any doubt about these suggested links of logic and science to subjectivity, Peirce himself draws the connecting line in the next paragraph of his lecture:

> Among vitally important truths there is one which I verily believe—and which men of infinitely deeper insight than mine have believed—to be solely supremely important. It is that vitally important facts are of all truths the veriest trifles. For the only vitally important matter is *my* concern, business, and duty— or yours. Now you and I—what are we? Mere cells of the social organism. Our deepest sentiment pronounces the verdict of our own insignificance. Psychological analysis shows that there is nothing which distinguishes my personal identity except my faults and limitations—or if you please, my blind will, which it is my highest endeavor to annihilate.[39]

The human or person does not exist outside the communal context ("the social organism"); to some community we owe the habits of thought and action that form our "deepest sentiment" and hence the most general horizon of our being. As such, that sentiment decrees our individual "insignificance." Peirce claims that "psychological analysis" supports his position, but certainly this is not the psychology of James, Wundt, Hamilton, or Bain. Peirce takes the common psychological insight that humans learn through reaction (Secondness) and changes it to claim that we learn through error ("faults and limitations"). As he argues in an early essay, our first encounter with a thing or situation usually results in some degree of error in our assessment or reaction to it, and this error creates a self-image by solidifying the nonself.[40] Here again, self-assertion is simultaneously self-negation, a characterizing trait of American Puritanism. Peirce equates this self-assertion to "blind will," an obvious criticism of William James, whose account of the self revolves so completely around a will that is clearly not blind, a will that purposefully subtends a person's consciousness and actions.

Peirce's next paragraph is especially important with regard to the Puritan imaginary and American mythos we are examining. Peirce gestures to the social consequences of rejecting his view of the self:

> To pursue "topics of vital importance" as the first and best can lead only to one or other of two terminations—either on the one hand what is called, I hope not justly, Americanism, the worship of business, the life in which the fertilizing stream of genial sentiment dries up or shrinks to a rill of comic tit-bits, or else on the other hand, to monasticism, sleepwalking in this world with no eye nor heart except for the other [world].[41]

This passage displays Peirce's fundamental concern for humans' capacity for relationship. What will be one's stance toward the Other? Will one be so caught up in one's own concerns—specifically the profit making that characterizes America's "worship of business"—that one cannot relate to others or can relate only superficially? Or will one be so fully self-denying that one sees others only in terms of that for which one has denied oneself, or not at all? Peirce advocates a middle position in which persons affirm themselves *through* denying themselves and through that denial affirm the greater realities of their community, the community of humankind, and the largest community of the cosmos. Chapter 5 discussed this same pattern of self-affirmation through self-denial and demonstrated its links to Puritan understandings of self and community. Peirce rejects the American culture that visibly follows the "gospel of greed" in favor of an imagined American culture that demands compassionate coexistence mediated by the gospel of Jesus. Actualizing the myth, he suggests, will require an interplay of logic and sentiment:

> The supreme commandment of the Buddhisto-christian religion is, to generalize, to complete the whole system even until continuity results and the distinct individuals weld together. Thus it is, that while reasoning and the science of reasoning strenuously proclaim the subordination of reasoning to sentiment, the very supreme commandment of sentiment is that man should generalize, or what the logic of relatives shows to be the same thing, should become welded into the universal continuum, which is what true reasoning consists in.[42]

Matters of the heart form the "cornerstone of our conduct," the ingrained habits of custom and tradition. Persons can unveil this reliance of human nature on matters of the heart through logic, the only science that "strenuously proclaim[s] the subordination of reasoning to sentiment." But if the essence of our being expresses the particularities—the idiosyncrasies, proclivities, and blindnesses—of our self and community, the "supreme commandment" of these particularities seeks their "immolation" in order to "become welded into the universal continuum."

Only logic can illuminate this highest calling of sentiment, and only logic prevents our interpreting the "welding" process as a glorification of sameness. Chapter 5 discussed in detail Peirce's theory of continuity (synechism) and his complex understanding of generality. Welding oneself into the cosmic continuum does not entail a complete loss of self but requires immolation of just those aspects of self that enforce the separation of persons and perpetuate the blindnesses that constitute the particularities of our communities. Peirce names this requirement for self-immolation the "supreme commandment of the Buddhisto-christian religion" because he is fascinated by the lectures he has heard on the Buddhist search for nirvana, and he considers this search the core of the Christian gospel. Importantly, both Christians and Buddhists need guidance in that search. Thus immolating the blindness of one's community mandates, paradoxically, the aid and consensus of that or some other community. Truth is produced within communities of inquiry but is only corroborated if those communities can engage with other communities without that truth requiring emendation. Since emendation is always required, however, truth is infinitely delayed in the continuous production of generality, that is, in the unceasing process of "welding" together small parts of the "great cosmos of ideas."

The Unthought and Multiculturalism

The mutations of concepts within this book are multiple. Peirce and James mutate European currents of thought about science and some of its attending concepts; they continue the ongoing mutation of America's Puritan imaginary; and each pragmatist philosophically mutates his society's image of the American self.

Peirce, like James, fully engages European debates about the nature of science and the possibilities and limitations of scientifically studying the human. Moreover, each pragmatist assumes the importance of the concepts of consciousness, causality, will, action, and belief; and each exerts himself in reconciling his commitment to human purposiveness with his desire to promulgate science. The resulting transpositions of those psychological concepts are similar enough to produce a discursive field, which we name American pragmatism. The differences between Peirce and James, however, are real and profound. To honor those differences amid asserting the construction of an indigenously American philosophy, I turned to the cultural spaces out of which pragmatism arises. In reading the pragmatists' texts against one another, I became convinced that the imaginary formations of America as a Puritan Christian nation importantly articulate the cultural space of pragmatism. In this concluding chapter my central goal has been to show this religious subtext. As such it bears repeating that Puritanism remains only a vague conditioning ground of pragmatism. Certainly much of the pragmatists' writings never mention anything apparently religious, and often when they do, the gestures seem rhetorical and unimportant, an unconscious by-product of their Victorian society. I contend, however, that a close examination of the pragmatists' concern for what counts as science, psychology, and the human demonstrates how their mutations of the concepts of consciousness, causality, will, action, and belief are guided by visions of the self that derive from their culture's Puritan imaginary.

The Puritan imaginary itself involves mutation, both historical and intellectual. The notion of the Puritan that influenced Peirce and James only vaguely links to seventeenth- and eighteenth-century Puritanism. The Puritan imaginary is not creedal, but mythic and evocative. In the prologue I compared the mythic function of the Puritan imaginary to three myths that, according to Mark Peterson, sustain the so-called declension narrative even in the face of ruthless critique.[43] I renamed those three myths the myth of origins (where did we—that is, Americans—come from?), the myth of the exemplary life (who are we [supposed to be]?), and the myth of community (what are our goals?). The first question is one of identity; the second, of ethics; and the third, of politics. The power of the Puritan imaginary, I have argued, is its ability to conjoin these three registers in a narrative that projects really and falsely (as a mirror image is both real and illusionary) a coherent story about America's past, present, and future. Holding the writings of Peirce and James up to the Puritan imaginary, it is evident that in them the question of politics is subsumed under (or repressed by) questions of identity and ethics. Or perhaps it is better to say that the political tenor of the writings of Peirce and James come through clearly in the fact that they answer the political question of the Puritan imaginary (what are our goals?) in ways eerily disjunctive to the social complexities and tensions that surround them.[44] Peirce's synechistic account of habit and James's tychistic account of will could be applied to (and emended in the face of) the economic and cultural (gender and race) contradictions of the late nineteenth century. Instead, Peirce and James absorb the Gilded Age's use of the Puritan to evoke a particular, ethical (not political) mode of being in the world. To them, the Puritan character displays paradoxical allegiances to head and heart, to self-assertion and self-abnegation, to private sentiment and public obligation. The pragmatists appropriate this paradox toward different ends, and in articulating this difference we have seen how Peirce functions as the operative unthought of James. James continually tries to resolve the Puritan paradox in an account of the self that praises individual will and universalizes or mythologizes the will's capacity for both self-sufficiency and world-saving choices. His attempted resolution of the Puritan paradox fails since his texts repeatedly reinstate it through his unwavering commitments to both head and heart (science and religion). Peirce's pragmaticism refuses to resolve the Puritan paradox of the self. In so doing Peirce rejects his peer's popular version of the American self and offers a theory of subjectivity that can be seen as both the condition of possibility and the opposite of James's. I contend that pragmaticism plays like a laughing imp between the lines of James's American self; through it Peirce insists on the unreality of the individual and the central importance of community for forming the ethical self through tradition and custom and for demanding from the self ascesis, or the disciplined construction of subjectivity through self-examination and public confession.[45]

Today, we may understandably reject Peirce's unclouded belief in a single process of science, his implicit assumption of progress, and his lack of any substantial social or political critique. Nonetheless, his pragmaticism joins the intellectual forces of formal logic, synechistic cosmology, psychological phenomenology, and antinominalist philosophy to present a vision of the self amenable to and healing of some postmodernist dilemmas. These dilemmas are many, but a familiar one opposes the poststructuralist affirmation of singularity and difference against the structuralist assumptions of commonality and sameness. The poststructuralist critique arises from a keen awareness that claims of commonality and sameness too often function to hide (repress and efface) difference and thus foreclose effective political challenge. But the pendulum's swing toward what Peirce would call "nominalist" assertions of singularity (wherein general terms are merely heuristic categories) also slips into political impotency.[46] Put simply, post-structuralists and deconstructionists (with whom I am in large agreement) nominalistically assert a radical difference, the subsequent social individualism of which can result in assertions of incommensurability. Yet claims for generality or commonality are rightly received suspiciously. I have tried to show how Peirce's pragmaticism posits the reality of difference through a theory of singularity (tychism) that rejects the nominalist assumption of the priority of the individual (or, politically, of individual rights). Instead, tychism only makes sense within and affirms the necessity and reality of continuity (synechism). Peirce warns, however, that continuity of community comes at the price of exacting duty and even an immolation of some particularities of the self in the mutual production of slowly agreed-upon and rigorously tested generalities. These generalities—the ground of Peirce's realism—are not commonalities or samenesses. Equally for the law of gravity and for the disputed truths of human being, actualization of a general is simultaneously its instantiation and its fragmentation.

Notes

Abbreviations

CP   Charles S. Peirce, *Collected Papers*, vols. 1–6 ed. Charles Hartshorne and Paul Weiss; vols. 7–8, ed. A. W. Burks (Cambridge, Mass.: Harvard University Press, 1931–35, 1958). Citations given by volume and paragraph (e.g., "8.36" refers to vol. 8, par. 36).

Discussions   William Hamilton, *Discussions on Philosophy and Literature, Education and University Reform*, 3d ed. (London: Blackwood, 1856)

DLPT   Alexander Bain. *Dissertations on Leading Philosophical Topics* (New York: Longmans, Green, 1903)

Ethics   Wilhelm Wundt, *Ethics: An Investigation of the Facts and Laws of the Moral* Life. Vol. 3, *The Principles of Morality and the Departments of the Moral Life*, 2d ed., trans. Margaret Floy Washburn (New York: Macmillan, 1907)

Ethik   Wilhelm Wundt, *Ethik: Eine Untersuchung der Tatsachen und Gesetze des Sittlichen Lebens*, Vierte umgearbeitete Auflage; Drei Bände: Dritter Band, *Die Prinzipien der Sittlichkeit und die Sittlichen Lebensgebiete* (Stuttgart: Ferdinand Enke, 1912)

EW   Hermann von Helmholtz, *Epistemological Writings: The Paul Hertz / Moritz Schlick Centenary Edition of 1921*, ed. Robert S. Cohen and Yehuda Elkana, trans. Malcolm F. Lowe (Boston: Reidel, 1977)

JERTAC   Joseph A. Conforti, *Jonathan Edwards, Religious Tradition, and American Culture* (Chapel Hill: University of North Carolina Press, 1995)

Life   Joseph Brent, *Charles Sanders Peirce: A Life* (Bloomington: Indiana University Press, 1993)

Metaphysics   William Hamilton, *Lectures on Metaphysics and Logic*. Vol. 1, *Metaphysics*, ed. Henry L. Mansel and John Veitch (Boston: Gould and Lincoln, 1868)

Outlines   Wilhelm Wundt, *Outlines of Psychology*, trans. Charles Hubbard Judd, 3d rev. English ed. from the 7th rev. German ed. (New York: Stechert, 1907)

PMT	William James, *Pragmatism and the Meaning of Truth* (Cambridge, Mass.: Harvard University Press, 1978)
PPP	Wilhelm Wundt, *Principles of Physiological Psychology*. Vol. 1, *Introduction: Part I. The Bodily Substrate of the Mental Life*, trans. from the 5th German ed. of 1902 by E. B. Titchener (New York: Macmillan, 1910; reprint, New York: Kraus, 1969)
Principles	William James, *The Principles of Psychology* (Cambridge, Mass.: Harvard University Press, 1983)
RLT	Charles Sanders Peirce, *Reasoning and the Logic of Things*, ed. Kenneth L. Ketner and Hilary Putnam (Cambridge, Mass.: Harvard University Press, 1992)
SW	Charles Sanders Peirce, *Charles S. Peirce: Selected Writings*, ed. Philip P. Wiener (New York: Dover, 1966)
SWHH	Hermann von Helmholtz, *Selected Writings of Hermann von Helmholtz*, ed. Russell Kahl (Middletown, Conn.: Wesleyan University Press, 1971)
UP	Jan Dawson, *The Unusable Past: America's Puritan Tradition, 1830–1930* (Chico, Calif.: Scholars, 1984)
VRE	William James, *The Varieties of Religious Experience: A Study in Human Nature* (New York: Modern Library, 1902)
WWJ	William James, *The Writings of William James*, ed. John J. McDermott (Chicago: University of Chicago Press, 1977)

Introduction

1. See the excellent collections of essays in Morris Dickstein, ed., *The Revival of Pragmatism: New Essays on Social Thought, Law, and Culture* (Durham, N.C.: Duke University Press, 1998), and in Chantal Mouffe, ed., *Deconstruction and Pragmatism* (New York: Routledge, 1996).

2. Richard Rorty, Introduction, in John P. Murphy, *Pragmatism: From Peirce to Davidson* (Boulder, Colo.: Westview, 1990), 4–5.

3. Frank Lentricchia, *Ariel and the Police: Michel Foucault, William James, Wallace Stevens* (Madison: University of Wisconsin Press, 1988), 106. Lentricchia narrates the political and apolitical character of James's value-laden pragmatism, noting memorably how James both "out-Marxes" and 'un-Marxes" Marx (128). For another literary critic's use of pragmatism, see Richard Poirier, *Poetry and Pragmatism* (Cambridge, Mass.: Harvard University Press, 1992).

4. See James Kloppenberg, "Pragmatism: An Old Name for Some New Ways of Thinking?" in Dickstein, *Revival of Pragmatism*, 111–17.

5. Edward C. Moore, *American Pragmatism: Peirce, James, and Dewey* (New York: Columbia University Press, 1961), vii.

6. A. J. Ayer, *The Origins of Pragmatism: Studies in the Philosophy of Charles Sanders Peirce and William James* (San Francisco: Freeman, Cooper, 1968), quoted in John E. Smith, *Purpose and Thought: The Meaning of Pragmatism* (New Haven, Conn.: Yale University Press, 1978), 1.

7. Bruce Aune, *Rationalism, Empiricism, and Pragmatism: An Introduction* (New York: Random House, 1970), 104.

8. H. S. Thayer, *Meaning and Action: A Critical History of Pragmatism* (New York: Bobbs-Merrill, 1968), 1.

9. Dickstein, *Revival of Pragmatism*, 1.

10. Robert J. Roth, *Radical Pragmatism: An Alternative* (New York: Fordham University Press, 1998), xiv. The single quote marks do not refer to a specific text, but function as an indication of how common is this characterization of pragmatism.

11. For two further assumptions of the American quality of pragmatism, see the following: Richard Rorty writes that pragmatism "names the chief glory of our country's intellectual tradition" in *Consequences of Pragmatism* (Minneapolis: University of Minnesota Press, 1982), 160. Martin Heidegger calls pragmatism "the American interpretation of Americanism" in *The Question concerning Technology and Other Essays*, trans. William Lovitt (New York: Harper and Row, 1977), 153. For an interesting essay that asks this same question tangentially, see "Do American Philosophers Exist? Visions of American Philosophy and Culture," in John J. Stuhr, *Genealogical Pragmatism: Philosophy, Experience, and Community* (Albany: State University of New York Press, 1997), 21–44.

12. My studies have included R. W. Emerson, John Fiske, Chauncey Wright, Francis E. Abbot, Oliver W. Holmes, Jr., Josiah Royce, and John Dewey.

13. The National Academy of Sciences was formed in 1863 specifically to function in an advisory capacity to the federal government.

14. See Paul F. Boller, Jr., *American Thought in Transition: The Impact of Evolutionary Naturalism, 1865–1900* (Chicago: Rand McNally, 1969), 2–22; Kenneth Ketner and Hilary Putnam, "Introduction: The Consequences of Mathematics," in *RLT* 4–36; and George H. Daniels, *Science in American Society: A Social History* (New York: Knopf, 1971).

15. Joseph L. Blau, *Men and Movements in American Philosophy* (New York: Prentice Hall, 1952), 9.

16. For a recent account of the Cambridge Metaphysical Club see Louis Menand, *The Metaphysical Club: A Story of Ideas in America* (New York: Farrar, Straus and Giroux, 2001), chap. 9.

17. As will become clear as the text proceeds, "mutation" of a question may entail placing it in a larger frame, investigating the stakes involved in asking the question, and/or emphasizing one aspect of the question over other or related aspects.

18. I was inspired in my development of the Puritan imaginary by Andrew Delbanco's chapter on "The Puritan Legacy" in Delbanco, *The Puritan Ordeal* (Cambridge, Mass.: Harvard University Press, 1989). I should note as well the influence of Sacvan Bercovitch, *The Puritan Origins of the American Self* (New Haven, Conn.: Yale University Press, 1975), and Paul K. Conkin, *Puritans and Pragmatists: Eight Eminent American Thinkers* (New York: Dodd, Mead, 1968). I use both of these texts in my chapters on Peirce and James. Bercovitch does not engage the pragmatists, though his argument is invaluable to me in giving a social context and thick description of the rhetorical poignancy of the term *Puritan*. Conkin's text reads as a traditional history of ideas and thus differs from my attempt to prioritize concepts and social intellectual formations over individual biographies. The latter difference also applies to two texts that I really do not engage but have read and appreciated: William A. Clebsch, *American Religious Thought: A History* (Chicago: University of Chicago Press, 1973), and Perry Miller, *Errand into the Wilderness* (Cambridge, Mass.: Harvard University Press, 1956). Indeed, Clebsch seems to me paradigmatic of scholarship on pragmatism in insisting on its American character while yet admitting that "being American" is "something at once obvious and elusive. . . . Rather than define it [being American], this book means to exemplify it" (3). Clebsch then goes on to list a number of traits that define being American (for example, "more voluntary than organic, more diverse than standard, more personal than institutional,

more practical than visionary or (in that sense) mystical" [3]), but he does not argue for them or give them any social, religious, or cultural explanation.

19. Bruce Fink, *A Clinical Introduction to Lacanian Psychoanalysis: Theory and Technique* (Cambridge, Mass.: Harvard University Press, 1997), 24.

20. By "matters of the heart," I mean ethics, as the term applies to reflections both on one's relations to other humans and to one's relation to God. Here it is best to have in mind Foucault's discussion of ethics as ascesis, or tasks of self-forming, and questions of the possibility and limitations of that task. See the interview "On the Genealogy of Ethics: An Overview of Work in Progress" in *The Foucault Reader*, ed. Raul Rabinow (New York: Pantheon, 1984), 340–72.

21. For an intriguing account of how the Puritan imaginary—as America's hegemonic self-image—specifically sustains racist words and practices, see Paul R. Griffin's *Seeds of Racism in the Soul of America* (Naperville, Ill.: Sourcebooks, 2000).

Prologue

1. William Lamont, *Puritanism and Historical Controversy* (Buffalo, N.Y.: McGill-Queen's University Press, 1996), 1. Lamont mentions Henry Parker's 1641 complaint about the term, as well as one from Thomas Fuller in 1655.

2. Raphael Samuel, "The Discovery of Puritanism, 1820–1914: A Preliminary Sketch," in *Revival and Religion since 1700: Essays for John Walsh*, ed. Jane Garnett and Colin Matthew (Rio Grande, Ohio: Hambledon, 1993), 201.

3. Margo Todd, *Christian Humanism and the Puritan Social Order* (New York: Cambridge University Press, 1987), 9.

4. Darren Staloff, *The Making of an American Thinking Class: Intellectuals and Intelligentsia in Puritan Massachusetts* (New York: Oxford University Press, 1998), 192.

5. Peter Lake, "Defining Puritanism—Again?" in *Puritanism: Transatlantic Perspectives on a Seventeenth-Century Anglo-American Faith*, ed. Francis J. Bremer (Boston: Massachusetts Historical Society, 1993), 4, 6.

6. Benedict Anderson, *Imagined Communities: Reflections on the Origin and Spread of Nationalism*, rev. ed. (New York: Verso, 1991), 6.

7. Ibid.

8. The other two parts are the symbolic and the real.

9. For the following discussion of the Lacanian imaginary, I draw upon Bruce Fink, *A Clinical Introduction to Lacanian Psychoanalysis*, (Cambridge, Mass.: Harvard University Press, 1997), 24–25, 32–33; and Alain Vanier, *Lacan*, trans. Susan Fairfield (New York: Other Press, 2000), 17–33. Fink carefully distinguishes the unification of self-understanding through the imaginary from the infusion of normative ideals that comes with the symbolic "overwriting" the imaginary (87–90). Vanier discusses this same point in terms of the "other" of the imaginary and the "Other" of the symbolic (26).

10. *JERTAC.*

11. *UP.*

12. *UP*, 2.

13. See Andrew Delbanco, *The Puritan Ordeal* (Cambridge, Mass.: Harvard University Press, 1989), chap. 8, which examines American literature and demonstrates how the word *Puritan* is used to signify a range of subjective and political positions.

14. Arminianism counters the strict, Calvinist doctrine of predestination with an emphasis on free will and belief in the possibility of universal salvation.

15. *UP*, 4.

16. *JERTAC*, 35. This revisionist understanding of the Second Great Awakening was first put forward by Jon Butler, "Enthusiasm Described and Decried: The Great Awakening as Interpretive Fiction," *Journal of American History* 69 (1982): 305–25. See also Frank Lambert, *Inventing the Great Awakening* (Princeton, N.J.: Princeton University Press, 1999). Lambert carries the arguments of Conforti and Butler back to the eighteenth century and maintains that the disjunction between the revivalistic events and their narrative interpretation was well known and debated even as it was occurring.

17. *UP*, 4.

18. I will discuss this further with regard to William Hamilton in chapter 3.

19. *JERTAC*, 3.

20. *UP*, 14.

21. *UP*, 13. Dawson reaches this conclusion through a reading of an 1843 essay by John Greenleaf Whittier.

22. *UP*, 26.

23. *UP*, 35–38.

24. *UP*, 43–44. Richard E. Wentz supports Dawson's account in his article, "John Williamson Nevin and American Nationalism," *Journal of the American Academy of Religion* 58, no. 4 (Winter 1990): 617–32. He quotes a historian of Mormonism who states that the religious language of the mid–nineteenth century combined "Enlightenment roots" and "romantic flowering" (619). Wentz correctly links the Romantic strain to transcendentalism, a philosophy of immanent influence to the young Peirce and James (620). Wentz's protagonist, Nevin, critiqued this mainstream American religiosity, calling it "Puritanism" and "false Protestantism." Wentz notes that Nevin gave "little critical attention to the justification of the usage" of the term *Puritanism* (620), but to me the presence of the term substantiates the accounts of Dawson and Conforti. *Puritanism* was an ideologically effective term and that in itself justified Nevin's employment of it.

25. Each of these meanings of *Puritan* is hegemonic and thus bolsters Paul Griffin's condemnation of Puritanism as fundamentally racist (and, by extension of his argument, sexist), as he asserts in his *Seeds of Racism* (Naperville, Ill.: Sourcebooks, 2000).

26. *UP*, 78.

27. *JERTAC*, 20–21.

28. *JERTAC*, 8, 27, 108–9.

29. *JERTAC*, 31–35. Conforti discusses Butler's finding in "Enthusiasm Described and Decried" that the first description of the First Great Awakening as the "broad, inclusive, and familiar" event we now take for granted occurs in Joseph Tracy's 1841 publication, *The Great Awakening: A History of the Revival of Religion in the Time of Edwards and Whitefield*.

30. *JERTAC*, 149.

31. Both quotations are from *JERTAC*, 148. A few pages later, Conforti comments on Barett Wendell's *Cotton Mather: The Puritan Priest* (1891): "It shows how descendants carefully picked the bones of ancestors and thereby fashioned a usable Puritan past" (155). Wendell depicts the Puritan life as "strenuous," a term that William James picks up in his lectures on pragmatism and to which I shall return in chapter 6. I wish to note, again, that in Conforti's and Dawson's histories, *Puritan* is a hege-

monic term which sustains the marginalization of non-hegemonic groups such as slaves, freed slaves, women, and immigrants.

32. *UP*, 77–78.

33. Consciousness, will, and character all are concepts I focus on in this book.

34. *UP*, 82–85.

35. *UP*, 86.

36. William James uses this phrase, among others, to describe the pragmatic character; see "The Present Dilemma in Philosophy," in *PMT*, 13.

37. Both quotations are from *JERTAC*, 159.

38. Mark A. Peterson, *The Price of Redemption: The Spiritual Economy of Puritan New England* (Stanford, Calif.: Stanford University Press, 1997), 6.

Chapter 1

1. These same priorities guided my choice of Wilhelm Wundt in chapter 2, and William Hamilton and Alexander Bain in chapters 3 and 4.

2. See n. 17 in the introduction for my explication of "mutation."

3. Robert S. Cohen and Yehuda Elkana, Introduction, in The editors list Helmholtz's contributions as including "cognitive and sensory psychology of hearing and vision, theoretical mechanics, electrodynamics, physical and chemical thermodynamics, electrochemistry, geometry, applied mathematics, medical experimentation and instrumentation, hydrodynamics, esthetics [*sic*] of musical theory and painting, atmospheric physics, epistemology, and more" (*EW*, x).

4. David Cahan, Introduction, in Helmholtz, *Science and Culture: Popular and Philosophical Essays*, ed. David Cahan (Chicago: University of Chicago Press, 1995), xii–xiv.

5. Russell Kahl, Introduction, in xliv–xlv.

6. Hermann von Helmholtz, *Popular Lectures on Scientific Subjects*, trans. E. Atkinson, 1st and 2d series (New York: Longmans, Green, 1908).

7. *Life,* 83–87. Brent discusses the so-called Cambridge Metaphysical Club, its relation to the origins of pragmatism, and the controversy in the secondary literature surrounding the existence and importance of this club.

8. Five of the eight volumes of Peirce's *Collected Papers* contain at least one reference to Helmholtz. See James quotes Helmholtz extensively in *The Principles of Psychology*, resulting in at least twenty-five separate references. See *Principles*.

9. Helmholtz, "An Autobiographical Sketch," in *Popular Lectures*, 2d series, 266–91.

10. See David Cahan, ed., *Hermann von Helmholtz and the Foundations of Nineteenth-Century Science* (Berkeley: University of California Press, 1993), which the editor calls a collection of essays purporting "to analyze the entire range of Helmholtz's scientific work and to place it within its appropriate scientific and philosophical contexts" (4). While none of the essays treats Helmholtz as a psychologist, a few indicate how his ideas were picked up and reworked by psychologists.

11. *CP,* 8.36. I have seen only one reference exploring the relation of Helmholtz to American pragmatism, a brief mention in R. Steven Turner, "Consensus and Controversy: Helmholtz on the Visual Perception of Space," in Cahan, *Helmholtz and the Foundations*. Turner simply notes that an empirical account of spatial perception, "whether derived from Helmholtz or from Wundt, proved congenial to the British associationist tradition and to the temper of American pragmatism" (198).

12. Indeed, considering Peirce's and Helmholtz's mutual emphasis on the study of signs, it is instructive to ponder why Helmholtz is not an alternative (and merely less successful) progenitor of semiotics. Peirce uses both *semeiotic* and *semiotic,* and I have chosen to retain the more Greek spelling both because it signifies that Peirce's system is not the Saussurian system and because Peirce wished to stress the etymology from the Greek *semeion* as opposed to the Latin *semi.* See Max H. Fisch, "Peirce's General Theory of Signs," in *Peirce, Semeiotic, and Pragmatism: Essays by Max H. Fisch,* ed. Kenneth L. Ketner and Christian J. W. Kloesel (Bloomington: Indiana University Press, 1986), 322. My thanks to Frank Crouch for drawing my attention to this reference.

13. For examples from just one classic text, see H. S. Thayer, *Meaning and Action* (New York: Bobbs-Merrill, 1968), 83–86, 120–32, 145–53, 190–200.

14. Carl Hausman, *Charles S. Peirce's Evolutionary Realism* (Cambridge, Mass.: Harvard University Press, 1994). Evolutionary realism is, according to Hausman, a special form of realism, which represents Peirce's desire to integrate German transcendentalism, Platonic idealism, and scholastic realism. Peirce's neologism for this intellectual assemblage is *pragmaticism.* Early in his writing career, Peirce is more of a nominalist. In the early 1890s he rejects the incipient nominalism of his essay "How to Make Our Ideas Clear" and begins to center his pragmatism on the reality of possibles, a position inspired by rereading Aristotle.

15. "The Conservation of Force: A Physical Memoir" (lecture delivered at a meeting of the Physical Society of Berlin on July 23, 1847. Footnotes and appendices added in 1881), in *SWHH,* 3; emphasis added.

16. Ibid., 4; emphasis added.

17. The German term *Kraft* was translated as "force" in the first half of the nineteenth century and as "energy" in the second half.

18. "Conservation of Force," in *SWHH,* 10–16. See also "The Aim and Progress of Physical Science," in *SWHH,* 228–29.

19. Kenneth L. Ketner and Hilary Putnam, Introduction, in *RLT,* 88. The editors speak of Peirce's "physical cosmology," developed in response to scientists' reactions to the laws of thermodynamics.

20. *RLT,* 197–217.

21. Helmholtz consistently defends Kant's nativist assumption that time is an a priori form of intuition, though many of the physicist's experiments aimed at critiquing a nativist notion of space.

22. Research on the specific energies of nerves, begun by his teacher Johannes Müller, investigated how seemingly identical nerves can each process different sensations, such as heat or pressure. Through such experiments, the law of causality was applied to the question of the relation between "inner" and "outer" worlds. How, in other words, do objects "cause" particular sensations, and how do these sensations "cause" particular conceptions?

23. "The Facts of Perception," in *SWHH,* 393; emphasis added. Lamarckism or Darwinism are hinted at in this quotation, but as far as I know, neither evolutionary theorist expressed the process of natural selection quite so bluntly in terms of the law of causality.

24. "The Facts of Perception," in *EW,* 142. Russell Kahl, in editing this essay in *SWHH,* 390, references the last sentence as a quotation from Goethe's *Faust,* part 2; I added in brackets the German cited by Kahl.

25. In this sentence it must be stressed that the real is material but not actual, as will be more fully explained in chapter 5.

26. See "The Aim and Progress of Physical Science," in *SWHH*, 228: "We experience the laws of nature as objective forces. They cannot be arbitrarily chosen by or defined in our minds, as one might devise various systems of classification of animals and plants. . . . Whenever the conditions under which the law operates present themselves, the result must follow without arbitrariness, without choice, without our intervention; it must follow from the very necessity which governs the things of the external world as well as our perceptions."

27. Helmholtz here alludes intriguingly to a mental process untouched by the law of causality, a process Wilhelm Wundt will expand into a full theory of psychical causality as a process that operates in parallel with physical causality. See chapter 2.

28. The discussion of this paragraph depends on Sabine S. Gehlhaar, *Die frühpositivistische (Helmholtz) und phänomenlogische (Husserl) Revision der Kantischen Erkenntnislehre* (Cuxhaven: Junghans-Verlan, 1991), 68–73. Hereafter cited as Gehlhaar.

29. Cohen and Elkana, Introduction, in *EW*, xx. For more on unconscious inferences, see "The Facts of Perception," in *EW*, 130; and Helmholtz, *Handbuch der physiologischen Optik*, 2nd ed. (Hamburg: Voss, 1886–96), 582. See also Timothy Lenoir, "The Eye as Mathematician: Clinical Practice, Instrumentation, and Helmholtz's Construction of an Empiricist Theory of Vision," in Cahan, *Helmholtz and the Foundations*, 124–25.

30. Synechism and tychism will be fully explained in chapter 5.

31. "The Endeavor to Popularize Science," in *SWHH*, 338.

32. Cohen and Elkana quote Cassirer on this point in their introduction, in *EW*, xix.

33. "The Relation of the Natural Sciences to Science in General," in *SWHH*, 125–26.

34. Ibid.

35. For more on Helmholtz's opinions on the specialization of knowledge and the changes of nineteenth-century German universities, see "The Relation of the Natural Sciences to Science in General," in *SWHH*, 122–23, 128.

36. It is interesting that Peirce frames his struggles with Kant as a conscious repositioning of the scholastic debates about nominalism and realism in the scientific milieu of the nineteenth century (see chapter 5). Peirce never develops a theory of history, but perhaps he intuits that history cannot assert either continuity or discontinuity, but is precisely the discipline that struggles with the relation of the one to the other. As Hans Blumenburg notes, "'Scientific revolutions,' if one were to choose to take their radicalness literally, simply cannot be the ultimate concept of a rational conception of history; otherwise that conception would have denied to its object the very same rationality it wanted to assert for itself." Hans Blumenburg, *The Legitimacy of the Modern Age*, trans. Robert M. Wallace (Cambridge, Mass.: MIT Press, 1983), 465. Put differently, the discontinuity of radical events (scientific revolutions) cannot become the rule for history since it would make history a narration (continuity) of discontinuity. Foucault also views history as an imbrication of continuity and discontinuity, which is why he resented being pegged as a historian of discontinuity.

37. For a concise statement of *praktikos* and *pragmatikos* and how each is applied to Kant's metaphysic, see John Murphy, *Pragmatism: From Peirce to Davidson* (Boulder, Colo.: Westview, 1990), 40.

38. Cohen and Elkana quote Helmholtz's *Physiological Optics* to this effect in *EW*, xx.

39. Immanuel Kant, *Critique of Pure Reason*, trans. Norman Kemp Smith (New York: St. Martin's, 1965), A99, A138/B177.

40. Gehlhaar, 18, quoting M. Schlick's commentary on Helmholtz: "Die Empfindungsqualitäten gehören als solche sicherlich allein dem Buwußtsein an, durchaus nicht dem Nervensystem." See also Kant, *Critique of Pure Reason*, A78/B103 and A41.

41. "The Facts of Perception," in *EW*, 122. See also: "That which remains alike [through time], without dependence upon anything else, through every alternation of time, we call *substance*. The relationship which remains alike between altering magnitudes, we call the *law* connecting them. *What we perceive directly is only this law*" (139; emphasis added).

42. Work on the specific energies of nerves was done by Helmholtz's teacher and mentor, Johannes Müller.

43. Gehlhaar, 19: "Kant untersucht die Bedingungen der Möglichkeit der Wahrnehmung, nicht aber die Wahrnehmung selbst."

44. "The Facts of Perception," in *EW*, 131.

45. Ibid., 122.

46. Kahl, in *SWHH*, xxxi. Kahl is referring to Helmholtz's essay "The Origin and Correct Interpretation of Our Sense Impressions." See also Kant, *Critique of Pure Reason*, A49/B67, for Kant's denial that a thing can be known through relations. For an interesting discussion that does not directly treat Kantian transcendentalism but nonetheless illuminates its role in struggling with these questions, see Graham Richards, "The Absence of Psychology in the Eighteenth Century," *Studies in History, Philosophy, and Science*, 23, no. 2 (1992): 195–211.

47. *SW*, 117.

48. Michel Foucault, *The Order of Things: An Archaeology of the Human Sciences* (New York: Vintage, 1970). See "The Relation of the Natural Sciences to Science in General," in *SWHH*, 123, for Helmholtz's supposition of the importance of organization as one of the two marks that distinguish his century's science from previous centuries; see 138 for the other mark, the connection of ideas, enabled by a zealous attention to facts and a prioritizing of cause and effect. He lists the following: "every lost fragment of an ancient author, every gloss of a pedantic grammarian, every allusion of a Byzantine court-poet, every broken tombstone of a Roman official found in some corner of Hungary or Spain or Africa. . . . Add to this, in history, the study of original documents; the critical examination of papers accumulated in the archives of states and towns; the combination of details scattered in memoirs, in correspondence, and in biographies; and the deciphering of hieroglyphics and cuneiform inscriptions—and add in natural history the increasingly comprehensive classification of minerals, plants, and animals, living as well as extinct. " See also: "This organization [of facts] consists, first of all, in rather mechanical arrangements of materials, such as are to be found in our catalogues, lexicons, registers, indexes, digests, scientific and literary annuals, law codes, systems of natural history, and the like" (129).

49. "The Relation of the Natural Sciences to Science in General," in *SWHH*, 142.

50. Ibid., 138–39.

51. Ibid., 140. See also "The Aim and Progress of Physical Science" (1869), in *SWHH*, 223–25, for the characteristics of the "good scientist"; 125 for the lack of immediate practical results for most investigations. For the social changes wrought by science, see "The Relation of the Natural Sciences to Science in General," in *SWHH*, 139, where he quotes Bacon's "knowledge is power." Then, noting that industrial

changes have enabled such social changes, he comments, "Even the proudest, most obstinate despotisms of our time have been forced to consider removing restrictions on industry and conceding to the industrial middle classes a due voice in national councils." For more on the difference between German science and the science of France and England, see "The Aim and Progress of Physical Science," in *SWHH,* 245, where he asserts that the German scientist has "a total lack of fear over the implications of the knowledge of the complete truth." In France and England, however, scientists "have almost always had to bow to social or ecclesiastical prejudice." The history of America's reception to evolutionary theories would suggest that Helmholtz would see America as being in line with England and France.

52. *CP,* 5.100–101. Peirce asks his audience whether our knowledge that a stone will fall to the ground when dropped is due to "mere chance" or to "some *active general principle.*" He suggests the latter and proves it by letting go of a stone and watching it fall to the ground. Then he challenges his audience: "I told you so!—if anybody doubts this still, a thousand other such inductive predictions are getting verified every day, and he will have to suppose every one of them to be merely fortuitous in order reasonably to escape the conclusion that *general principles are really operative in nature.* That is the doctrine of scholastic realism." Peirce frames this discussion with a bet. In 5.95 he bets his audience a hundred to one that the stone will fall to the ground when released. Since no one takes up the bet, Peirce calls their professed nominalism a hypocrisy and gains empirical weight for his realism.

53. *CP,* 1.170: "How can one mind act upon another mind? How can one particle of matter act upon another at a distance from it? The nominalists tell us this is an ultimate fact—it cannot be explained. . . . what is meant is that we come up, bump against actions absolutely unintelligible and inexplicable, where human inquiries have to stop. . . . It is one of the peculiarities of nominalism that is continually supposing things to be absolutely inexplicable. That blocks the road of inquiry. But if we adopt the theory of continuity we escape this illogical situation."

54. *CP,* 6.348: "Get rid, thoughtful Reader, of the Ockhamistic prejudice of political partisanship that in thought, in being, and in development the indefinite is due to a degeneration from a primary state of perfect definiteness. The truth is rather on the side of the scholastic realists that the unsettled is the primal state, and that definiteness and determinateness, the two poles of settledness, are, in the large, approximations, developmentally, epistemologically, and metaphysically."

55. That real laws create real relations between events is the kernel of Peirce's logic of relatives, which is part of his theory of continuity, or synechism. I shall return to these claims in chapter 5, but the theory asserts the ontological status of laws as that of *esse in futuro,* on which see *CP,* 5.48 and 6.368. The end of *CP,* 6.368 states: "If, however, we admit that the law has a real being, not of the mode of being of an individual, but even more real, then the future necessary consequent of a present state of things is as real and true as that present state of things itself." For the place of mind and chance in Peirce see, for example, "The Doctrine of Necessity," in *SW,* 176.

56. *CP,* 1.180–202. He defines mathematics as that which "studies what is and what is not logically possible, without making itself responsible for its actual existence." Philosophy is a "*positive science,* in the sense of discovering what really is true; but it limits itself to so much of truth as can be inferred from common experience."

57. The metaphysical categories of first, second, and third are more general than the phenomenological categories. The icon is the Firstness of Thirdness (thirdness works phenomenologically through icon, index, and symbol), or what John Sheriff calls a "Third-Firstness." See John K. Sheriff, *Charles Peirce's Guess at the Riddle:*

Grounds for Human Significance (Bloomington: Indiana University Press, 1994), 28. The precise meaning of *icon*, however, has been a matter of some discussion in Peirce studies. See Hausman, *Peirce's Evolutionary Realism*, 88–90.

58. *Principles*, 249, 446–47. James may also have been drawing on J. S. Mill, whose account of causality discusses the complex network of factors that result in any single action. Peirce argues against Mill, noting that his phrasing of this insight— that nature is uniform—requires a deterministic view of the universe. See *RLT*, 198; *CP*, 1.92, 6.410–13.

Chapter 2

1. Biographical information was obtained primarily from Daniel B. Klein, *A History of Scientific Psychology: Its Origins and Philosophical Backgrounds* (New York: Basic, 1970), 816–20.

2. *Outlines*, 17. See also Klein, *History of Scientific Psychology*, 817.

3. Klein, *History of Scientific Psychology*, 826.

4. *PPP*, 3.

5. Ibid., 4.

6. Ibid., 16; emphasis added.

7. Ibid., 5; emphasis added.

8. *Ethics*, 23. I could only find the second edition translated, indicating a quite different reception of Wundt than of Helmholtz in America. For the German, see *Ethik*, 24: "Äußerlich wird dieser Zusammenhang [der Individualwille und Gesamtwille] durch alle die Momente der Kultur und Sitte bezeugt, in denen das übereinstimmende Fühlen und Denken einer Gemeinschaft sich ausprägt. Sprache, mythologische und religiöse Anschauungen, Lebensgewohnheiten und Normen des Handelns weisen hier auf gemeinsame geistige Erlebnisse hin, die an Umfang alles, was der einzelne für sich zurückbehalten mag, überragen." Washburn translates *Wille* as "consciousness" (unless Wundt changed his phrasing after the second edition), an obfuscation, in my opinion. Later in the same chapter, however, Wundt does connect volition and consciousness: "Das Kriterium für die Unterscheidung zwischen Individual- und Gesamtwille und innerhalb des letzteren wieder zwischen deren weiteren und engeren Gestaltungen ist für uns demnach kein hypothetisches oder metaphysisches, sondern ein tatsächliches, psychologisches, kein außerhalb des Bewußtseins liegendes, sondern ein vollbewußtes. Wille und Vorstellungsinhalt sind individuell, insoweit sie der individuellen Persönlichkeit spezifisch eigentümlich sind; sie gehören zu einem Gesamtbewußtsein, insoweit sie einer Gemeinschaft von Individuen gemeinsam sind" (*Ethik*, 36).

9. See the quotation from *PPP* on p. 41.

10. *Outlines*, 6. In light of this text's effort toward and interest in the history of psychology, it seems odd that Graham Richards places Wundt in a list of "German proto-Psychologists" that also includes Beneke, Herbart, Lotze, and Fechner. See Richards, "Absence of Psychology," 204. For more on the newness of using empirical methods in psychology, see Wundt's *Lectures on Human and Animal Psychology*, trans. J. E. Creighton and E. B. Titchener from the German 2d ed. of 1892 (New York: Macmillan, 1894; reprinted in *Significant Contributions to the History of Psychology 1750–1920*, ed. Daniel N. Robinson [Washington, D.C.: University Publications of America, 1977], 9).

11. *Outlines*, 5–6.

12. Ibid., 314.

13. Ibid., 315.

14. Ibid., 316–17.

15. He displays this deduction in *PPP*, 102: "If, then, experience teaches us that the molecular processes within our nervous system may have psychical concomitants, we can only say that we are here in presence of a fact which lies altogether beyond the cognisance of a molecular mechanics of nerve-substance, and consequently beyond the cognisance of any strictly physiological inquiry. It would fall within the scope of physiology only if we were able in some way to interpret the psychical processes themselves as molecular processes, i.e. in the last resort, as modes of motion or as physical energies. This, however, we cannot do: the attempt fails at once, under whatever guise it may be made. Psychical processes refuse to submit to any one of our physical measures of energy; and the physical molecular processes, so far as we are able to follow them, are seen to be transformed, variously enough, into one another, but never directly into psychical qualities. In saying this, we do not, of course, reject the idea that psychical processes may be regularly attended by an interchange of physical forces, which as such forms a proper object of co-ordinate investigation by the molecular mechanics of the nervous system; nor do we deny, what would naturally follow, that psychical symptoms may be taken as indicative of definite physiological molecular processes, and that these in their turn, if it ever happens that we know more about them, may be taken, under certain circumstances, as indicative of psychical conditions. But such a relation between the two departments is entirely compatible with their separate independence, with the impossibility, at any time or by any means, of the reduction of the one to the other." See also *Ethik*, 46–47: "So ergibt sich für die gesamte objektive Vorstellungswelt unseres Bewußtseins die notwendige Idee eines Parallelismus der Vorstellungen und der ihnen engsprechenden Bewegungsvorgänge ihres hypothetischen Substrats, der Materie. . . . Doch dieser Parallelismus bezieht sich nicht, wie es sich Spinoza dachte, auf zwei unabhängig voneinander gegebene unendliche Wirklichkeiten, sondern auf eine einzige, die wir in der Form der Vorstellungen so, wie sie uns unmittelbar gegeben ist, auffassen, in der Form der materiellen Bewegungsvorgaenge so, wie wir sie nach ihrer begrifflichen Verarbeitung und nach Abstraktion von den in der Erfahrung stets an sie gebundenen Gefühls- und Willensreaktionen voraussetzen."

16. *Outlines*, 367; cf. 252, 357.

17. Ibid., 10.

18. The quoted phrases are from Wundt, *Lectures on Human and Animal Psychology*, 237.

19. *Ethics*, 5. "Wenn wir von den einzelnen allein wirklichen Vorgängen unserer unmittelbaren seelischen Erfahrung absehen und bloß darauf reflektieren, daß wir Tätigkeiten und Ereignisse in uns wahrnehmen, so nennen wir vielmehr eben diese Abstraktion das Bewußtsein. Dieses drückt also lediglich die Tatsache aus, daß wir ein inneres Leben führen, ist aber von den einzelnen Vorgängen dieses Lebens ebensowenig verschieden, wie das physische Leben eine besondere Kraft ist, die außerhalb der sämtlichen physischen Lebensprozesse ein selbständiges Dasein hat." (*Ethik*, 2–3). For more about how psychological terms are formed by abstraction from the mental process, see *PPP*, 19 and 25, where Wundt calls such terms "class-concepts" (as opposed to substantial categories).

20. See *Ethik*, 11: "Sowohl die entscheidenden Gefühlsmotive wie die vor diesen zurücktretenden, die etwa an einem der Entscheidung vorangehenden Kampf der Motive beteiligt waren, setzen übrigens stets weiter zurückliegende Bedingungen voraus. Die Willensmotive erscheinen so überall als die letzten Ausläufer einer

Kausalreihe, die unserer Wahrnehmung nur unvollständig zugänglich ist, weil sie sich schließlich in die gesamte Vorgeschichte des individuellen Bewußtseins und in die diese Geschichte bestimmenden Bedingungen zurückverliert. Jede, auch die einfachste Willenshandlung ist so Endglied einer unendlichen Reihe, von der uns nur die letzten Glieder gegeben sind." Washburn translates this as follows: "All the feelings that motivate an action presuppose other causal conditions just as much as the motives that finally decide it. Feelings and desires are thus simply the last members of a causal series that is only to a very limited extent accessible to our introspection, since it ends by taking in the whole previous history of the individual consciousness and the sum total of the conditions which originally determined the latter. And so we see that every voluntary act, even the simplest, is the end of an infinite series, of which the last links alone are open to our observation" (*Ethics*, 10).

21. *Outlines*, 24.

22. Klein, *History of Scientific Psychology*, 849.

23. Wundt states that the psychology of his time is too entranced by a "deep-rooted, abstract doctrine of the will." He is implying both Schopenhauer and the eighteenth-century faculty psychologists. See *Outlines*, 216.

24. *PPP*, 28: "When . . . we ruled out all the movements that may possibly go on without the participation of consciousness, there remains but one class that bears upon it the constant and unmistakable signs of an expression of mental life,—the class of *external voluntary actions*."

25. *Outlines*, 18. For the concomitance of feelings, ideas, and volition, see *PPP*, 15: "This whole group of subjective experiences, in which feelings are the determining factors, may be brought under the title of *Gemuthsbewegungen und Willenshandlungen*. Of these, *Gemuthsbewegungen* is the wider term, since it covers volitional as well as affective processes." Feelings always accompany volition but not all feelings actually result in volition. For more on this point, see Wundt, *Lectures on Human and Animal Psychology*, 223.

26. For more on the connection of will and consciousness, see *Ethik*, 7: "Bewußtsein und Wille sind, soweit wir beide aus der subjektiven Wahrnehmung kennen und aus der objektiven Beobachtung anderer Wesen zu erschließen vermögen, untrennbar aneinander gebunden. Auch ist der Wille keine Funktion, die bald dem Bewußtsein zukommt und bald fehlt, sondern er ist eine integrierende Eigenschaft desselben." "So far as we know them in introspection and can infer them from external perception, consciousness and will are inseparably united. But will is not merely a function which sometimes accrues to consciousness and is sometimes lacking: it is an integral property of consciousness" (*Ethics*, 7).

27. *PPP*, 11; emphasis added.

28. Wundt, *An Introduction to Psychology*, trans. Rudolf Pinter (London: George Allen and Co., Ltd., 1912; reprint, New York: Arno, 1973). Attention is "that psychical perception of a narrow region of the content of consciousness" (16).

29. Wundt, *Lectures on Human and Animal Psychology*, 249.

30. Ibid.

31. Arthur L. Blumenthal, Introduction, in Wilhelm Wundt, *The Language of Gestures*, trans. J. S. Thayer, C. M. Greenleaf, and M. D. Silberman (The Hague: Mouton, 1973), 11.

32. Wundt, *Introduction to Psychology*, 17.

33. *Outlines*, 228.

34. Ibid., 251. See also Blumenthal, Introduction, in Wundt, *Language of Gestures*, 16.

35. *Ethics*, 41. "Bei geistigen Ereignissen vermögen wir höchstens die allgemein Richtung zu bestimmen, in der sie erfolgen, nie die besondere Gestaltung, die sie annehmen werden" (*Ethik*, 41).

36. *Outlines*, 90.

37. Ibid., 208.

38. Wundt, *Lectures on Human and Animal Psychology*, 210: "Feeling and conation always accompany our sensations and ideas; they determine our actions, and it is mainly from them that our whole mental life receives its bias and stamp of individuality." The final "them" in the sentence might refer to "actions" or to the preceding "feeling and conation"; I read it as the latter.

39. Ibid., 231.

40. Ibid., 234.

41. *Ethics*, 21. "Wie das Ich der Will in seiner Sonderung von den einzelnen Bewußtseinsinhalten, so ist die Persönlichkeit das Ich, als sich mit der Mannigfaltigkeit dieser Inhalte wieder erfüllt hat." Wundt's next section refers to the "selbstbewußtsein Persönlichkeit" (*Ethik*, 23).

42. *Ethics*, 38. "Seiner selbst sich besinnen heißt: der Persönlichkeit bewußt sein, und besonnen handeln heißt: mit dem Bewußtsein der Bedeutung handeln, welche die Motive und Zwecke für den Charakter des Wollenden besitzen" (*Ethik*, 39).

43. *Outlines*, 319.

44. *Ethics*, 48. "Die geistige Kausalität is die unmittelbare, uns direkt gegeben als Beziehung von Motiven und Zwecken; sie bedarf keiner diesem Tatbestand der psychischen Erlebnisse hinzugefuegten Voraussetzung." A few pages later Wundt argues that psychical causality is the more general of the two types of causality, such that physical causality is in fact a subordinate form of psychical causality ("Damit bleibt die mechanische eine Unterform der geistigen Kausalität" (*Ethik*, 47).

45. See n. 19 for this term.

46. *Ethics*, 56. "Unter Charakter verstehen wir demgemäß den aus der vorangegangenen geistigen Kausalität resultierenden Gesamterfolg, der sich selbst wieder an jeder neuen Wirkung als Ursache beteiligt" (*Ethik*, 54).

47. *Ethics*, 57; emphasis added. "Je gleichförmiger die Bedingungen des Charakters beschaffen sind, und je mehr sie sich in der individuellen Anlage zu festen sittlichen Tendenzen verdichtet haben, um so eher sind wir daher imstande, nicht nur nachträglich die erfolgten Handlungen aus dem Charaketer abzuleiten, sondern aus der Kenntnis desselben mit Wahrscheinlichkeit vorauszusagen, wie er auf bestimmte Motive reagieren werde. *Gerade bei diesen höchsten Formen gewinnt so die geistige Kausalität eine bis zu einem gewissen Grade dem Naturmechanismus gleichende Unveränderlichkeit*" (*Ethik*, 54; emphasis added).

48. Both quotations are from Wundt, *Lectures on Human and Animal Psychology*, 427.

49. *Ethics*, 26.

50. *Ethics*, 80. "Die objektive besteht darin, daß durch die altruistische Richtung des Handelns eine extensivere Wirkung des sittlichen Willens möglich wird, die den gemeinschaftlichen sozialen und humanen Zwecken zugute kommt. Die subjektive und vielleicht gewichtigere liegt darin, daß jedes unegoistische Handeln für uns eine Charakterprobe ist, an der wir den allgemeinen Wert der individuellen Persönlichkeit messen" (*Ethik*, 81–2).

51. Ralph Barton Perry, *The Thought and Character of William James*, briefer version (New York: Braziller, 1954), 142.

52. John O'Donnell, quoted in Ludy T. Benjamin, Jr., et. al., "Wundt's American Doctoral Students," *American Psychologist*, 47, no. 2 (1992), 123.

53. I am especially thinking of the Darwinian theories, though the effect and threat of Darwin's texts would not have been nearly so profound if the dominance of a similar (i.e., positivist or mechanistic) *Naturwissenschaft* were not already permeating society on all levels.

54. Wundt was first reader for a number of American doctoral students who wrote in Germany on ethical, philosophical, and theological themes: James F. Latimer, who wrote on Reid and Hamilton; Gottfried Fritschel (a naturalized U.S. citizen), who became a theologian at Wartburg Seminary in Iowa; James T. Bixley, who wrote on Spencer's *Ethics* and then became a Unitarian minister and published articles on Darwin, Huxley, and Spencer; Edward A. Pace, who wrote on "the relativity principle of Spencer's psychological theory of evolution"; and William H. Squires, who wrote on Jonathan Edwards and then taught psychology, logic and pedagogy at Hamilton College after leaving the ministry. This information is from Benjamin et al., "Wundt's American Doctoral Students," 126.

55. *Principles*, 182.

56. Ibid., 142.

57. Peirce attributes James's inability to broaden the notion of science to his peer's nominalism. Nominalism, as described in chapter 1, tends to block the road of inquiry by assuming some aspects of experience to be inexplicable. James ends "The Mind-Stuff Theory" chapter with just such an assumption. See *Principles*, 182: "The spiritualistic reader may nevertheless believe in the soul if he will; whilst the positivistic one who wishes to give a tinge of mystery to the expression of his positivism can continue to say that nature in her unfathomable designs has mixed us of clay and flame, of brain and mind, that the two things hang indubitably together and determine each other's being, but how or why, no moral may ever know." James walks between these two imagined readers, both of whom render "spiritual" things free from "scientific" (empirical) inquiry.

58. *Principles*, 142–45.

59. *Ethics*, 5. See p. 47 and n. 19.

60. *PMT*, 172–173. Chapter 6 will discuss radical empiricism in more detail; basically, the theory makes three claims: that experience generates all knowledge worthy of debate; that the relations between experiences are just as real as the experiences themselves; and that those real relations nullify any need for a trans-experiential frame of inquiry. In asserting that the relations between experiences are as real as the particular experiences themselves, James "radically" redefines *empiricism* and presents the traditional mind-body problem as a pseudoproblem.

Chapter 3

1. John Veitch, *Blackwood's Philosophical Classics: Hamilton* (Philadelphia: Lippincott, n.d.), 2–3.

2. J. S. Mill, *An Examination of Sir William Hamilton's Philosophy and of the Principal Philosophical Questions Discussed in His Writings*, 6th ed. (New York: Longmans, Green, 1889), 1.

3. Porter was the son-in-law of the New Haven theologian Nathaniel William Taylor.

4. Porter points to three articles in the *Edinburgh Review*: "On the Philosophy of the Unconditioned; in Reference to Cousin's Infinito-Absolute" (1829), "Philosophy

of Perception" (1830), and "Logic: The Recent English Treatises on that Science" (1833). See the appendix, note B, in John Veitch, *Memoir of Sir William Hamilton, Bart.* (London: Blackwood, 1869), 421.

5. Ibid.

6. Ibid., 422.

7. Porter, in Veitch, *Memoir of Sir William Hamilton*, 423.

8. In addition to the prologue and its cited sources, see Bruce Kuklick, *Churchmen and Philosophers: From Jonathan Edwards to John Dewey* (New Haven, Conn.: Yale University Press, 1985), chaps. 4–7.

9. *JERTAC*, 37, 48.

10. Porter, in Veitch, *Memoir of Sir William Hamilton*, 423. Porter also writes "Hamilton found us just as we were becoming interested in what the French and Germans could teach us. . . . While he has not by any means been the only teacher of this generation—while his own writings have directed and encouraged us to study the philosophers of the Continent—yet his influence has been most potent to repress what might otherwise have been magniloquent [*sic*] pretension [in the reception of German philosophical systems]" (427). Porter's letter states that Hamilton's *Lectures on Metaphysics and Logic* became standard textbooks in "many of the colleges and higher seminaries" (424), and that he himself used the *Lectures on Metaphysics* in his classes from the time they appeared in print (427). He opines that no American was an actual student of Hamilton, so that his influence was transmitted solely through his writings, "and yet there is no part of the country where his writings have not produced a deep and permanent impression" (425), a statement that suggests Hamilton's influence has more broad than the elite of New England, though Porter's letter gives no evidence for this.

11. Kuklick traces the study of Scottish philosophy at Harvard through Levi Hedge (who relied on Thomas Brown), James Walker (a disciple of Dugald Stewart), and Francis Bowen (*Churchmen and Philosophers*, 131). According to Kuklick, Bowen "edited Hamilton for his students and conceded much to German ideas," and he taught at Harvard through the 1870s, that is, through the years that Peirce and James attended the college (131). Kuklick offers no bibliographical reference for this lineage.

12. *CP*, 8.290. The only sustained argument with Hamilton comes in *CP*, 2, the volume on logic, in which Peirce reflects on the differences between Whatley and Hamilton.

13. *VRE*, 2. Despite this declaration, James's pragmatic writings do not engage Hamilton as deeply as they do Bain; his discursive move from psychology to philosophy parallels an interest that moves from issues of consciousness and knowledge (epistemology) to issues of the effects of consciousness (volition, belief, and action).

14. Mill, *Examination of Sir William Hamilton's Philosophy*, 637–38.

15. For this point see H. O. Mounce, "The Philosophy of the Conditioned," *Philosophical Quarterly* 44, no. 175 (April 1994): 180, 189.

16. See William Hamilton, *Lectures on Metaphysics and Logic*.Vol. 1. *Metaphysics*, 7th ed., ed. Henry Mansel and John Veitch (London: Blackwood, 1882), 246–63 (attention), 404–19 (phrenology), 419–46 (brain studies).

17. Veitch, *Memoir of Sir William Hamilton*, 39–46. Even so, Veitch quotes a colleague of Hamilton's at Oxford, whose opinion is that Hamilton's examination was "not a brilliant one." His reputation was for absorbing others' knowledge, instead of pressing forward to new territories of thought.

18. *Metaphysics*, 91.

19. Hypothetical realism, or "cosmothetic idealism," asserts that "the mind is conscious or immediately cognizant of nothing beyond its subjective states," though the

mind also irresistibly posits (hypothesizes) an external world beyond those states. See "Philosophy of Perception," in *Discussions*, 56.

20. *Metaphysics*, 97.

21. Hamilton, *Philosophy of Sir William Hamilton, Bart.*, arranged and ed. O. W. Wright (New York: Appleton, 1853), 34. Mill treats Hamilton's position on the relativity of knowledge in chap. 3 of his *Examination of Sir William Hamilton's Philosophy* (17–44).

22. *Metaphysics*, 207. See also Mounce, "Philosophy of the Conditioned," who interprets Hamilton as asserting that humans do not learn about objects (say, a piece of velvet) from our sensations (in our hand), but rather the opposite. We learn about our sensations from the objects that give rise to them. "Our attention is on the surface [the velvet], not on the mode in which we are aware of it, the sensations themselves" (175–76).

23. *Metaphysics*, 58.

24. Hamilton, *Philosophy*, 352.

25. Ibid., 353.

26. Ibid.

27. "The Philosophy of the Unconditioned; in Reference to Cousin's Infinito-Absolute," in *Discussions*, 12.

28. Ibid., 14.

29. William Hamilton, *Lectures on Metaphysics and Logic*. Vol. 2. *Logic*, ed. Henry Mansel and John Veitch (Boston: Gould and Lincoln, 1864), 61–62.

30. Hamilton, "Appendix I. Philosophical (A.)," in *Discussions*, 596–97.

31. Ibid., 597–602.

32. Ibid., 598.

33. "Philosophy of the Unconditioned," in *Discussions*, 14–15.

34. The first and second points are noted by Mounce in "Philosophy of the Conditioned." Mounce argues for the "coherence" of Hamilton's realism over against that of J. S. Mill, despite the fact that Mill's critique of Hamilton (and Hamilton's student Henry Mansel) was instrumental in the latter's declining reputation. The third point can be found in "Philosophy of the Unconditioned," in *Discussions*, 14–15.

35. *Discussions*, 619. The discussion of causality is most thoroughly presented in *Discussions*, 605–28. See also *Metaphysics*, 548–58.

36. *Metaphysics*, 556.

37. Ibid.

38. *Metaphysics*, 133, 139. See Mill's *Examination of Sir William Hamilton's Philosophy*, 144.

39. Hamilton, "The Philosophy of Perception," in *Discussions*: "*Consciousness* and *immediate knowledge* are thus terms universally convertible; and if there be an immediate knowledge of things external, there is consequently the *consciousness of an outer world*" (51).

40. William James argues against this in *Principles*, saying it is perfectly possible to "know" something without "knowing that I know it" (264). James misses Hamilton's claim, which is to critique faculty psychology. James certainly would assent to this critique, though he does show greater sensitivity to the variety of "knowledges," some of which are tacit, passive, or unconscious.

41. Both quotations are from "Philosophy of Perception," in *Discussions*, 49.

42. *Metaphysics*, 132.

43. "Philosophy of Common Sense," in Hamilton, *Philosophy*, 26.

44. *Metaphysics*, 185: "I am still bold enough to maintain, that consciousness

affords not merely the only revelation, and only criterion of philosophy, but that this revelation is naturally clear,—this criterion, in itself, unerring." See also *Metaphysics*, 199.

45. See Mill's discussion of the founding of consciousness on belief in *Examination of Sir William Hamilton's Philosophy*, 74–77.

46. "Philosophy of Perception," in *Discussions*, 86.

47. *Metaphysics*, 9. See also *Discussions*, 41–42.

48. *Metaphysics*, 3, 7. See also *Discussions*, 42, and Hamilton, *Philosophy*, 9.

49. Hamilton, "On the Study of Mathematics. As an Exercise of Mind," in *Discussions*, 260–323. This essay presents an extended critique of the Cambridge University policy of emphasizing mathematics over "other branches of liberal education" (321). The essay purports to be a review of the logician William Whewell's treatise *Thoughts on the Study of Mathematics as Part of a Liberal Education*, but Hamilton barely examines the book. I say that his position on mathematics is unexpected because many of his British contemporaries view mathematics and logic on a continuum, even if slightly different in their goals (certainly this is Peirce's position a generation later). Hamilton, however, insists that logic is "practically valueless in mathematics" (282). His argument is that where logic is the form of reasoning that leads us to reason correctly, mathematics, according to Aristotle and to math's own history, progresses without recourse to reason or dispute. "The art of reasoning *right* is assuredly not to be taught by a process [mathematics] in which there is no reasoning *wrong*. We do not learn to swim in water by previous practice in a pool of quicksilver" (283).

50. See *CP*, 8.12, 6.212, 6.100, 5.350, and 1.74 for some of Peirce's comments on truth now and in the long run.

Chapter 4

1. Daniel B. Klein, *A History of Scientific Psychology* (New York: Basic, 1970), 792. Klein notes that Bain's father was a weaver and that Bain himself worked as a weaver for a time to assist the family.

2. Alexander Bain, *Education as a Science* (New York: Appleton, 1897).

3. Bain began the journal *Mind* in 1876. He also was a close friend of J. S. Mill, with whom he edited Mill's *Logic* and debated the findings of Darwin.

4. Klein, *History of Scientific Psychology*, 791–95. Bain's other strong scientific influence was Darwin, whose *Origin of Species* was published the same year as *The Emotions and the Will* (1859). Bain never became an evolutionist, though he received Darwin's work with critical admiration. Darwin refers to Bain's psychology of emotions in his *The Expression of the Emotions in Man and Animals* (1872), and Bain responds to this reference in later editions of his psychological treatises.

5. For the division of the psychological powers of association into lower, material and upper, spiritual levels, see "Association Controversies," originally published in *Mind* and reprinted in *DLPT*, 49–54.

6. Daniel N. Robinson, Preface, in Alexander Bain, *The Emotions and the Will*, vol. 5 of *Significant Contributions to the History of Psychology, 1750–1920*, ed. Daniel N. Robinson (Washington, D.C.: University Publications of America, 1977), xxxvi.

7. Alexander Bain, *Mental Science: A Compendium of Psychology and the History of Philosophy. Designed as a Text-book for High-schools and Colleges* (New York: Appleton, 1868), 372.

8. Bain, "Association Controversies," in *DLPT*, 38. For the "disburdening" of psychology from metaphysics, see Bain, *The Senses and the Intellect*, 4th ed. (New York: Appleton, 1902), viii.

9. Bain, *Mental Science*, 143.

10. Bain, *Logic. Part First: Deduction* (New York: Longmans, Green, 1924), 1. Hereafter cited as Bain, *Deduction*. In effect, then, Bain asserts that psychology borders physiology and logic. Peirce will make the same assertion and conclude from it that a separate science of psychology is unnecessary, while Bain uses this fact as an argument in favor of scientizing psychology.

11. Bain, "The Respective Spheres and Mutual Helps of Introspection and Psychophysical Experiment in Psychology," in *DLPT*, 247.

12. Bain, *Logic. Part Second: Induction*, 3d ed. (New York: Longmans, Green, 1912), 275. Hereafter cited as Bain, *Induction*.

13. For the points covered in this paragraph, see Bain, *Senses and the Intellect*, 1, 9; Bain, *Induction*, 276; and Bain, *Mind and Body: The Theories of Their Relation* (New York: Appleton, 1901), 130–33.

14. Bain, *Mind and Body*, 128.

15. Ibid., 196.

16. For the second reference, see p. 82, and n. 35.

17. Bain, "The Meaning of 'Existence' and Descartes's 'Cogito,'" in *DLPT*, 2.

18. Bain, *Senses and the Intellect*, 8.

19. Bain, *Mind and Body*, 45.

20. Ibid., 48. For other discussions of relativity as transition or change, see Bain, *Deduction*, 54; and Bain, *Induction*, 280.

21. Bain, "The Empiricist Position," in *DLPT*, 142.

22. Bain, *Emotions and the Will*, 599–605; and Bain, "Definition and Problems of Consciousness," in *DLPT*, 239. For another phrasing of this definition, see Bain, *Senses and the Intellect*, 349.

23. Bain, *Senses and the Intellect*, 73.

24. Bain, *Emotions and the Will*, 57.

25. Ibid., 558. See also Bain, *Deduction*, 267.

26. Bain, "Empiricist Position," in *DLPT*, 141.

27. Bain, *Emotions and the Will*, 557–59.

28. Bain, "Definition and Problems of Consciousness," in *DLPT*, 231, 238.

29. See Edward S. Reed, "The Separation of Psychology from Philosophy: Studies in the Sciences of Mind 1815–1879," in *The Nineteenth Century*, ed. C. L. Ten (New York: Routledge, 1994), 297–356.

30. Bain, *Senses and the Intellect*, 400; see 398–405 for a full discussion of this point.

31. Bain, *Emotions and the Will*, 570; Bain, *Deduction*, 21. Again, this is Bain's law of relativity.

32. Bain, *Deduction*, 12.

33. Bain, *Emotions and the Will*, 296.

34. Ibid., 568; see also Bain, *Mental Science*, 220, 371.

35. Bain, *Mental Science*, 372. This theological reference is at best ironic.

36. Bain, *Induction*, 278; see also Bain, *Mental Science*, 372.

37. Bain, *Induction*, 376.

38. Bain, *Emotions and the Will*, 3, 184; Bain, *Mental Science*, 109; Bain, "Physiological Expression in Psychology," in *DLPT*, 178; and Bain, *Senses and the Intellect*, 322.

39. Bain, *Mental Science*, 2.

40. Bain, *Emotions and the Will*, 8.

41. Bain, *Emotions and the Will*, 327; see also 339. Bain's wording here almost replicates Wundt's.

42. Bain, *Deduction*, 28.

43. Bain, *Emotions and the Will*, 37. Again, this wording is nearly the same as Wundt's.

44. Bain, *Induction*, 114.

45. Bain, "Empiricist Position," in *DLPT*, 148; Bain, *Induction*, 113; and Bain, *Deduction*, 19.

46. Bain, *Induction*, 8.

47. Ibid., 10. Recall that the Law of Relativity is also derived from Succession.

48. Ibid., 15.

49. Ibid., 16. This quotation resonates with Peirce's synechism, or doctrine of continuity, but, as chapter 5 will detail, Peirce's concomitant theory of tychism, or chance, troubles this assumption of a predictable uniformity in nature. Thanks to Frank Crouch for this point.

50. Bain, *Senses and the Intellect*, 536.

51. Bain, *Induction*, 19.

52. Bain, "Empiricist Position," in *DLPT*, 146.

53. For references to these discussions, see Bain, *Induction*, 20–40; and Bain, "Empiricist Position," in *DLPT*, 146–47. Bain does not attribute conservation of energy to Helmholtz, though he does recognize it as coming from the domain of physics.

54. Ibid., 21.

55. Bain, *Induction*, 36.

56. Bain, *Emotions and the Will*, 544: "We may produce any amount of mystery, incomprehensibility, insolubility, transcendentalism, by insisting on keeping up a phraseology, or a theoretical representation, that is unadapted to the facts." The discussion proceeds to explain the insufficiency of the terms *liberty, freedom, free will*, and *necessity* as applied to the question of the limitations inherent to human action.

57. Bain, *Mental Science*, 187–88, presents the case against an innate notion of cause; *Emotions and the Will*, 584, states how human assumption of the order of the world engenders the concept of causality.

58. Bain, *Emotions and the Will*, 473, draws upon James Herschel to connect the concept of causality to that of effort or resistance.

59. Bain, "On Moral Causation," in *DLPT*, 9–19.

60. Bain, *Emotions and the Will*, 543; Bain, *Mental Science*, 113.

61. Bain, *Emotions and the Will*, 543.

62. Bain, *Mental Science*, 113; see also Bain, *Senses and the Intellect*, 451–54.

63. *CP*, 5.12. See James's note on Bain and belief in *Principles*, 949.

Chapter 5

1. *Life*, xiv. Most of the biographical information in this section comes from Brent's text.

2. I should stress that the elitism conveyed in this sentence was not limited to intellectual privilege. According to Brent (*Life*, 62–64), the Peirce family upheld a strident anti-abolitionism in a culture of abolitionist struggle. Brent claims that Peirce's

only mention of the Civil War is in an 1862 letter to the superintendent of the Coast Survey, anxiously asking if his position with the survey exempted him from the military draft. It is neither coincidental nor inconsequential that American pragmatism was developed by Cambridge elites (though James was as liberal as Peirce was conservative, he was no egalitarian or advocate for the poor). In *Seeds of Racism* (Naperville, Ill.: Sourcebooks, 2000), 16–20, Paul R. Griffin poignantly argues that Puritan theology, which I attest Peirce and James took for granted as culturally normative (not as religiously orthodox), was profoundly racist in even its most basic tenets of creation and sin. He contends that the abolitionist struggle itself was condescending and racist, aimed more at saving the soul of white America from the sin of slavery than at constructing an equal society or participatory democracy.

3. *Life*, 38–58.

4. Ibid., 151; the phrase is from a letter of Simon Newcomb to Johns Hopkins's president, Daniel Gilman.

5. Ibid., chaps. 2 and 3.

6. Peirce wrote articles for the *Nation* and for the Smithsonian Institution and managed to arrange a few lecture series in the Boston area, again with James's aid. Peirce depended on James so profoundly that in 1909 he began calling himself Charles *Santiago* Sanders Peirce. See *Life*, 315.

7. Various references to the importance of community can be found in *SW*, 17, 69, 83, 88, 241.

8. Peirce, "What Pragmatism Is" (1905), in *SW*, 184.

9. *CP*, 2.428 (1893).

10. *CP*, 3.432 (1896).

11. *CP*, 2.45 (1902).

12. *CP*, 2.43 (1902).

13. *CP*, 5.192 (1903). For more references on the grounding of psychology in logic, see *CP*, 2.51, 2.210, 3.432, 5.110, 5.172. Disagreement persists within Peircean scholarship about which science is primary in Peirce's classification, though all agree that it is not psychology. For instance, Beverley Kent insists on logic; Kenneth Ketner and Hilary Putnam vie for mathematics; and Carl Hausman argues for phenomenology. The disagreement stems from internal inconsistencies within Peirce's various unpublished manuscripts, which span some forty years of thought. I am most convinced by the claims for mathematics, though I think that the distinctions between mathematics and logic are ultimately negligible. See Beverley Kent, *Charles S. Peirce: Logic and the Classification of the Sciences* (Kingston, Ontario: McGill-Queen's University Press, 1987); Kenneth L. Ketner and Hilary Putnam, Introduction, in *RLT*; and Carl R. Hausman, *Charles S. Peirce's Evolutionary Realism* (Cambridge, Mass.: Harvard University Press, 1994).

14. This is a distinction between providing conditions of truth (logic) and providing criteria of relevance (psychology/sociology). Peirce would agree with this distinction, though the terminology is more akin to Davidson and Putnam than to the pragmatist.

15. *CP*, 4.1 (1898).

16. Ibid. Peirce ends *CP*, 4.1, by indexing the contemporary importance of nominalism in the debate between Ernst Mach (a nominalist) and E. C. Hegeler (a realist); additionally, Peirce attributes the formulation of a realist position for science to F. E. Abbot's *Scientific Theism*. Abbot was a member of the Cambridge Metaphysical Club, the philosophy discussion group of the 1870s that met informally in Cambridge and that James names the site of Peirce's early articulations of pragmatism. There is some

question as to the real existence and importance of these meetings. See Max Fisch, Introduction, *Writings of Charles S. Peirce: A Chronological Edition*, vol. 3, *1872–1878,* ed. Christian J. W. Kloesel (Bloomington: Indiana University Press, 1986), xxix–xxxvii; Fisch, "Was There a Metaphysical Club in Cambridge?" in *Studies in the Philosophy of Charles S. Peirce*, ed. Edward C. Moore and Richard S. Robin (Amherst: University of Massachusetts Press, 1964), 5–7; *Life*, 82–89; Mark Mendell, "The Problem of the Origin of Pragmatism," *History of Philosophy Quarterly*, 12, no. 1 (Jan. 1995): 111–31; and Louis Menand, *The Metaphysical Club* (New York: Farrar, Straus and Giroux, 2001).

17. Helmholtz recognized a general trend of evolution (growth of knowledge and control), and this might be interpreted as a sort of final causality. I presume that Helmholtz's disposition toward evolution was as mechanistic as Darwin's, but since his texts leave this point ambiguous, I will admit that final causality may be implied in to his theories, albeit much less so than in the pragmatists' texts.

18. As opposed to indicating a lack within law by being *merely* regulative. See Peirce's parallel counter to the nominalists' attribution that concepts are *mere* words in *CP,* 8.191 (c. 1904): "The external world . . . does not consist of existent objects merely, nor merely of these and their reactions; but on the contrary, its most important reals have the mode of being of what the nominalist calls 'mere' words, that is, general types and would-bes. The nominalist is right in saying that they are substantially of the nature of words; but his 'mere' reveals a complete misunderstanding of what our everyday world consists of."

19. *CP,* 1.25 (1903). Peirce continues, "We naturally attribute Firstness to outward objects, that is we suppose they have capacities in themselves which may or may not be already actualized, which may or may not ever be actualized, although we can know nothing of such possibilities [except] so far as they are actualized." Here, again, Peirce stresses that reality exceeds the human perception of reality, while still acknowledging that human perception is required for our *knowledge* of reality.

20. *CP,* 1.531 (1903).

21. *CP,* 1.24 (1903).

22. *CP,* 1.26 (1903).

23. *CP,* 5.48 (1903): "A law of nature, then, will be regarded by him [the scholastic realist] as having a sort of *esse in futuro*. That is to say they will have a present reality which consists in the fact that events *will* happen according to the formulation of those laws." As a mode of being, *esse in futuro* never translates into present tense in logic, but always remains a future conditional, a would-be. Peirce states this with an example in his 1905 essay, "Issues of Pragmaticism" (*CP,* 5.453): "For if the reader will turn to the original maxim of pragmaticism . . . , he will see that the question is, not what *did* happen [when one tries to scratch a diamond], but whether it would have been well to engage in any line of conduct whose successful issue depended upon whether that diamond *would* resist an attempt to scratch it." The issue here is conduct, or the embodiment of Thirdness in habit. See also *CP,* 2.146, 2.667, 2.667n. 3.459, 5.467, 5.517 n. 1, 6.327, 8,104, 8.113, 8.225, and 8.236–38. For more on Peirce and the would-be character of Thirdness, see Hausman, *Peirce's Evolutionary Realism*, 7, 50, 60.

24. Along these lines, Hausman notes that a third or a general "should not be thought of apart from a telos. With respect to being a habit, a third or general is what it is by virtue of its influence on its future instances" (*Peirce's Evolutionary Realism*, 175; see also 201). I agree with this, except that I am uneasy with the notion of "telos." I would distinguish purpose from purposiveness and attribute the latter to Peirce.

Moreover, though Peirce does embrace a commonsense realism, which accepts our perceptions of the world as true, he also asserts that chance is an active and separate force in nature.

25. *CP*, 4.1 (1898).

26. I should note that Peirce does differentiate between definiteness and determinateness, though this distinction is not necessary to my argument. See *CP*, 5.447–48, 4.431. I should also acknowledge that the virtuality of Thirdness only logically precedes its particular actualizations, while the pure virtuality of Firstness ontologically precedes its actualization into Secondness and generalization into Thirdness. The virtuality of Thirdness ontologically depends on the virtuality of Firstness: Not every may-be becomes a would-be—not every first becomes a third—but every would-be was once a may-be.

27. *CP*, 6.169 (1902). See also Michael Raposa, *Peirce's Philosophy of Religion* (Bloomington: Indiana University Press, 1989), 41–46. Beverley Kent notes that Peirce was goaded to theorize about continuity by J. J. Sylvester, when the two taught on the same faculty at Johns Hopkins. She suggests that texts of Wilhelm Wundt and William Whewell also acted as spurs. See Kent, *Logic and the Classification of the Sciences*, 12.

28. *CP*, 1.164 (1889).

29. Peirce attributes to William James an "almost unexampled incapacity for mathematical thought" (*CP*, 6.182). Since I share that incapacity, my treatment of synechism will be rather more metaphysical than mathematical or logical. Though I do hope to indicate the magnitude, complexity, and importance of synechism for Peirce's pragmaticism, my chief goal is to demonstrate how continuity is a real general and, thus, what are some of the consequences of accepting the primacy of the virtual. For a full treatment of synechism see Ketner and Putnam, Introduction, in *RLT*. See also helpful notes in Hausman, *Peirce's Evolutionary Realism*, 180 n. 20, 183.

30. *CP*, 6.123 (1892). See also *CP*, 6.166 (1903): "The Kanticity is having a point between any two points. The Aristotelicity is having every point that is a limit to an infinite series of points that belong to the system." The editors of *CP* indicate that Peirce is drawing from Aristotle's *Physics* and *Metaphysics*.

31. *CP*, 4.121 (1893). See Immanuel Kant, *Critique of Pure Reason*, trans. Norman Kemp Smith (New York: St. Martin's, 1965), A169, A659, B211, B687.

32. Hausman, *Peirce's Evolutionary Realism*, 187. See also Ketner and Putnam, Introduction, in *RLT*, 41.

33. William I. McLaughlin, "Resolving Zeno's Paradoxes," *Scientific American*, Nov. 1994, 86. Putting the definition in terms of writing is interesting and stems, I think, from the implicit recognition that thought or consciousness itself is a process conjoined through relations of infinitesimals. Since writing actualizes thought, the impossibility of writing an infinitesimal quantity highlights the inherently vague or virtual quality of infinitesimals.

34. Ketner and Putnam, Introduction, in *RLT*, 37–54. See also McLaughlin, "Resolving Zeno's Paradoxes," 84–89. It is a sign of Peirce's sustained obscurity that despite his almost lifelong engagement with Zeno's paradoxes, and especially his attempt to solve them via infinitesimals, McLaughlin does not mention him, though he does reference A. N. Whitehead. McLaughlin notes that "mathematicians of the nineteenth century invented a technical substitute for infinitesimals: the so-called theory of limits. So complete was its triumph that some mathematicians spoke of the 'banishment' of infinitesimals from their discipline. By the 1960s, though, the ghostly

tread of infinitesimals in the corridors of mathematics became quite real once more, thanks to the work of the logician Abraham Robinson of Yale University" (86). I am indebted to Vivisvani Soni for patiently trying to translate nonstandard analysis—of which the theory of infinitesimals is a part—into language I can understand. For a discussion of how infinitesimals relate to consciousness, especially to how consciousness can be finite but still not have a determinable beginning, see James Hoopes, *Consciousness in New England: From Puritanism and Ideas to Psychoanalysis and Semiotic* (Baltimore, Md.: Johns Hopkins University Press, 1989), 198–99.

35. McLaughlin, "Resolving Zeno's Paradoxes," 87.

36. Ketner and Putnam, Introduction, in *RLT*, 44: "In nonstandard analysis we say that two points P and Q whose distance is infinitesimal are 'identical modulo the infinitesimals' and we symbolize this by using a wiggly equals sign: $P \approx Q$. If P is a point, the collection of all points Q such that $P \approx Q$ is called the *monad* of P."

37. Ibid., 41–42.

38. *CP*, 4.1 (1898).

39. See Peirce, "Critical Review of Berkeley's Idealism" (1871), in *SW*, 82–83; and "Issues of Pragmaticism" (1905), in *SW*, 215. Peirce's development of synechism is a long and intricate argument for why it is rational to accept the world as we experience it and why we can expect our habits to be challenged when that experience is insufficient, namely, because we are beings who are both guided by purpose and driven to seek purpose in the world around us.

40. *CP*, 1.414–15 (1890).

41. *CP*, 1.412 (1890).

42. *CP*, 1.414 (1890).

43. *RLT*, 261. See also *CP*, 6.202 (1898). In *CP*, 8.252, an 1897 letter from Peirce to James, Peirce writes: "I am much encouraged at your thinking well of 'tychism.' But tychism is only a part and corollary of the general principles of Synechism. That is what I have been studying these last 15 years, and I become more and more encouraged and delighted with the way it seems to fit all the wards of your lock."

44. Peirce, "The Doctrine of Necessity" (1892), in *SW*, 170.

45. Ibid., 176–77.

46. *CP*, 5.587 (1898). See also *CP*, 1.9 and 1.152–75.

47. *RLT*, 260.

48. *CP*, 1.155 (c. 1897).

49. *CP*, 1.144 (c. 1897).

50. *CP*, 1.135 (1899). He writes: "Upon this first, and in one sense this sole, rule of reason, that in order to learn you must desire to learn, and in so desiring not be satisfied with what you already incline to think, there follows one corollary which itself deserves to be inscribed upon every wall of the city of philosophy: Do not block the way of inquiry." *CP*, 1.135–40 are, according to the editors, from an unpaginated manuscript entitled "F. R. L." (c. 1899).

51. *CP*, 1.137, 1.140 (1899).

52. *CP*, 1.138 (1899).

53. *CP*, 1.139 (1899). *Retroduction* is Peirce's early term for *abduction*. Both mean "hypothesis" and work alongside deduction and induction. *CP*, 5.144 (1903), suggests that Peirce took "abduction" from Aristotle's *apagoge* in his *Prior Analytics*. See also *CP*, 4.541 n. 1 (1906), and *CP*, 1.89 (1896).

54. See Peirce, "Issues of Pragmatism," written for the *Monist* in 1905 (*CP*, 5.438–63), in which Peirce lists six characteristics of critical commonsensism, in an attempt to demonstrate how pragmaticism is a modification of Kant's *Critik* by the lessons of

Scottish commonsensism. See also "Pragmaticism and Critical Common-Sensism," (1905), in *CP*, 5.497–501, and "Consequences of Critical Common-Sensism" (1905), in *CP*, 5.502–37.

55. Phrased this way, one can see clearly how Peirce's sense of "habit" functions to embrace and uphold the status quo. His theory of fallibilism should function as a corrective to this tendency, but was not effective in Peirce's own life.

56. *CP*, 5.505 (1905). Peirce at places suggests that pragmatism is a modification of Kant (*CP*, 5.1, 5.3, 5.12). He was proud of his profound knowledge of Kant's work. See *CP*, 1.4: "I devoted two hours a day to the study of Kant's *Critic of the Pure Reason* [*sic*] for more than three years, until I almost knew the whole book by heart, and had critically examined every section of it."

57. *CP*, 5.511 (1905). The emphasis is in the original, but I note it again, for in other places Peirce asserts that reflection on self-control motivates his whole development of pragmatism.

58. Peirce stresses that the doubt that motivates criticism must be real, that is, it must have its source in a perceived sense of error, failure, or inadequacy. Otherwise, the doubt is nothing but a false Cartesian strategy and cannot hope to address real issues and problems. In light of the elitism and racism that were deeply ingrained in Peirce, however, one wonders what social impetus would be strong enough to spur real doubt. Does *any* disagreement with one's position engender doubt and necessitate critical reflection? Or are some disagreements either labeled as exterior to one's community of inquiry (and therefore justifiably dismissed) or as themselves demonstrative of "error, failure, or inadequacy" (as when pleas from marginalized quarters of society are dismissed as ludicrous impropriety)?

59. Again, Peirce would be thinking of dogmatism in terms of intellectual debates, not social ones.

60. Peirce's well-known essay "The Fixation of Belief" (1877) treats doubt extensively and critiques the "paper-doubt" of Descartes. See *SW*, 92–112. Examples of truths that no one thinks to doubt might include the sun rising in the East or 2+2=4. Of course, each of these "truths" is true only due to specific presuppositions—and that is exactly Peirce's point: those presuppositions are so widely shared that usually no one has a reason to question them. If anyone were to indicate a reason to question them, Peirce insists that the community of inquiry has a duty to listen and consider the intervention seriously. Donna Haraway's dictum that "facts are theory-laden; theories are value-laden; values are history-laden" is one with which I think Peirce would agree, though as applied to biology or geography more than to, for example, interpretations of the Boer War or regulations on who can vote. Peirce and Haraway both assert that life can usually be lived and scientific experiments developed and performed without having to consciously acknowledge that dictum. Only when internal dissent arises must methods and assumptions be re-examined, for dissent is real doubt, and any one person's real doubt throws doubt on everyone's assumed certainty. See Haraway, "In the Beginning Was the Word," in Haraway, *Simians, Cyborgs, and Women: The Reinvention of Nature* (New York: Routledge, 1991), 77.

61. Peirce, "How to Make Our Ideas Clear" (1878), in *CP*, 5.407.

62. Peirce, "Some Consequences of Four Incapacities" (1868), in *SW*, 69.

63, Ibid., 56 n. 5.

64. Strictly speaking, Peirce uses the term *representamen* to designate the most general semeiotic elements; signs are a subset of representamen and always contain a mental aspect. See *CP*, 1.540 and 2.274. He writes in the latter (1902), "If a sunflower, in turning towards the sun, becomes by that very act fully capable, without

further condition, of reproducing a sunflower which turns in precisely correspond-ing ways toward the sun, and of doing so with the same reproductive power, the sun-flower would become a Representamen of the sun. But *thought* is the chief, if not the only, mode of representation." Again I stress that, for Peirce, thought is not human thought; rather human thought is a selected subset of Thought, the realm of virtuality or pure Firstness.

65. *CP,* 5.448 n. 1.

66. *CP,* 5.484, from "Pragmatism" (c. 1906).

67. This phrase comes from *CP,* 4.219, though Peirce is discussing geometry, not cosmology, in this passage. However, Hausman takes up this passage and uses it helpfully to interpret Peirce's cosmological thought experiment in the last of his 1898 Cambridge lectures. See Hausman, *Peirce's Evolutionary Realism,* 189.

68. *CP,* 1.414 (1890).

69. *CP,* 1.292 (1908): "A medad [pure firstness] would be a flash of mental 'heat lightning,' absolutely instantaneous, thunderless, unremembered, and altogether without effect."

70. *CP,* 1.541(1903): "A REPRESENTAMEN is a subject of a triadic relation TO a sec-ond, called its OBJECT, FOR a third, called its INTERPRETANT, this triadic relation being such that the REPRESENTAMEN determines its interpretant to stand in the same triadic relation to the same object for some interpretant."

71. For a full classification of signs, see *CP,* 2.227–73, "The Division of Signs," which the editors date c. 1897. To be precise, I should say that each rabbit example is a symbol or conventional sign, demonstrating iconic, indexical, and strictly symbolic qualities, respectively. Words and sentences all are symbolic; gestures may be sym-bolic (the "ok" sign) or indexical (a pointing finger).

72. *CP,* 2.228 (1897). Peirce calls this sense of idea "Platonic" and Hausman makes much of Peirce's repositioning of Platonism. See Hausman, *Peirce's Evolutionary Realism,* 152–53, 167–68.

73. Hausman, *Peirce's Evolutionary Realism,* 9.

74. This distinction is only partially helpful, however, for every component of reality is both mental and material. My term, *material interpretant* tries to acknowl-edge that the memories (habits, instincts) of the sensory-motor system are more physi-cal than the cognitive memory (habits) of consciousness, though formally the se-meiotic process works the same way in both venues and, indeed, the two venues are never wholly separate. I should also note here that Peirce indicates three types of interpretants: immediate, dynamical, and logical. I will return to this division in the next section.

75. *CP,* 5.54 (1903). Asserting a "propositional form" is simply Peirce's way of indexing the logical quality of inferences.

76. The percept as the ground of perceptual judgments is my extrapolation. See *CP,* 4.539 (1906), which claims that the percept is the immediate object of all knowl-edge. I would suggest that Peirce would be more consistent to write "perceptual judg-ment" here, instead of "percept."

77. *CP,* 5.142 (1903). Peirce notes here that perceptual judgments are always ve-racious, though to varying degrees: "There is no meaning in saying that they [per-ceptual judgments] have any other truth than veracity, since a perceptual judgment can never be repeated. At most we can say of a perceptual judgment that its relation to other perceptual judgments is such as to permit a simple theory of the facts." Such a theory would be formed by conjoining perceptual judgments to subsequent hypoth-eses and actions and modifying it in response to future judgments. This process, Peirce

states, distinguishes material truth from logical correctness, where "the *latter* refers to a single line of argument and the *former* to all the arguments which could have a given proposition or its denial as their conclusion." Peirce concludes by asserting that this reasoning should be carefully weighed "because pragmatism largely depends upon it."

78. Reading this sentence through lenses shaped by the hermeneutic of suspicion (that is, the writings of Marx, Nietzsche, and Freud), one can understand how the class and intellectual elitism of Peirce and James convert into theories of truth that Gramsci would call hegemonic, that is, sustaining the power and privilege of the dominant classes, not through coercion but through persuasion and the construction of common sense. In line with Griffin's argument in *Seeds of Racism*, the tenet that America is a "classless" society (a notion that is clearly false) is congruent with (and justified by) the Puritan tenets that assert both an equality of all souls before God and a hierarchical and role-bound creation. Thus Peirce and James are both particularly American in theorizing truth and science in ways that seem to critique while still upholding the disparities and injustices of American society with regard to race, class, and gender.

79. "Issues of Pragmaticism" (1905), *CP,* 5.442. Note the inclusion of "women"; Peirce was by no means a feminist and yet the feminist abolitionist and writer Margaret Fuller was a regular guest at Benjamin Peirce's dinner table, and his first wife, Melusina Fay, was a feminist activist who promulgated the conviction that the Holy Spirit was the feminine aspect of the Godhead. See *Life,* 60–66.

80. *JERTAC,* 148. Conforti's chapter is titled "Colonial Revival: Edwards and Puritan Tradition in American Culture, 1870–1903," and this span also marks the years during which pragmatism was developed and widely disseminated.

81. Inspired by Griffin's *Seeds of Racism,* let me note that these concepts—as well as the "virtue" of self-control—are not neutral but are marked by assumptions about race and class. The fact that those in power often justify the marginalization of others through condemning their "lack of control" should make us wary of advocating for this character trait in the absence of a social commentary about who is able to label something "self-control" (versus, for example, resistance or self-protection) and about those social structures that limit, block, or otherwise frustrate the growth of self-control.

82. *CP,* 6.294 (1893): "Here, then, is the issue. The gospel of Christ says that progress comes from every individual merging his individuality in sympathy with his neighbors. On the other side, the conviction of the nineteenth century is that progress takes place by virtue of every individual's striving for himself with all his might and trampling his neighbor under foot whenever he gets a chance to do so. This may accurately be called the Gospel of Greed." Peirce's critiquie of greed anticipates and is resonant with that of Henry Ward Beecher, the man who was hailed in 1897 as "the Puritan of Puritans: (as was discussed in the prologue).

83. "What Pragmatism Is" (1905), in *SW,* 183.

84. *CP,* 5.442 (1905).

85. Peirce, "How to Make Our Ideas Clear" (1878), in *SW,* 124: "Consider what effects, which might conceivably have practical bearings, we conceive the object of our conception to have. Then, our conception of these effects is the whole of our conception of the object."

86. "What Pragmatism Is," in *SW,* 186.

87. "What Pragmatism Is," *CP,* 5.429. For a direct reference to James's *Will to Believe,* see *CP,* 5.3. For a reference of the same sort to Caldioni, the Italian pragmatist, see *CP,* 8.212.

88. Peirce uses the gospel phrase in *CP*, 5.465, an unpublished manuscript in which he notes that pragmatism deploys the methods of "all the successful sciences": "this experimental method being itself nothing but a particular application of an older logical rule, 'By their fruits ye shall know them.'" In a footnote added in 1893 to "How to Make Our Ideas Clear" (*CP*, 5.403 n. 3), Peirce stresses, "We must certainly guard ourselves against understanding this rule in too individualistic a sense." Any individual may by herself accomplish very little, but when viewed according to the collective efforts of the community, the accomplishment takes on greater importance.

89. As I noted, read pessimistically, one can imagine using this theory about action and conduct to keep "unruly sorts" (like freed slaves and women) in their proper (domesticated) places.

90. Stephen Innes, *Creating the Commonwealth: The Economic Culture of Puritan New England* (New York: W.W. Norton, 1995), 132–59.

91. *CP*, 7.364–65, emphasis added. This references two paragraphs from alternative pages to his 1902 *Minute Logic*, chap. 2, "Classification of the Sciences." For mind as inner and outer association, see *CP*, 4.157. For more on the electrical current example, see John K. Sheriff, *Charles Peirce's Guess at the Riddle* (Bloomington: Indiana University Press, 1994), 24–27.

92. *CP*, 7.364 (1902).

93. *CP*, 7.363 (1902).

94. *CP*, 7.366 (1902).

95. *CP*, 8.303 (1909). Note how this definition is reminiscent of Wundt's constellation of volition, feeling and action. See chapter 2.

96. *CP*, 1.377 (1890) and 8.303 (1909), respectively. For primisense, altersense, and medisense, see *CP*, 7.551 (c. 1900).

97. "Some Consequences of Four Incapacities" (1868), in *SW*, 56.

98. *CP*, 7.553 (c. 1900); cf. 7.547, 554.

99. *CP*, 7.554 (c. 1900).

100. See my prologue's discussion of the Puritan imaginary, and also Andrew Delbanco, *The Puritan Ordeal* (Cambridge, Mass.: Harvard University Press, 1989), chap. 8.

101. Delbanco, *Puritan Ordeal*, 248.

102. Innes, *Creating the Commonwealth*, 132–59. See also Everett Emerson, *Puritanism in America, 1620–1750* (Boston: Twayne, 1977), 13, 56 (for the importance of the communal gaze), and 93–94, 146 (for the already mythic character of this ideal community). For the various shades of "individual" and their suspicious reception by American myth makers, see Richard P. Gildrie, *The Profane, the Civil, and the Godly: The Reformation of Manners in Orthodox New England, 1679–1749* (University Park: Pennsylvania State University Press, 1994), 8–10.

103. Innes, *Creating the Commonwealth*, 132–59. See also Margo Todd, "Puritan Self-Fashioning," in Bremer, ed., *Puritanism: Transatlantic Perspectives on a Seventeenth-Century Anglo-American Faith*, ed. Francis J. Bremer (Boston: Massachusetts Historical Society, 1993), 57–87; and Michael G. Ditmore, "Preparation and Confession: Reconsidering Edmund S. Morgan's *Visible Saints*," *New England Quarterly* 67, no. 2 (June 1994), 318–19.

104. Again, one should bear in mind the elitism implied by Peirce's vision, which assumes that persons *can* increase their self-control, obviating social, cultural and political limits and obstacles to that "virtue."

105. The phrase *moral tenor* is from Paul Conkin's preface to his *Puritans and Pragmatists* (New York: Dodd, Mead, 1968), v. Conkin admits that "in no literal,

doctrinal sense were the pragmatists also Puritans" but sets up his book as demonstrating the moral similarities between the two. His project is vastly different from mine in neither theorizing the nineteenth-century Puritan imaginary nor examining in any depth the non-American interlocutors of Peirce and James.

106. *CP*, 4.68 (1893). The paragraph subsequent to this quotation returns to discussing the relation of inference to truth.

107. John P. Diggins, *The Promise of Pragmatism: Modernism and the Crisis of Knowledge and Authority* (Chicago: University of Chicago Press, 1994), 101. This is from Diggens's chapter on Henry Adams. Interestingly, Diggens does not treat Peirce's concept of "evolutionary love" or agapism with any depth, though he does ponder why Peirce compares a scientist's love for his method with a man's love for his wife (199), in that only the former should be open to criticism.

108. Material evidence for this turn includes increased museum exhibits and spectacles at the world fairs. This attention to the East affected mainly the educated elite, though museum exhibits were constructed for the sake of disciplining (through entertaining and "educating") the working classes. See, for instance, Timothy J. Jackson Lears, *No Place of Grace: Antimodernism and the Transformation of American Culture, 1880–1920* (Chicago: University of Chicago Press, 1981), 225–41; and Timothy Mitchell, *Colonising Egypt* (Berkeley: University of California Press, 1988).

109. *CP*, 1.673 (1898); "What Is Christian Faith" (1893), in *SW*, 355; "Letters to Lady Welby" (1908), in *SW*, 401; and "The Concept of God" (1906), in *Philosophical Writings of Peirce*, ed. Justus Buchler (New York: Dover Publications, 1955), 376–77.

110. "The Concept of God," in Buchler, *Philosophical Writings*, 376. This facet of Peirce resonates with Spinoza's depiction of God as the substance that fractures along the lines of *conatus* into an infinity of attributes. Substance, for Spinoza, like love, for Peirce, is "the essence of every scent."

111. The patriarchal, if not sexist, slant of this statement is obvious.

112. "The Concept of God," in Buchler, *Philosophical Writings*, 377.

113. *CP*, 5.421 (1905).

114. Peter Ochs, *Peirce, Pragmatism, and the Logic of Scripture* (Cambridge: Cambridge University Press, 1998), 166–75. An organism has a greater momentum or inertia than the filaments that make up the organism (as Deleuze might say, a body is without organs, or is a body despite organs).

115. Peirce, "Some Consequences of the Four Incapacities" (1868), in *SW*, 41: "Let us not pretend to doubt in philosophy what we do not doubt in our hearts."

116. *CP*, 6.270 (1892). See also *CP*, 5.264–317.

117. John Calvin, *Institutes of the Christian Religion*, trans. Henry Beveridge (Grand Rapids, Mich.: Eerdmans, 1983), vol. 1, bk. 1, chap. 1, 37. Calvin explicitly discusses the creation of humanity in the image of God in vol. 1, bk. 1, chap. 15, 162–70.

118. *CP*, 7.570 (c. 1892).

119. Innes, *Creating the Commonwealth*, 29; emphasis added. This same subordination of individual to community is described in other recent Puritan scholarship. See, e.g., Todd, "Puritan Self-Fashioning."

120. Sacvan Bercovitch, *The Puritan Origins of the American Self* (New Haven, Conn.: Yale University Press, 1975), 13.

121. *CP*, 2.444 (c. 1893).

122. *RLT*, 186.

123. "Issues of Pragmaticism" (1905), in *SW*, 206–7.

124. For more on the endless series implied in self-control as related to Royce and causality, see *CP*, 8.122 n. 19 (1902).

125. *CP*, 4.611 (1908).

126. *CP*, 8.320 (1906). The editor notes that it is unclear whether or not this letter ever was sent. Peirce is discussing the necessitarians (thinkers who advocate a physical determinism) and the possibilities for human freedom.

127. *CP*, 8.315 (1909).

128. *CP*, 5.432: "Accordingly, the pragmaticist does not make the *summum bonum* to consist in action, but makes it to consist in that process of evolution whereby the existent comes more and more to embody those generals which were just now said to be *destined* [in the sense of not coming about by accident, but formed through ethical reflection, *CP*, 5.430], which is what we strive to express in calling them *reasonable*. In its higher stages, evolution takes place more and more largely through self-control, and this gives the pragmaticist a sort of justification for making the rational purport to be general."

129. *CP*, 5.533 (1905).

130. *CP*, 5.402n3 (1906).

131. Peirce recites this poetically in an 1893 addition to *CP*, 5.402 n. 2, which draws on typical nineteenth-century imagery of progress and Christian eschatology: "Individual pleasure is not our end; we are all putting our shoulders to the wheel for an end that none of us can catch more than a glimpse at—that which the generations are working out."

132. Innes, *Creating the Commonwealth*, 120–25.

133. Joseph L. Blau, *Men and Movements in American Philosophy* (New York: Prentice-Hall, 1952), 41.

134. *CP*, 1.55 (1903).

135. *CP*, 1.57 (1903).

136. This statement illuminates the political and social conservatism of American pragmatism.

Chapter 6

1. This privileged upbringing was not inconsequential to the development of American pragmatism. Though James and his family were abolitionists and broad-minded, in no way can they be called social activists or even social critics. James's attention to the individual and his reflections on training the virtues of consciousness, will, and belief retain a quality of abstraction from the gritty realities of the Gilded Age. He discourses on war, on foreign policy, and on education, but not on immigration policies, labor conflicts, feminist struggles, or other tensions that might challenge his optimistic perceptions about the power of will and belief.

2. James received the contract to write *Principles* in 1878, and it was to be published in 1880. Instead, it was published in the same year James's father died, in 1890. Every biography of James treats to some degree the pressure William felt from his father to enter a career of science, as well as the resistance of William, whose interests always hovered around the aesthetic. See, for example, Paul Jerome Croce, "Out of the James Household," in Croce, *Science and Religion in the Era of William James* (Chapel Hill: University of North Carolina Press, 1995), 23–81; Ralph Barton Perry, *The Thought and Character of William James,* vol. 1. *Inheritance and Vocation* (Boston: Little, Brown, and Company, 1935), parts 1–2; and Howard

M. Feinstein, *Becoming William James* (Ithaca, N.Y.: Cornell University Press, 1984), 103–81.

3. See James's 1892 essay, "Plea for Psychology as a Natural Science," reprinted in *Collected Essays and Reviews,* ed. Ralph Barton Perry (New York: Longmans, Green, 1920), 316–27. This was composed only two years after *Principles* was published. James writes no such argument after 1900, by which time psychological laboratories are being set up at Johns Hopkins and other academic locations.

4. Both sociology and ethics (particularly Christian ethics) were new fields of knowledge or discourses. Whereas Harvard had long offered courses in moral philosophy and theology, courses in ethics were approved only in James's day.

5. See chap. 5.

6. James often quips that pragmatism is a method for deciding "what difference the difference [between philosophical positions] makes."

7. "The Automaton Theory," in *Principles,* 144.

8. *Principles,* 8: "This book, assuming that thoughts and feelings exist and are vehicles of knowledge, thereupon contends that psychology when she has ascertained the *empirical correlation* of the various sorts of thought or feeling with definite conditions of the brain, can go no farther—can go no farther, that is, as *a natural science*" (emphases added).

9. *Principles,* 142, 143.

10. Ibid., 6.

11. Ibid., 144–45.

12. See chap. 2.

13. "The Knowing of Things Together," in *WWJ,* 168.

14. "Does 'Consciousness' Exist?" in *WWJ,* 170. The other article, "The Notion of Consciousness," was composed and presented originally in French; *WWJ* provides a translation by Salvadore Saladino. The article covers the same issues as "Does 'Consciousness' Exist?" but in a more condensed form.

15. "A World of Pure Experience," in *WWJ,* 195.

16. "Does 'Consciousness' Exist?" in *WWJ,* 177–78.

17. See ibid., 170 n. 34, in which James claims no thinker behind the flow of thoughts. In his assumption of a knowing subject, which in some respects stands before the epistemological problem, James differs from both Henri Bergson (whose work he admired) and Peirce. Though Peirce is quite suspicious of Bergson's *elan vital* due to its lack of logical rigor, he shares the latter's interest in developing a metaphysics that encompasses questions of epistemology.

18. This sentence displays James's perspectivalism, a character of his thought that remains quite popular in that it allows for a liberal valuing of difference. I will show that this valuation can occur only in the context of individual will.

19. "Does 'Consciousness' Exist?" in *WWJ,* 170.

20. Ibid., 172.

21. Ibid., 173.

22. "The Experience of Activity," in *WWJ,* 288.

23. For example, he says in the article at hand that the thermometer may refute our claim that "it is cold," but this "does not abolish cold as a specific nature from the universe" (ibid., 288–89). In terms of action, we can imagine the cool limpidity of fall in the hot humidity of summer, but if we act on our imagination, we will be thought mad. Likewise, in "Does 'Consciousness' Exist" James discusses at length the differences between physical and imagined fire, while still claiming that both refer to the same reality.

24. Ibid., 289.

25. Ibid., 289 n. 183.

26. *Principles*, 279. This sentence is starkly sexist and classist and implicitly racist. In his *Seeds of Racism* (Naperville, Ill.: Sourcebooks, 2000), Paul R. Griffin argues that the cultural normativity of Puritan theology in America strongly supports and encourages white, male, bourgeois assumptions like this—even in liberal-minded persons, such as William James.

27. *Principles,* 279.

28. Ibid., 281–82. Note how this position might function recursively to heighten a marginalized person's social ostracism. A person can act in the world (through will), but without reciprocal recognition, the acts will be isolated and socially impotent (albeit, for James, no less real and momentous for that).

29. Ibid., 285.

30. Ibid., 289, 288.

31. Ibid., 289.

32. See chap. 2.

33. All quotations in this paragraph are from *Principles*, 289–290 n. 5; the words are James's translation of Wundt. Bracket in the last quotation also is James's.

34. Ibid., 319.

35. This claim is one of a list of five characteristics of thought: (1) each thought is an "owned" part of consciousness; (2) within that consciousness, thought constantly changes; (3) within that consciousness, thought is continuous; (4) thought concerns objects independent of thought; and (5) of those objects, thought selects parts of interest.

36. *Principles*, 320.

37. Ibid.

38. Ibid., 320–21.

39. Ibid., 321.

40. Ibid.

41. Ibid. See James Livingston, *Pragmatism and the Political Economy of Cultural Revolution, 1850–1940* (Chapel Hill: University of North Carolina Press, 1994), whose excellent account of pragmatism arising during specific shifts within late nineteenth-century capitalism has everything to do with possession or ownership. I am indebted to his account. See also Griffin, *Seeds of Racism*, whose argument can be read as corroborating Livingston in asserting that Puritan theological tenets of hierarchical creation lie behind these cultural assumptions about possession, and thus as suggesting the racist (and, by extension, sexist and classist) assumptions that are not only inherent to but also constitutive of American pragmatism.

42. *Principles*, 1171–72. It should be noted that this chapter is in the second volume of *Principles* and that the two volumes were written over a decade. To justify my claim of continuity, I rely on James's early footnote, which extensively quotes Wundt (see n. 33) explicitly connecting apperception to the working of the will.

43. "The Stream of Consciousness," in *Principles,* 246. See also 452, where James clarifies the relation between thought and feeling by restoring "the *vague* to its psychological rights."

44. Ibid., 249.

45. Ibid., 255.

46. This phrase originated with Umberto Eco, though he was using it to reinterpret Peirce's "interpretant." See Eco, *A Theory of Semiotics* (Bloomington: Indiana University Press, 1975).

47. "A World of Pure Experience," in *WWJ*, 212.

48. Ibid., 206.

49. This argument was made fully in chap. 5.

50. "The Stream of Consciousness," in *WWJ*, 73; emphasis added in last phrase.

51. Moreover, since for Peirce, actualization is the development or performance of a habit, any entity—including rocks, gases, and flowers—is able to accomplish actualization, since an entity is by definition a bundle of habits that persists by developing further habits and acting upon established ones.

52. "The Stream of Consciousness," in *WWJ*, 72; emphasis added.

53. Ibid., 73.

54. "Habit," in *WWJ*, 16. James's entire account of habit in this chapter of *Principles* may be read as much more deterministic than other more voluntarist accounts of ethical action and character. I read this chapter as a direction that James abandoned for the sake of asserting greater control over one's life and surroundings, a stance he takes in direct opposition to Schopenhauer's determinism and in favor of Renouvier's optimistic account of will, which led to his famous "will to believe."

55. Statements like this show how James assumes a freedom and level of opportunity that was literally unimaginable for much of the populace at the time. The combination of James's optimistic views and his unwillingness (or inability?) to test them in the social and cultural milieu surrounding him led many twentieth-century commentators to dismiss the pragmatic project. See, for example, John P. Diggins, *The Promise of Pragmatism* (Chicago: University of Chicago Press, 1994).

56. Paul K. Conkin, *Puritans and Pragmatists* (New York: Dodd, Mead, 1968), 344. Conkin continues: "He [James] never quite fit into the New England setting. He was too swayed by diverse, often European influences, and too immune to Puritan spirituality. His moral zeal and interest in religion did not make him religious in any redemptive sense." I disagree with most of this quotation. James fit precisely into his New England setting, as one of a generation of privileged young men caught in the fulcrum of mid–nineteenth-century intellectual and economic changes. He was no more influenced by European forces than was Peirce or others of the Cambridge Metaphysical Club; indeed, it has been the assumption of this book that the deep reliance of American intellectuals on German and British scholarship raises the honest question of what makes nineteenth-century American scholarship anything but derivative. Finally, as the remainder of this chapter will show, James is not immune to the Puritan imaginary so much as he is interested in transforming it (by mutating the very understanding of "redemption") in a way that he thinks makes sense for a liberal, democratic, post-Darwinian society that yet was still clinging to the necessity of God. Conkin is right, however, to note that, for James, religion is mainly "moral zeal."

57. Croce, *Science and Religion*, 229.

58. This word is used by William James as one qualifier of the pragmatic character; see "The Present Dilemma in Philosophy," in *PMT*, 13.

59. *PMT*, 142. See also *Principles*, 302; and "The Moral Philosopher and the Moral Life," in *WWJ*, 628.

60. *PMT*, 13. Being tender-minded includes being "Rationalistic (going by 'principles'), Intellectualistic, Idealistic, Optimistic, Religious, Free-willist, Monistic, Dogmatical." Being tough-minded includes being "Empiricist (going by 'facts'), Sensationalistic, Materialistic, Pessimistic, Irreligious, Fatalistic, Pluralistic, Skeptical." James asserts in this first lecture that pragmatism sets out to reconcile the best of these two lists—and, in fact, that is what he accomplishes—though as the lectures proceed, he grants an increasingly positive valence to being tough-minded, to the point of claiming this title for the true pragmatic spirit.

61. *VRE*, 20.

62. See James Hoopes, *Consciousness in New England* (Baltimore, Md.: Johns Hopkins University Press, 1989), 81–87; Bruce Kuklick, *Churchmen and Philosophers* (New Haven, Conn.: Yale University Press, 1985), 31–32; and Harold Simonson, *Jonathan Edwards: Theologian of the Heart* (Grand Rapids, Mich.: Eerdmans, 1988), chaps. 1–3. Edwards's confidence on this point cost him his Northampton parish and resulted in his exile to the Indian mission at Stockbridge. Since true conversion always effects changes in dispositions and habits, Edwards felt assured in reversing his grandfather Solomon Stoddard's long-held Northampton policy of keeping both baptism and the Lord's Supper open to all who wanted it. Instituting a required, mild confession before allowing admission to the Lord's Supper resulted in the parish's outrage and collective vote to seek another pastor.

63. Of course Edwards would always contextualize (or assume the context of) such experience within the boundaries of church discipline or correct doctrine, but this historical fact did not prevent Gilded Agers from using his works as they saw fit. See Edwards, "Personal Narrative," in Simonson, *Jonathan Edwards:*, 27–44. Edwards's writings on revivalism (both those in response to the Northampton revival of 1734–35 and the larger movement of the Great Awakening, 1740–42) walked the line between defending the emotionalism of the revivalists and yet denouncing itinerants (who rejected the institutional church) and irrationalists (antinomians).

64. *VRE*, 238.

65. Ibid., 229.

66. Ibid., 330, 248. "Delightful conviction" is Edwards's phrase.

67. Jonathan Edwards, *Selected Writings of Jonathan Edwards*, ed. Harold P. Simonson (New York: Ungar, 1970), 170 ("Freedom of the Will"), 182–83 ("The Nature of True Virtue").

68. Conkin, *Puritans and Pragmatists*, 320. See also Perry Miller and Thomas H. Johnson, eds., *The Puritans* (New York: American Book, 1938), 19–22 (on Puritan humanism) and 41–48 (on the consequences of using reason to inquire after God for biblical interpretation and church authority); and George M. Marsden, *Fundamentalism and American Culture: The Shaping of Twentieth-Century Evangelicalism 1870–1925* (New York: Oxford University Press, 1982), 14–21.

69. *Principles*, 295–302.

70. Ibid., 300: "In each kind of self, material, social, and spiritual, men distinguish between the immediate and actual, and the remote and potential, between the narrower and the wider view, to the detriment of the former and advantage of the latter."

71. Ibid., 301.

72. In the edition I employ, the editor, George A. Miller, has corrected the original index for pagination errors and has rekeyed the pagination for his edition; the index entries, however, are James's. It should be made clear that James's interest in issues of God and morality did not appear *ex nihilo* after the publication of *Principles* (1890). A number of addresses written in the 1880s treat religious and moral themes, including "Scientific View of Temperance" (1881), in *The Works of William James: Essays, Comments, and Reviews* (Cambridge, Mass.: Harvard University Press, 1987), 19–21; "Reflex Action and Theism" (1881), republished in *The Will to Believe and Other Essays in Popular Philosophy*, ed. Frederick H. Burkhardt, Fredson Bowers, Ignas K. Skrapskelis (Cambridge, Mass.: Harvard University Press, 1979), 90–113; "The Dilemma of Determinism" (1884), republished in *The Will to Believe*, 114–40; and the Introduction (1884), in *The Literary Remains of the Late Henry James,* ed. William James (New York: Houghton, Mifflin, 1897), 7–119.

73. "The Continuity of Experience," in *WWJ*, 299–300.

74. "The Essence of Humanism," in *WWJ*, 306.

75. "Philosophical Conceptions," in *WWJ*, 348–49.

76. Compare this example to Peirce's examples of the meaning of *hard* ("How to Make Our Ideas Clear," in *SW*, 124–36; see note on 136) and the probabilism of situations of chance, such as those insurance companies handle (*CP*, 5.19–24).

77. "Philosophical Conceptions," in *WWJ*, 354.

78. Ibid., 357.

79. James comes close to stating just this later in his life: "God is real since he produces real effects" (*VRE*, 507). It should be noted that his lectures in *Pragmatism* do initially speak of the pragmatic method as attempting "to interpret each [metaphysical] notion by tracing its respective practical consequences" (*PMT*, 28), a formulation much closer to Peirce's. However, the fact that James collects his responses to critics of *Pragmatism* in a volume titled *The Meaning of Truth* (now published in one volume with *Pragmatism*) indicates James's particular emphasis.

80. I say "somewhat" because James does recognize that novelty or surprise leads to forming new habits of expectation. As has been discussed, however, James does not adequately reconcile this realization with his functional dualism, though some passages resolve the issue into a classical dualism by distinguishing between "facts" (things of the world separate from consciousness) and "truths" (purely human appropriations of the world).

81. James actually states, "Our esteem for facts has not neutralized in us all religiousness. It is itself almost religious. Our scientific temper is devout" (*PMT*, 14). For his assertion that pragmatism synthesizes both lists, see *PMT*, 23. James works to reconcile or synthesize the scientific and religious disposition, while Peirce asserts them as co-existing but contradictory temperaments.

82. *PMT*, 42. In one sense this brings James closer to Peirce, whose pragmatism also concerns consequences or effects. In another sense, it highlights their differences, for Peirce critiques what he perceives to be James's implicit hedonism in a "satisfaction" theory of truth. Truth *is* what satisfies, agrees Peirce, but the realm of satisfaction is communal and logical, not individual and existential.

83. This phrase is from James's 1891 address to the Yale Philosophical Club, "The Moral Philosopher and the Moral Life," and James specifically aligns the "strenuous mood" with Puritanism. See *WWJ*, 628. See also "The Absolute and the Strenuous Life," in *PMT*, 289. For his clearest statements on the pragmatist's relation to God and religion, wherein he compares his meliorism to "a healthy-minded buoyancy" and admits the appeal of its pluralism to the tough-minded, see *PMT*, 137–42.

84. *PMT*, 41.

85. Ibid., 62.

86. Ibid., 138.

87. "The Moral Philosopher and the Moral Life," in *WWJ*, 619.

88. James's understanding of habit as the "great fly-wheel of society" plays a role in this position. In his chapter on habit in *Principles*, he recognizes that class, nationality, and even family patterns weigh like gravity on individuals. Despite these inevitable differences, he still believes that humans generally experience the same things, hence his belief in the possibility of a "religion of humanity." See *WWJ*, 11, 16, 74. It is frustrating that James repeatedly approaches the material for solid social commentary, but never quite enters into it.

89. "Address at the Emerson Centenary in Concord," in *WWJ*, 583.

90. For this point see also *WWJ*, 697, 716, which are selected from James's *Psychology: A Briefer Course* (1892), and in which James specifically connects the will to special causality and thus reveals its consequences for a religious and moral life.

91. *VRE*, 31–32.

92. Ibid., 488–89.

93. Conkin, *Puritans and Pragmatists*, 266–75; Croce, *Science and Religion*, part 1; Feinstein, *Becoming William James*, bk. 3; and Perry, *Thought and Character of William James*, part 2.

94. John E. Smith, "Jonathan Edwards: Piety and Practice in the American Character," *Journal of Religion* 54 (1974): 166. Smith uses James as an example of the mythic character he wants to attribute to Edwards.

95. It is important to note the differences between James and Edwards since the philosophical commentaries on Edwards often give quick comparisons of his psychology of religious experience to James's *Varieties of Religious Experience* or of the two thinkers' empiricisms—without at all commenting upon the profound differences between them. See Simonson, *Jonathan Edwards*; Miller and Johnson, Introduction, in Miller and Johnson, *The Puritans*; M. X. Lesser, *Jonathan Edwards* (Boston: Twayne, 1992); Michael Raposa, "Jonathan Edwards' Twelfth Sign," *International Philosophical Quarterly* 33, no. 2 (June 1993): 158; and Smith, "Jonathan Edwards," 173.

96. Interestingly, Raposa downplays the communal aspect of Edwards in his comparison of Peirce and Edwards.

Conclusions

1. This is discussed most thoroughly in Sacvan Berkovitch, *The Puritan Origins of the American Self* (New Haven, Conn.: Yale University Press, 1975); see also, Perry Miller and Thomas H. Johnson, Introduction, in *The Puritans* (New York: American Book, 1938); Timothy Jackson Lears, *No Place of Grace* (Chicago: University of Chicago Press, 1981); and Ross Posnock, *The Trial of Curiosity: Henry James, William James, and the Challenge of Modernity* (New York: Oxford University Press, 1991).

2. James Livingston, *Pragmatism and the Political Economy of Cultural Revolution* (Chapel Hill: University of North Carolina Press, 1994), 158–72. Livingston views James as a thinker who has been too easily ignored in favor of the more logical Dewey or the more profound Peirce. James's rhetorical complicity with the changing face of capitalism in his time does not render him shallow or naive, Livingston insists. Quite the contrary, Jamesian pragmatism grasps the contradictions for subjectivity inherent in the shift to corporate capitalism and exploits those contradictions for the sake of creating new possibilities for the self. Livingston portrays James as construing the self as multiple, fluid, and full of possibility. The pragmatist's combination of the dance of exuberant possibility with the constraint of efficient practicality, according to Livingston, effectively cancels out and preserves the Romantic and positivistic tendencies of James's day. Livingston, however, omits a discussion of will in James and the way in which the will, as demonstrated in chapter 6, individualizes the fluidity of the self that Livingston rightly emphasizes.

3. "What Makes a Life Significant," in *WWJ*, 648.

4. Ibid., 649.

5. Specifically, the goals of "laboring classes"; that is, James stands at a privileged distance from the working classes and romanticizes them for and to his own purposes.

6. *WWJ*, 649.

7. *VRE*, 488–89.

8. As alluded to in n. 5, this type of assimilation, ordered will, and attention can elucidate the implicit conservatism and racism of both the Puritan imaginary and American pragmatism. In *Seeds of Racism* (Naperville, Ill.: Sourcebooks, 2000), 32–38, Paul R. Griffin argues that abolition movements were inspired by the emphasis during the Second Great Awakening on the doctrine of perfectionism and "the notion of moral government and agency" (32). Griffin argues that the effect of abolition was to unify white America, not to eradicate racism. If he is correct (and I find his argument persuasive), then one can see the analogy to this kind of social movement in James. Just as abolition, in a sense, used the plight of slavery for the gains of white nationalism, so James is here using the plight of workers for the gains of bourgeios virtue.

9. *Principles*, 281–82.

10. *WWJ*, 648.

11. Ibid., 650.

12. Ibid.

13. Ibid. In reading passages such as this, one can understand the critique of pragmatism as a "bourgeois" philosophy. James seems aware of the alienation of bourgeois existence and acknowledges the toil and pain of the working classes, and yet his insights do not bear fruit in terms of a change of his habits, either personally (that is, biographically) or theoretically (by embarking on social analysis and critique).

14. Berkovitch, *Puritan Origins of the American Self*, 185.

15. Ibid., 185–86.

16. Ibid., 144. "Early New England rhetoric provided a ready framework for inverting later secular values—human perfectibility, technological progress, democracy, Christian socialism, or simply (and comprehensively) the American Way—into the mold of sacred teleology" (136).

17. Miles Orvell, *The Real Thing: Imitation and Authenticity in American Culture, 1880–1940* (Chapel Hill: University of North Carolina Press, 1989), xvii. Orvell is discussing how the notion of "the real thing" continuously bounces between material and religious or metaphysical frameworks.

18. As chapter 5 discussed, Peirce often advocates a separation of natural science and ethics in that the two inquiries require incommensurable dispositions. Nevertheless, he fully maintains the possibility of a scientific philosophy and, even, a scientific inquiry into ethics and religion. The separation lies less between scientific and nonscientific methods as between appropriate scientific methods. Too, the separation counsels recognition that inquiry into a phenomenon differs from believing in and practicing that phenomenon. The next section on Peirce will clarify this position.

19. Berkovitch, *Puritan Origins of the American Self*, 169.

20. Paul K. Conkin notes, "Peirce remained in large part aloof from practical political and social issues. Like Jonathan Edwards, he wanted to get at the root of all modern ills and only on occasion noted the surface symptoms" (*Puritans and Pragmatists* [New York: Dodd, Mead, 1968], 258). Conkin makes a number of similar gestures toward a comparison of Edwards and Peirce, but none is presented as an argument. Evidence abounds for a fruitful assemblage of Edwards and Peirce, some of which will be inserted in the following discussion, but in chapter 6 I chose to com-

pare Edwards and James since the two men fill similar social and intellectual positions. Because Peirce is not (or, arguably, is only recently becoming) a mythic personality, it is more fruitful to align his alternative vision of the American self with less well known currents within the same Puritan imaginary.

21. Gilles Deleuze, *Foucault*, trans. Sean Hand (Minneapolis: University of Minnesota Press, 1988), 97. Michael Foucault discusses the unthought in *The Order of Things* (New York: Vintage, 1970), 322–28.

22. "Some Consequences of Four Incapacities," in *SW*, 56. What Peirce conveys by this assertion is that thought is semeiosis, and semeiosis (and hence thought) is public and corporate.

23. Foucault, *Order of Things*, 326.

24. *Life*, 263.

25. Ketner and Putnam, "Introduction: The Consequences of Mathematics," in *RLT*, 19, 24–25. The rest of this paragraph draws from their account.

26. *CP*, 1.661.

27. See, for example, James Hoopes, *Consciousness in New England* (Baltimore, Md.: Johns Hopkins University Press, 1989); and Miller and Johnson, "This World and the Next," in *The Puritans*.

28. *CP*, 1.662; bracketed phrases inserted by the editors.

29. He also sidesteps any discussion of his own social and political positions, relegating the term *radical* to the intellectual (especially scientific) spheres and the term *conservative* to the tendency toward community inertia, regardless of class or other qualifiers of community. Today we may recognize that sentimental conservatism added to social power forms an adequate recipe for hegemony, and I think Peirce's pragmatism bears out this concern. Still, I think Peirce's theories might be usefully steered toward cultural critique.

30. The columns of tender-minded and tough-minded qualities are presented as opposites defining "The Present Dilemma in Philosophy," in *PMT*, 13.

31. *CP*, 1.663.

32. *CP*, 1.664.

33. *CP*, 1.665.

34. *CP*, 1.666.

35. *CP*, 1.670.

36. Chapter 5 discussed in detail Peirce's appropriating the scholastic nominalist debates for his nineteenth-century concerns.

37. *CP*, 1.672.

38. *CP*, 7.558.

39. *CP*, 1.673.

40. "Questions concerning Certain Faculties," in *SW*, 28–29.

41. Ibid.

42. Ibid.

43. Mark A. Peterson, *The Price of Redemption* (Stanford, Calif.: Stanford University Press, 1997), 6.

44. I have tried to point out some criticisms of Peirce and James in my notes and have referred readers to other texts, such as Livingston, *Pragmatism and the Political Economy of Cultural Revolution*; and Griffin, *Seeds of Racism*. Livingston would argue against my criticisms, I think, in suggesting that James's pragmatism displays and popularizes a self perfectly aligned to the needs and hopes of a newly formed corporate capitalism. See especially 158–80. In my view, attending to what one kind reviewer of my manuscript called the "dark side" of pragmatism (the ways it upholds

racism, sexism, and classism) would require a separate and worthy book, one that would be a logical sequel to this text. In this book I have desired only to establish two claims: (1) the non-American genealogy of American pragmatism and (2) the work of the Puritan imaginary in mutating German and Scottish thought into something uniquely American.

45. Gilles Deleuze and Felix Guattari effect a material transformation of Peirce's categories in a way that shows the political and philosophical usefulness of Peirce in our postmodernist times. See *A Thousand Plateaus: Capitalism and Schizophrenia*, trans. Brian Massumi (Minneapolis: University of Minnesota Press, 1987), 531. See also Gilles Deleuze, *Cinema 2: The Time Image*, trans. Hugh Tomlinson and Robert Galeta (Minneapolis: University of Minnesota Press, 1989), 30–34.

46. Feminists have been ruminating over this dilemma for some time. On the one hand, the category of "woman" or even "women" may be problematic in evoking a false sense of commonality. On the other hand, some general category is necessary for rallying political action.

Bibliography

Anderson, Benedict. *Imagined Communities: Reflections on the Origin and Spread of Nationalism.* Rev. ed. New York: Verso, 1991.

Aune, Bruce. *Rationalism, Empiricism, and Pragmatism: An Introduction.* New York: Random House, 1970.

Ayer, A. J. *The Origins of Pragmatism: Studies in the Philosophy of Charles Sanders Peirce and William James.* San Francisco: Freeman, Cooper, 1968.

Bain, Alexander. *Dissertations on Leading Philosophical Topics.* New York: Longmans, Green, 1903.

———. *Education as a Science.* New York: Appleton, 1897 (preface dated 1878).

———. *The Emotions and the Will.* Vol. 5 of *Significant Contributions to the History of Psychology, 1750–1920.* Ed. Daniel N. Robinson. Washington, D.C.: University Publications of America, 1977.

———. *Logic. Part First: Deduction.* New York: Longmans, Green, 1924 (preface dated 1870).

———. *Logic. Part Second: Induction.* 3d ed. New York: Longmans, Green, 1912.

———. *Mental Science: A Compendium of Psychology and the History of Philosophy. Designed as a Text-book for High-schools and Colleges.* New York: Appleton, 1868.

———. *Mind and Body: The Theories of Their Relation.* New York: Appleton, 1901.

———. *Practical Essays.* New York: Appleton, 1884.

———. *The Senses and the Intellect.* 4th ed. New York: Appleton, 1902.

Benjamin, Ludy T., et al. "Wundt's American Doctoral Students." *American Psychologist.* 47, no. 2 (1992): 123–31.

Berkovitch, Sacvan. *The Puritan Origins of the American Self.* New Haven, Conn.: Yale University Press, 1975.

Blau, Joseph L. *Men and Movements in American Philosophy.* New York: Prentice Hall, 1952.

Blumenburg, Hans. *The Legitimacy of the Modern Age.* Trans. Robert M. Wallace. Cambridge, Mass.: MIT Press, 1983.

Bremer, Francis J., ed. *Puritanism: Transatlantic Perspectives on a Seventeenth-Century Anglo-American Faith.* Boston: Massachusetts Historical Society, 1993.

Brent, Joseph. *Charles Sanders Peirce: A Life*. Bloomington: Indiana University Press, 1993.

Boller, Paul F., Jr. *American Thought in Transition: The Impact of Evolutionary Naturalism, 1865–1900*. Chicago: Rand McNally, 1969.

Bolton, M. P. W. *Inquisitio Philosophica: An Examination of the Principles of Kant and Hamilton*. London: Chapman and Hall, 1856; reprint, London: Routledge/ Thoemmes, 1993.

Butler, Jon. "Enthusiasm Described and Decried: The Great Awakening as Interpretive Fiction," *Journal of American History* 69 (1982): 305–25.

Cahan, David, ed. *Hermann von Helmholtz and the Foundations of Nineteenth Century Science*. Berkeley: University of California Press, 1993.

Calvin, John. *Institutes of the Christian Religion*. Trans. Henry Beveridge. Grand Rapids, Mich.: Eerdmans, 1983.

Carden, Allen. *Puritan Christianity in America: Religion and Life in Seventeenth-Century Massachusetts*. Grand Rapids, Mich.: Baker, 1990.

Clebsch, William A. *American Religious Thought: A History*. Chicago: University of Chicago Press, 1973.

Colapietro, Vincent M. *Peirce's Approach to the Self: A Semiotic Perspective on Human Subjectivity*. Albany: State University of New York Press, 1989.

Commager, Henry Steele. *The American Mind: An Interpretation of American Thought and Character since the 1880s*. New Haven, Conn.: Yale University Press, 1950.

Conforti, Joseph. *Jonathan Edwards, Religious Tradition, and American Culture*. Chapel Hill: University of North Carolina Press, 1995.

Conkin, Paul K. *Puritans and Pragmatists: Eight Eminent American Thinkers*. New York: Dodd, Mead, 1968.

Croce, Paul Jerome. *Science and Religion in the Era of William James: Eclipse of Certainty, 1820–1880*. Chapel Hill: University of North Carolina Press, 1995.

Daniel, E. Valentine. *Fluid Signs: Being a Person the Tamil Way*. Berkeley: University of California Press, 1984.

Daniels, George H. *Science in American Society: A Social History*. New York: Knopf, 1971.

Dawson, Jan C. *The Unusable Past: America's Puritan Tradition, 1830–1930*. Chico, Calif.: Scholars, 1984.

Delbanco, Andrew. *The Puritan Ordeal*. Cambridge, Mass.: Harvard University Press, 1989.

Deleuze, Gilles. *Bergsonism*. Trans. Hugh Tomlinson and Barbara Habberjam. New York: Zone, 1991.

———. *Cinema 2: The Time Image*. Trans. Hugh Tomlinson and Robert Galeta. Minneapolis: University of Minnesota Press, 1989.

———. *Foucault*. Trans. Sean Hand. Minneapolis: University of Minnesota Press, 1988.

Deleuze, Gilles, and Felix Guattari. *A Thousand Plateaus: Capitalism and Schizophrenia*. Trans. Brian Massumi. Minneapolis: University of Minnesota Press, 1987.

———. *What Is Philosophy?* Trans. Hugh Tomlinson and Graham Burchell. New York: Columbia University Press, 1994.

Deleuze, Gilles, and Claire Parnet. *Dialogues*. Trans. Hugh Tomlinson and Barbara Habberjam. New York: Columbia University Press, 1987.

Dickstein, Morris, ed. *The Revival of Pragmatism: New Essays on Social Thought, Law, and Culture*. Durham, N.C.: Duke University Press, 1998.

Diggins, John P. *The Promise of Pragmatism: Modernism and the Crisis of Knowledge and Authority*. Chicago: University of Chicago Press, 1994.

Ditmore, Michael G. "Preparation and Confession: Reconsidering Edmund S. Morgan's *Visible Saints*." *New England Quarterly*, 67, no. 2 (1994): 298–319.

Eco, Umberto. *A Theory of Semiotics*. Bloomington: Indiana University Press, 1975.

Edwards, Jonathan. *Selected Writings of Jonathan Edwards*. Ed. Harold P. Simonson. New York: Ungar, 1970.

Emerson, Everett. *Puritanism in America, 1620–1750*. Boston: Twayne, 1977.

Feinstein, Howard M. *Becoming William James*. Ithaca, N.Y.: Cornell University Press, 1984.

Fink, Bruce. *A Clinical Introduction to Lacanian Psychoanalysis: Theory and Technique*. Cambridge, Mass.: Harvard University Press, 1997.

Fisch, Max. "Was There a Metaphysical Club in Cambridge?" In *Studies in the Philosophy of Charles S. Peirce*. Ed. Edward C. Moore and Richard S. Robin. Amherst: University of Massachusetts Press, 1964, 3–32.

———, ed. *Pragmatism and Purpose: Essays Presented to Thomas A. Goudge*. Buffalo, N.Y.: University of Toronto Press, 1981.

Foster, Lawrence. *Women, Family, and Utopia: Communal Experiments of the Shakers, the Oneida Community, and the Mormons*. Syracuse, N.Y.: Syracuse University Press, 1991.

Foucault, Michel. *The Foucault Reader*. Ed. Paul Rabinow. New York: Pantheon, 1984.

———. *The Order of Things: An Archaeology of the Human Sciences*. New York: Vintage, 1970.

Garnett, Jane, and Colin Matthew, eds. *Revival and Religion since 1700: Essays for John Walsh*. Rio Grande, Ohio: Hambledon, 1993.

Gehlhaar, Sabine S. *Die frühpositivistische (Helmholtz) und phänomenlogische (Husserl) Revision der Kantischen Erkenntnislehre*. Cuxhaven Junghans-Verlan, 1991.

Gildrie, Richard P. *The Profane, the Civil, and the Godly: The Reformation of Manners in Orthodox New England, 1679–1749*. University Park: Pennsylvania State University Press, 1994.

Griffin, Paul R. *Seeds of Racism in the Soul of America*. Naperville, Ill.: Sourcebooks, 2000.

Guelzo, Allen C. "From Calvinist Metaphysics to Republican Theory: Jonathan Edwards and James Dana on Freedom of the Will." *Journal of the History of Ideas* 56, no. 3 (1995): 399–418.

Hamilton, William. *Discussions on Philosophy and Literature, Education and University Reform*. 3d ed. London: Blackwood, 1856.

———. *Lectures on Metaphysics and Logic*. Vol. 2, *Logic*. Ed. Henry Mansel and John Veitch. Boston: Gould and Lincoln, 1864.

———. *Lectures on Metaphysics and Logic*. Vol. 1, *Metaphysics*. Ed. Henry Mansel and John Veitch. Boston: Gould and Lincoln, 1868.

———. *Philosophy of Sir William Hamilton, Bart*. Ed. O. W. Wright. New York: Appleton, 1853.

Haraway, Donna. *Simians, Cyborgs, and Women: The Reinvention of Nature*. New York: Routledge, 1991.

Hausman, Carl. *Charles S. Peirce's Evolutionary Realism*. Cambridge, Mass.: Harvard University Press, 1994.

Heidegger, Martin. *The Question concerning Technology and Other Essays*. Trans. William Lovitt. New York: Harper and Row, 1977.

Helmholtz, Hermann von. *Epistemological Writings: The Paul Hertz/Moritz Schlick Centenary Edition of 1921.* Ed. Robert S. Cohen and Yehuda Elkana. Trans. Malcolm F. Lowe. Boston: Reidel, 1977.

―――. *Handbuch der physiologischen Optik.* 2d ed. Hamburg: Voss, 1885–94.

―――. *Popular Lectures on Scientific Subjects.* Trans. E. Atkinson. 1st and 2d series. New York: Longmans, Green, 1908.

―――. *Science and Culture: Popular and Philosophical Essays.* Ed. David Cahan. Chicago: University of Chicago Press, 1995.

―――. *Selected Writings of Hermann von Helmholtz.* Ed. Russell Kahl. Middletown, Conn.: Wesleyan University Press, 1971.

Hollinger, David A. *Science, Jews, and Secular Culture: Studies in Mid–Twentieth-Century American Intellectual History.* Princeton, N.J.: Princeton University Press, 1996.

Hoopes, James. *Consciousness in New England: From Puritanism and Ideas to Psychoanalysis and Semiotic.* Baltimore, Md.: Johns Hopkins University Press, 1989.

Innes, Stephen. *Creating the Commonwealth: The Economic Culture of Puritan New England.* New York: Norton, 1995.

James, Henry, Sr. *The Literary Remains of the Late Henry James.* Ed. William James. New York: Houghton, Mifflin, 1897.

James, William. *Collected Essays and Reviews.* Ed. Ralph Barton Perry. New York: Longmans, Green, 1920.

―――. *Pragmatism and the Meaning of Truth.* Cambridge, Mass.: Harvard University Press, 1978.

―――. *The Principles of Psychology.* Cambridge, Mass.: Harvard University Press, 1981.

―――. *The Varieties of Religious Experience: A Study in Human Nature.* New York: Modern Library, 1902.

―――. *The Will to Believe and Other Essays in Popular Philosophy.* Ed. Frederick H. Burkhardt, Fredson Bowers, and Ignas K. Skrupskelis. Cambridge, Mass.: Harvard University Press, 1979.

―――. *The Writings of William James.* Ed. John J. McDermott. Chicago: University of Chicago Press, 1977.

―――. *The Works of William James: Essays, Comments, and Reviews.* Cambridge, Mass: Harvard University Press, 1987.

Joas, Hans. *Pragmatism and Social Theory.* Chicago: University of Chicago, 1993.

Kant, Immanuel. *Critique of Pure Reason.* Trans. Norman Kemp Smith. New York: St. Martin's, 1965.

Kent, Beverley. *Charles S. Peirce: Logic and the Classification of the Sciences.* Kingston, Ontario: McGill-Queen's University Press, 1987.

Ketner, Kenneth L., and Christian J. W. Kloesel, eds. *Peirce, Semeiotic, and Pragmatism: Essays by Max H. Fisch.* Bloomington: Indiana University Press, 1986.

Klein, Daniel B. *A History of Scientific Psychology: Its Origins and Philosophical Backgrounds.* New York: Basic, 1970.

Kuklick, Bruce. *Churchmen and Philosophers: From Jonathan Edwards to John Dewey.* New Haven, Conn.: Yale University Press, 1985.

Lanbert, Frank. *Inventing the Great Awakening.* Princeton, N.J.: Princeton University Press, 1999.

Lamont, William. *Puritanism and Historical Controversy.* Buffalo: McGill-Queen's University Press, 1996.

Lears, Timothy J. Jackson. *No Place of Grace: Antimodernism and the Transforma-tion of American Culture, 1880–1920*. Chicago: University of Chicago Press, 1981.

Leary, David E., ed. *Metaphors in the History of Psychology*. New York: Cambridge University Press, 1990.

Lentricchia, Frank. *Ariel and the Police: Michel Foucault, William James, Wallace Stevens*. Madison: University of Wisconsin Press, 1988.

———. *Modernist Quartet*. Cambridge: Cambridge University Press, 1994.

Lesser, M. X. *Jonathan Edwards*. Boston: Twayne, 1992.

Livingston, James. *Pragmatism and the Political Economy of Cultural Revolution, 1850–1940*. Chapel Hill: University of North Carolina Press, 1994.

McLaughlin, William. "Resolving Zeno's Paradoxes." *Scientific American*, Nov. 1994, 84–89.

Marsden, George. *Fundamentalism and American Culture: The Shaping of Twenti-eth-Century Evangelicalism 1870–1925*. New York: Oxford University Press, 1982.

———. *Religion and American Culture*. Philadelphia: Harcourt Brace, 1990.

Menand, Louis. *The Metaphysical Club: A Story of Ideas in America*. New York: Farrar, Straus and Giroux, 2001.

Mendell, Mark. "The Problem of the Origin of Pragmatism." *History of Philosophy Quarterly* 12, no. 1 (1995): 111–131.

Mill, John Stuart. *An Examination of Sir William Hamilton's Philosophy and of the Principal Philosophical Questions Discussed in His Writings*. 6th ed. New York: Longmans, Green, 1889.

Miller, Perry. *Errand into the Wilderness*. Cambridge, Mass.: Harvard University Press, 1956.

———. *Jonathan Edwards*. New York: Sloane, 1949.

Miller, Perry, and Thomas H. Johnson, eds. *The Puritans*. New York: American Book, 1938.

Mitchell, Timothy. *Colonising Egypt*. Berkeley: University of California Press, 1988.

Moore, Edward C. *American Pragmatism: Peirce, James, and Dewey*. New York: Columbia University Press, 1961.

Mouffe, Chantal, ed. *Deconstruction and Pragmatism*. New York: Routledge, 1996.

Mounce, H. O. "The Philosophy of the Conditioned." *Philosophical Quarterly* 44 (1994): 175–89.

Murphy, John P. *Pragmatism: From Peirce to Davidson*. Boulder, Colo.: Westview, 1990.

Murray, J. Clark. *Outline of Sir William Hamilton's Philosophy: A Textbook for Stu-dents*. Boston: Gould and Lincoln, 1870.

Ochs, Peter. *Peirce, Pragmatism, and the Logic of Scripture*. Cambridge: Cambridge University Press, 1998.

Orvell, Miles. *The Real Thing: Imitation and Authenticity in American Culture, 1880–1940*. Chapel Hill: University of North Carolina Press, 1989.

Pease, Donald E., ed. *National Identities and Post-Americanist Narratives*. Durham, N.C.: Duke University Press, 1994.

Peirce, Charles Sanders. *Collected Papers of Charles Sanders Peirce*. Ed. Charles Hartshorne and Paul Weiss. Vols. 1–6. Cambridge, Mass.: Harvard University Press, 1931–35.

———. *Collected Papers of Charles Sanders Peirce*. Ed. Arthur Burks. Vols. 7–8. Cambridge, Mass.: Harvard University Press, 1958.

————. *Charles S. Peirce: Selected Writings*. Ed. Philip P. Wiener. New York: Dover, 1966.

————. *Philosophical Writings of Peirce*. Ed. Justus Buchler. New York: Dover, 1955.

————. *Reasoning and the Logic of Things*. Ed. Kenneth L. Ketner and Hilary Putnam. Cambridge, Mass.: Harvard University Press, 1992.

————. *Writings of Charles S. Peirce: A Chronological Edition*. Vol. 3: 1872–1878. Ed. Christian J. W. Kloesel. Bloomington: Indiana University Press, 1986.

Perry, Ralph Barton. *The Thought and Character of William James*. Briefer version. New York: Braziller, 1954.

————. *The Thought and Character of William James*. Vol. 1, *Inheritance and Vocation*. Boston: Little, Brown, 1935.

————. *The Thought and Character of William James*. Vol. 2, *Philosophy and Psychology*. Boston: Little, Brown, 1935.

Peterson, Mark A. *The Price of Redemption: The Spiritual Economy of Puritan New England*. Stanford, Calif.: Stanford University Press, 1997.

Poirier, Richard. *Poetry and Pragmatism*. Ed. Edward W. Said. Cambridge, Mass.: Harvard University Press, 1992.

Posnock, Ross. *The Trial of Curiosity: Henry James, William James, and the Challenge of Modernity*. New York: Oxford University Press, 1991.

Putnam, Hilary. *Pragmatism: An Open Question*. Cambridge: Blackwell, 1995.

Putnam, Hilary, and Ruth Anna Putnam. "What the Spilled Beans Can Spell: The Difficult and Deep Realism of William James." *New York Times Literary Supplement*, June 21, 1996, 14–15.

Raposa, Michael. "Jonathan Edwards' Twelfth Sign." *International Philosophical Quarterly* 33, no. 2 (1993): 153–62.

————. *Peirce's Philosophy of Religion*. Bloomington: Indiana University Press, 1989.

Richards, Graham. "The Absence of Psychology in the Eighteenth Century: A Linguistic Perspective." *Studies in History, Philosophy, and Science* 23, no. 2 (1992): 195–211.

Rorty, Richard. *Consequences of Pragmatism*. Minneapolis: University of Minnesota Press, 1982.

Roth, Robert J. *British Empiricism and American Pragmatism: New Directions and Neglected Arguments*. New York: Fordham University Press, 1993.

————. *Radical Pragmatism: An Alternative*. New York: Fordham University Press, 1998.

————. "Radical Pragmatism and a Theory of Person." *International Philosophical Quarterly* 36, no. 3 (1996): 335–49.

Sabean, David Warren. "Production of the Self during the Age of Confessionalism." *Central European History* 29, no. 1 (1996): 1–18.

Seltzer, Mark. *Bodies and Machines*. New York: Routledge, 1992.

Sheriff, John K. *Charles Peirce's Guess at the Riddle: Grounds for Human Significance*. Bloomington: Indiana University Press, 1994.

————. *The Fate of Meaning: Charles Peirce, Structuralism, and Literature*. Princeton, N.J.: Princeton University Press, 1989.

Simonson, Harold P. *Jonathan Edwards: Theologian of the Heart*. Grand Rapids, Mich.: Eerdmans, 1988.

Skagestaad, Peter. *The Road of Inquiry: Charles Peirce's Pragmatic Realism*. New York: Columbia University Press, 1981.

Smith, John E. *America's Philosophical Vision*. Chicago: University of Chicago Press, 1992.

———. "Jonathan Edwards: Piety and Practice in the American Character." *Journal of Religion* 54 (1974): 166–80.

———. *Jonathan Edwards: Puritan, Preacher, Philosopher*. Notre Dame, Ind.: University of Notre Dame Press, 1992.

———. *Purpose and Thought: The Meaning of Pragmatism*. New Haven, Conn.: Yale University Press, 1978.

Staloff, Darren. *The Making of an American Thinking Class: Intellectuals and Intelligentsia in Puritan Massachusetts*. New York: Oxford University Press, 1998.

Stuhr, John J. *Genealogical Pragmatism: Philosophy, Experience, and Community*. Albany: State University of New York Press, 1997.

Ten, C. L. *The Nineteenth Century*. New York: Routledge, 1994.

Thayer, H. S. *Meaning and Action: A Critical History of Pragmatism*. New York: Bobbs-Merrill, 1968.

Tocqueville, Alexis de. *Democracy in America*. Trans. George Lawrence. Ed. J. P. Mayer. New York: Harper and Row, 1969.

Todd, Margo. *Christian Humanism and the Puritan Social Order*. New York: Cambridge University Press, 1987.

Vanier, Alain. *Lacan*. Trans. Susan Fairfield. New York: Other Press, 2000.

Veitch, John. *Blackwood's Philosophical Classics: Hamilton*. Philadelphia: Lippincott, n.d.

———. *Memoir of Sir William Hamilton, Bart*. London: Blackwood, 1869.

Verhave, Thom. "Network Theories of Memory: Before Wundt and Herbart." *Psychological Record* 43 (1993): 547–52.

Wentz, Richard E. "John Williamson Nevin and American Nationalism," *Journal of the American Academy of Religion* 58, no. 4 (Winter 1990): 617–32.

West, Cornel. *The American Evasion of Philosophy: A Genealogy of Pragmatism*. Madison: University of Wisconsin Press, 1989.

White, Sheldon H. "Hilgard's Vision of Psychology's History." *American Psychological Society* 5, no. 4 (1994): 192–193.

Wiley, Norbert. *The Semiotic Self*. Chicago: University of Chicago Press, 1994.

Woodward, William R., and Mitchell G. Ash, eds. *The Problematic Science in Nineteenth-Century Thought*. New York: Praeger, 1982.

Wundt, Wilhelm M. *Elements of Folk Psychology: Outlines of a Psychological History of the Development of Mankind*. Trans. Edward Leroy Schaub. New York: Macmillan, 1921.

———. *Ethics: An Investigation of the Facts and Laws of the Moral Life*. Vol. 3, *The Principles of Morality and the Departments of the Moral Life*. 2d ed.Trans. Margaret Floy Washburn. New York: Macmillan, 1907.

———. *Ethik: Eine Untersuchung der Tatsachen und Gesetze des Sittlichen Lebens*. Vierte umgearbeitete Auflage; Drei Bände: Dritter Band, *Die Prinzipien der Sittlichkeit und die Sittlichen Lebensgebiete*. Stuttgart: Ferdinand Enke, 1912.

———. *Grundzüge der Physiologischen Psychologie*. Zweite Band. 6th ed. Leipzig: Wilhelm Engelmann, 1910.

———. *Grundzüge der Physiologischen Psychologie*. Dritter Band. 6th ed. Leipzig: Wilhelm Engelmann, 1911.

———. *An Introduction to Psychology*. Trans. Rudolf Pinter. London: George Allen, 1912; reprint, New York: Arno, 1973.

———. *The Language of Gestures*. Trans. J. S. Thayer, C. M. Greenleaf, and M. D. Silberman. English ed. from 4th German ed. The Hague: Mouton, 1973.

————. *Lectures on Human and Animal Psychology*. Trans. J. E. Creighton and E. B. Titchener. English ed. from 2d German ed. New York: Macmillan, 1894; reprinted in *Significant Contributions to the History of Psychology 1750–1920*. Ed. Daniel N. Robinson. Washington, D.C.: University Publications of America, 1977.

————. *Outlines of Psychology*. Trans. Charles Hubbard Judd. 3d rev. English ed. from the 7th rev. German ed. New York: Stechert, 1907.

————. *Principles of Physiological Psychology*. Vol. 1, *Introduction: Part I. The Bodily Substrate of the Mental Life*. Trans. E. B. Titchener. English ed. from 5th German ed. New York: Macmillan, 1910; reprint, New York: Kraus, 1969.

Zakai, Avihu. *Exile and Kingdom: History and Apocalypse in the Puritan Migration to America*. New York: Cambridge University Press, 1992.

Index